AF867607

The Principle of Compensation in International Arbitration

by

Amirhossein Kousha, Ph.D

MAJD PUBLICATIONS

MAJD PUBLICAIONS OÜ
(17530423)

The Principle of Compensationin International Arbitration

Amirhossein Kousha, Ph.D

First Edition, 2026
Published by
Majd Publications OU
Tallinn, Estonia
Subjects: International Commercial Arbitration; Compensation and Damages; Iran–United States Claims Tribunal; Expropriation of Foreign Property; International Investment Law; Valuation of Damages; Interest Awards; State Responsibility; Claims Settlement; International Dispute Resolution
ISBN (Soft Cover): 978-9916-4-4026-1
DDC: 341.522 (International Arbitration)
DDC: 341.6 (International Dispute Settlement) — Alternative
LCC: K2400–K2408 (International Commercial Arbitration)
LCC: KZ3695–KZ3698 (International Claims and Compensation) — Secondary Classification
Website: www.majdpub.com
E-mail: info@majdpub.com
European Union

Table of Cases

•*Dadras International and Per-Am Construction Corporation v the Islamic Republic of Iran and Thran Development*, [1995] case no. 213,215, 31 _IUSCTR_ 127 4.2.4.2.2,4.3.1

•*DIC of Delaware v. the Islamic Republic of Iran*, [1985] case no.225, 8 _IUSCTR_ 1444.3.1

•*Eastman Kodak Company v the Islamic Republic of Iran*, [1991] case no.227, 27 _IUSCTR_ 3 2.5

•*Ebrahimi Shahin Shaine v. the Islamic Republic of Iran*, 1994] case no. 44&46, 30 _IUSCTR_ 1702.3.1, 3.4,5.2.1.1.1, 5.2.1.1.1.1, 6.6

•*Endo Laboratories, Inc. v the Islamic Republic of Iran*, [1987] case no. 366, 17 _IUSCTR_ 1143.5.2

•*Economy Forms Corporation v the Islamic Republic of Iran*, [1983] case no.165, 3 _IUSCTR_ 421.6.2, 4.3.1

•*Edgar Protiva v the Islamic Republic of Iran*, [1995] case no.316, 31 IUSCTR_6.4•*Esfahanian v Bank Tejarat*, [1983] case no.157, 2 -IUSCTR- 157 1.7

•*Exxon Corporation v. the Islamic Republic of Iran*, [1987] case no.154, 17 _IUSCTR_ 3. 6.5

•*Exxon Research and Engineering Co v. National Iranian Oil Company*, [1987] case no.155, 15 _IUSCTR_ 3 6.5

•*First Travel Corporation v. the Islamic Republic of Iran*, [1985] case no.34, 9 _IUSCTR_ 360 6.7.3

•*FMC Corp. v the Ministry on National Defence*, [1987] case No.353, 4 _IUSCTR_ 111..........4.3.1

•*Ford Aerospace Communications v the Islamic Republic of Iran*, [1987] case no.93, 14_IUSCTR_ 2553.5.3

•*General Electric Company v the Islamic Republic of Iran*, [1991] case no386. 26 _IUSCTR_ 1483.5.3, 4.2.4.1.1, 4.3.1.1

•*General Dynamics Corp. v the Islamic Republic of Iran*, [1984] case no.238, 5 -IUSCTR- 3861.6.2.1

•*General Dynamics Tel., Inc. v. the Islamic Republic of Iran*, [1985] case no.285, 9 IUSCTR_ 1534.2.1.3

•*Pereira, William v. the Islamic Republic of Iran*, [1984] case no.1, 5 IUSCTR_ 198 4.2.1.2

•*Petrolane Inc. v the Islamic Republic of Iran*, [1991] case no.22, 27 IUSCTR_ 222.2., 3.2.1.3, 4.3.2, 5.2.1.1.2.2

•*Phelps Dodge International Corp. v. the Islamic Republic of Iran*, [1986] case no.99, 10_IUSCTR_ 1212.3.1, 2.3.2, *3.4, 5.2.1.1.1.1.*

•*Phillips Petroleum Company v. the Islamic Republic of Iran and NIOC*, [1989] case no.39, 21 -IUSCTR- 221.6.1.1, 2.3.1, 2.3.2, 2.5, 3.2, 3.2.1.1,

•5.2.1.1.2, 5.2.1.1.2.1, 5.2.1.2.1, 6.5

•*Pomeroy Corporation v. the Islamic Republic of Iran*, [1983] case no.41, 2 _IUSCTR- 3912.2.3, 4.3.1, 6.7

•*Questech, Inc. v the Islamic Republic of Iran*, [1985] case no.59, 9 _IUSCTR_ 107 3.5.1

•*Reading & Bates Drilling Company v the Islamic Republic of Iran*, [1988] case no.10633, 18 _IUSCTR_ 164 6.3

•*Reliance Group, Inc. v National Oil Company*, [1987] case no.115, 16 _IUSCTR_ 257...4.2.1.3, 6.5

•*Rexnord, Inc. v. the Islamic Republic of Iran*, [1983] case no.132, 2 _IUSCTR_ 64.2.1.2

•*Richard D. Harza. V. The Islamic Republic of Iran*, [1986] case no.97, 11 - IUSCTR- 764.2.4.1

•*R.J. Reynolds Tobacco Co. v. the Islamic Republic of Iran*, partial award [1984] case no.35, 7-IUSCTR- 1811.6.2, 1.6.2, 1.6.2.1.1.3, 6.5, 6.6

•*R.J. Reynolds Tobacco Co. v. the Islamic Republic of Iran*, [1985] case no.35, 8 -IUSCTR- 55 (Iran_U.S. Claims Tribunal) 6.7.5

•*Rockwell International Systems, Inc. v the Islamic Republic of Iran*, [1989] case no.430, 23 _IUSCTR_ 150 4.2.4.2.1

•*Saghi v. the Islamic Republic of Iran*, [1993] case no.298, 29 _IUSCTR_ 203.2.1.2, 5.2.1.2.1

•*Sea-Land Service, Inc. v. the Islamic Republic of Iran*, [1984] case no.33, 6 _IUSCTR_ 149Intro, 2.4, 3.2, 3.3, 3.4

•*Schering Corp v the Islamic Republic of Iran*, [1984] case no.38, 5 _IUSCTR_ 361 3.2

•*SEDCO, Inc. v. the Islamic Republic of Iran and National Iranian Oil Company*, [1985] case no.129, 9 _IUSCTR_ 2482.4

•*SEDCO, Inc. v. the Islamic Republic of Iran and National Iranian Oil Company*, [1986] case no.129, 10 -IUSCTR- 1801.6.1.2,

•*SEDCO, Inc. v. National Iranian Oil Company*, [1987] case no.129, 15 _IUSCTR_ 234.3.2

•*SEDCO, Inc v Iran Marine Industrial CO.*, [1989] case no. 128&129, 21 _IUSCTR- 315.2.1.2.1

•*Seismograph Service Corporation v. National Iranian Oil Company and The Islamic Republic of Iran*, [1989] case no.443, 22 _IUSCTR_ 34.3.1

•*SeaCo, Inc. v. the Islamic Republic of Iran*, [1992] case no. 260, 28 _IUSCTR_ 198 3.2.1.1

•*Shannon &Wilson, Inc. v. Atomic Energy Org. of Iran*, [1985] case no.217, 9 -IUSCTR- 397 1.6.2.1.1.1

•*Sola Tiles, Inc. v the Islamic Republic of Iran*, [1985] case no.317, 14 _IUSCTR_ 223 5.2.1.1.1

•*Starrett Housing Corporations, Srarrett System, Inc. and Starrett Housing International, Inc. v. the Islamic Republic of Iran, [1987] case no.24, 16_IUSCTR_ 113 2.2.1, 2.5, 3.2.1.1, 3.2.1.2, 4.2.1.2, 4.2.1.3, 5.2.1.1.2.2, 6.6*

•*Sylvania Technical Systems, Inc. v. the Islamic Republic of Iran*, [1985] case no.64, 8 _IUSCTR_ 2984.2.4.1.1, 4.3.1, 6.7.3

•*T.C. S. B., Inc. v. the Islamic Republic of Iran*, [1984] case no.140, 5 _IUSCTR_ 1612.4,4.2.1.2

•*The Stanwick Corp. v. the Islamic Republic of Iran*, [1990] case no.66, 24 _IUSCTR_ 1026.3

•*Tippett, Abbett, McCarthy, Stratton v TAMSA_AFFA Consulting of Iran*, [1984] case no.7, 6 _IUSCTR_ 219 2.2.1, 3.2.1., 3.2.1.2, 4.2.1.2

•*Uiterwyk Corp. v the Islamic Republic of Iran*, [1988] case no.381, 19 _IUSCTR_ 106 6.3

• *Watkins-Johnsons Company v. the Islamic Republic of Iran*, [1989] case no.370, 22 _IUSCTR_ 2183.5.3

• *Westinghouse Electric. Corporation v. the Islamic Republic of Iran*, [1997] case no.389, 33 _IUSCTR_ 604.2.1.2

• *William J. Levitt v the Islamic Republic of Iran*, [1987] case no.209, 14 _IUSCTR_ 1913.4, 4.2.1.3, 4.3.1, 4.3.2, 4.2.4.2.2

• *Woodward-Clyde Consultants v the Islamic Republic of Iran*, 1983] case no.67, 3 _IUSCTR_ 2394.2.4.2

International Arbitration

•-*AutopistaConcesionada de Venezuela, C.A.(Aucoven) v Bolivarian Republic of Venezuela, ARB/00/5, [2003] 10 ICSID Reports 309 (ICSID)3.4*

•-*Cf Joseph Charles Lemire v Ukraine, ARB/06/18, [2000] 6 _ICSID Reports_ 59 (ICSID).Intro*

•-*Chorzow Factory case, (Germany v. Poland) Merits, [1928] 17 Series A (Permanent Court of International Justice).*

1ntro, 2.3, 3.2.1.1-4.3

•*CME Czech Republic B.V. v. The Czech Republic, [2006] 9 ICSID Reports 113 (ICSID).3.4*

•*Compañía del Desarrollo de Santa Elena, S.A. v. Republic of Costa Rica, ARB/96/1, [1997] 5 ICSID Reports 296 (ICSID)6.6*

•*Gabčikovo-Nagymaros Project, Hungary v Slovakia, Judgment, Merits, ICJ GL No 92, [1997] ICJ Rep 7, [1997] ICJ Rep 88, (1998) 37 ILM 162, ICGJ 66 (ICJ 1997), 25 September 1997, International Court of Justice [ICJ])Intro*

•-*Hadley v. Baxandale,* [1854] 156 Eng. Rep.145. Court of Exchequer *3.3*

•-*Middle East Cement Co v Arab Republic of Egypt, ARB/99/6, [2002] 7 ICSID Reports 174 (ICSID).Intro, 606*

•-*Mohamed Abdulmohsen Al-Kharafi & Sons Co v Libya, 2013 Cairo Regional Center for International Commercial Arbitration, enligne: <https://www.italaw.com/sites/default*

•*/files/case-documents/italaw1554.pdf>.Intro*

•-*Saudi Arabia v Arabian American Oil Company(Aramco), 1958, 27, I.L.R 117, 165, 1958 1.6.2.1.1.2*

•-*Sapphire International Petroleums Ltd. v National Iranian Oil Company, [1963] 35, I.L.R ,136, (ad hoc Tribunal) 3.4*

•-*SD Myers, Inc. v Government of Canada, [2002] 8, ICSID Reports, 4 (ICSID, NAFTA arbitration) 4.2.4.1, 4.2.4.2.1*

•-*The State of Kuwait v The American Independent Oil Company (Aminoil'), [1982] 21, International Legal Materials 976-1053, (ad hoc arbitration). 6.6*

•-*Wena Hotels Ltd. v. Arab Republic of Egypt, ARB/98/4, [2000] 6, ICSID Repoprts ,(ICSID).6.6*

•-*YUKOS Universal LTD. (ISLE OF MAN) v The Russian Federation, 2014 Permanent Court of Arbitration,* PCA Case No. 2005/04-AA 227*enligne: <https://pcacases.comweb/sendAtta ch/420>1.8, 2.3.3*

List of Acronyms

BIT: Bilateral Investment Treaty

CISG: United Nations Convention on Contracts for the International Sale of Goods, Vienna ,1980

DCF: Discounted Cash Flow

FMV: Fair Market Value

ICC: International Chamber of Commerce

ICSID: International Center for Settlement of Investment Disputes

ILC: International Law Commission

IUSCT: Iran-United States Claims Tribunal

I.U.S.C.T.R: Iran-United States Claims Tribunal Report

NAFTA: North America Free Trade Agreement

NBV: Net Book Value

PCIJ: Permanent Court of International Justice

UNCITRAL: United Nations Commission on International Trade Law

UNIDROIT: International Institute for the Unification of Private Law

UPICC: Unidroit Principles of Commercial Contracts

Table of Contents

Foreword

International arbitration is encountering a growing number of disputes arising from complicated multiple contracts and actions in international investment.As these contracts deal with state parties, they are governed by international law. The problem in adopting public international law, as the system of law governing commercial relationships, is not a problem of principle, but of practice. Public international law, being concerned primarily with the relationships between states, is not particularly well equipped to deal with detailed contractual issues such as mistake, misrepresentation, time of performance, force majeure, or the measure of damages. The same criticism may be directed at the choice of 'general principles of law' as the governing law of a contract. The general principles of law recognized by civilizednations have been defined as the general principles of municipal jurisprudence, in particular of private law, insofar as they are applicable to relations of States.

Theproblem with the general principles is that they are just that: they deal with topics including theprinciple of good faith in treaty relations, abuse of rights, and the concept of state andindividual responsibility. They are excellent as generalisations, but may lack sufficient detailfor contractual relations.

The Principles of International Commercial Contracts (UPICC) are a widely accepted codification of transnational law set out by The International Institute for the Unification of Private Law (UNIDROIT), which present a set of detailed and practical legal rules to govern commercial relations.

The framers designed UNIDROIT's Principles of International Commercial Contracts (UPICC) to settle private international commercial disputes, not international disputes between states and investors, which usually relate to expropriation issues. A crucial question emerges: can general principles of law codified in the UPICC serve as substantive law in investor-state or interstate arbitrations?

The present book, which is the result of a Ph.D. thesis presented at the University of Montreal, sheds light on the above questions now commonly faced by international commercial tribunals and practitioners. It explores the application of the principle of compensation in the practice of the Iran–United States Claims Tribunal (IUSCT). This study examines how the IUSCT, established in 1981, applies compensation rules and the relationship of those rules to the UPICC.Those who have participated in major international trade arbitrations know that questions linked to the assessment of damages give rise to bitter controversies, whose stakes can be considerable and depend more often on the resolution of pure questions of law. This paper studies these questions in detail, shedding light on the jurisprudence of the Iran–United States Claims Tribunal. This study thoroughly examines critical issues concerning the application of the principle of compensation in the practice of the Tribunal with a clear focus on the related rules in UPICC, which addresses issues of damages.

IUSCT practice, involving more than 800 awards and decisions in investor-state disputes over more than 35 years, contains substantial jurisprudence in this field. This study proceeds through case studies and comparisons of the tribunal's jurisprudence with UPICC's principle of compensation and related rules in the Convention on Contracts for the International Sale of Goods, Vienna 1980. It explores the tribunal's interpretation and application of the principle of compensation and the extent of the UPICC's influence on the reasoning in its awards. The tribunal's implicit—and more recently explicit— adoption of UPICC principles not only bolsters the UPICC's authority, but also brings predictability and certainty to the application of UPICC rules and provides a useful model for other international tribunals. Thisstudy of the IUSCT awards strongly concludes that the UPICC, as a widespread and influential codification of the general principles of international commercial contract law, is superbly suited for application as substantive law in arbitrating international investment disputes.

I am particularly grateful to Professor Emmanuel Darankoum, of the Centre de droit des affaires et du commerce international (CDACI) of the University of Montreal, for his guidance and support throughout my work on this study and for his unfailing generosity in sharing his experience, expertise, and precious time. Finally, I would like to acknowledge with gratitude, the assistance of Dr. Abbas Hoseini Nik and the team at Majd Publications, without their efforts this book have not been possible.

Amirhossein Kousha
Doctoraten droit (LL. D.)

Introduction

Rapid global development in the 20th and early 21st centuries has transformed commercial relations between traders throughout the world. Frequently, parties from several countries, with different legal traditions, have engaged in a joint contract. The huge growth, both in the value and volume of transactions and in their diversity and complexity, has resulted in increased specialization with ever more complex and sophisticated contracts[1]. Foreign investors, following new opportunities, often place their funds and trust as aliens in other countries. Thus, when disputes arise, it may be very hard to find and agree on the applicable law. Seeking for answers has led scholars to look for ways to systematize, harmonize, and even unify commercial rules in the emerging field of transnational commercial law.

Nowadays, we inhabit a world of multiple normative communities. Many of normative communities such as traders and businessmen articulate norms without formal state power behind them. Indeed, legal pluralists have long noted that law does not reside solely in the coercive commands of a sovereign power. Rather, law is constantly constructed through the contest of these various norm generating communities[2]. Alongside the domestic-international dichotomy that marked international law for a very long time, transnational law offers itself as a supplementary and challenging category within interdisciplinary research on globalization and law[3]. Therefore, one can

1.Roy GOODE, « Rule, practice, and pragmatism in transnational commercial law », (2005) 54-3 *Int. Comp. Law Q.* 539-562.p.540

2.Paul SCHIFF BERMAN, « Global Legal Pluralism », (2007) 80-13 *South. Calif. Law Rev.* 1155-1238.p.1158

3.Peer ZUMBANSEN, « Transnational Law », dans Jan SMITH (dir.), *Encyclopedia of Comparative Law*, Edward Elgar, 2006, p. 738-754.p.739

consider that the purpose of transnationalisation is to remove the dispute from the ambit of a possibly inadequate national law[4]. For the first time, Jessup in 1956, has advanced the concept of transnational law in meaning of "all law which regulate actions and events that transend national frontiers"[5].Today, transnational law seeks to codify and extract commercial law from various sources in order to harmonize international commercial law. A hybrid of national and international law has emerged as a third legal order, popularly known as the lex mercatoria(or new merchant law), which mixes characteristics of both, to govern international commercial relations and disputes[6]. lex mercatoria, spontaneously generated bythe international community in the shadow of national legal orders. This new lex mercatoria is composedof commercial customs, but also includes a variety of other internationalnorms that are regularly respected by international commercial actors[7].

This modern version of merchant law consists of rules and practices that have evolved within the international business communities and draws on sources of law, including public

---

4.Gabrielle KAUFMANN-KOHLER, « Arbitral Precedent: Dream, Necessity or Excuse? », (2007) 23-3 *Arbitr. Int.* 357-378.p.364

5.Philip C. JESSUP, « The Concept of Transnational Law: An Introduction », (1963) 3-1 *Columbia J. Transnatl. Law* 1-17. P.8

6.Thomas E. CARBONNEAU, « arbitral law-making », (2004) 25 *Michigan Journal of International law* 1183-1208.p.1203 , Abul F. MANIRUZZAMAN, « The Lex Mercatoria And International Contracts: A Challenge for International Commercial Arbitration ? », (1999) 14 *AM U INTL REV* 657-697.p.661

7.Gilles CUNIBERTI, « Three Theories of Lex Mercatoria », (2014) 52-6 *Columbia J. Transnatl. Law* 369-434.p.372, , Alec STONE SWEET, « The new Lex Mercatoria and transnational governance », (2006) 13-5 *J. Eur. Public Policy* 627-646.p.634

international law generally and the general principles of law specifically.[8] This approach provokes long discussions on the necessity, for the needs of international trade, of applying in international commercial contracts a neutral law independent of various doctrinal conceptions[9]. The trend to harmonization leads to efforts to find and extract general principles standard to some or most legal systems.

The new lex mercatoria is a response to the commercial demands of globalization. However, as Berger argues, it has developed in this way because of the trend towards a 'global civil society' that erodes national boundaries in markets and reduces states' power to steer national or international economic factors.[10] In general terms, uniform law refers to any intelligible set of rules intended to govern aspects of commerce. The lex mercatoria, or merchant law, posits transnational rules consisting of usages and principles that would constitute a judicial order specific to the operators of international commerce. It is by nature uncodified, non-statutory, and non-conventional.[11]

In the past three decades, transnational commercial actors have generated their own institutions. Institution building has proceeded on two linked fronts. The first is the intensive effort to 'unify' or standardize the general principles of a stable 'a-national' contract law;

8.Nigel BLACKABY et Constantine PARTASIDIES, *Redfern And Hunter on International Arbitration*, Sixth, New York, Oxford University Press, 2015.p.206

9.Emmanuel S. DARANKOUM, « L'application des Principes d'UNIDROIT par les arbitres internationaux et par les juges étatiques », (2002) 36 *Rev. Jurid. Thémis* 425-480.p.429

10.Klaus P. BERGER, « The New Law Merchant and the Global Market: A 21st Century View of Transnational Commercial Law », (2000) 91-3 *INT ARB REV.*1-22, p.14

11.Louis MARQUIS, *International Uniform Commercial Law*, England, Ashgate, 2005.p.26

and various standardized, model contracts are in fact increasingly used[12]. Second, a robust system of private, competing transnational arbitration houses has evolved, providing traders with a range of alternatives to litigating transnational contract disputes in state courts. In consequence, national courts and legislators have adapted, most notably, by reducing the scope of their authority to regulate both contracting and arbitration. It is through these processes that the new Lex Mercatoria has achieved meaningful (but not absolute) autonomy from traditional, public sources of law, such as national statute and public international law, though how to understand this autonomy is actively debated[13]. Despite the ongoing debate on its actual content, the concept of a modern lex mercatoria largely autonomous from national laws-is now widely accepted[14]. Unfortunately there is no agreement on what the lex mercatoria comprises. To some it is merely another label for transnational commercial law and thus encompasses all kinds of harmonization, formal and informal. To others, it is the product of so-called spontaneous international law-making through international trade usage as evidenced by rules of trade associations, standard-term contracts and general principles and rules and restatements formulated by international agencies.

The opponents of the new lex mercatoria argue that, as it is based on custom and general principles of law, it is not a complete system and that, being subject to rules of public policy and mandatory rules of national law, it is not an autonomous body of principles. Professor Goode makes an effort to refute the importance of these objections. He argues that while it may be true that the lex mercatoria is not a complete legal system, that is not to say that its choice as the applicable law is wholly ineffective but merely that if its principles do

---

12.A. STONE SWEET, préc., note 7.p.633

13.Ralf MICHAELS, « The true lex mercatoria: Law beyond the state », (2007) 14-2 *Indiana J. Glob. Leg. Stud.* 447-468.p.448

14.G. CUNIBERTI, préc., note 7.p.383

not cover a particular question in dispute reference would have to be made to some applicable national law. He also argues that while it is also true that the lex mercatoria may be subject to rules of public policy and rules of mandatory national law, "it does not follow that the lex mercatoria lacks normative force, merely that it is subordinate to higher norms. Professor goode advocates to confine the lex mercatoria to international trade practice. To equate the lex mercatoria with the entirety of transnational commercial law deprives us of a useful label to denote that part of transnational commercial law which derives from the international practice of merchants[15].

Ole Lando has identified eight elements to lex mercatoria -- namely, public international law, uniform laws, the general principles of law, the rules of international organizations, uncodified customs and usages, codifications of customs and usages by international organizations, standard-form contracts, and reported arbitral awards[16]. These principles are specific to international commerce or are common to all or many states that participate in it. These principles are genuine sources of the lex mercatoria because they are in use in international trade. Their function is primarily to fill any gaps that other sources may have left[17].

The proposed method of transnational law will provide the classification of lex mercatoria sources based on either a legislative or an adjudicatory approach.[18] First, the legislative approach involves codified

15.R. GOODE, préc., note 1.p.547

16.Ole LANDO, « The Lex Mercatoria International Commercial Arbitration », (1985) 34 *Int. Comp. Law Q.* 747-768.,p.753

17.Liu CHENGWEI et Marie Stefanini NEWMAN, *Remedies for Non-performance - Perspectives from CISG, UNIDROIT Principles and PECL*, Juris Net Llc, 2008.p.8

18.N. BLACKABY et C. PARTASIDIES, préc., note 8., 208, professor Redfern has proposed the following methods, list approach and functional approach. In fact, these are different names for identical approaches, that is, legislative rules of the lex mercatoria from international instruments. Establishing through academic research, the existence of general principles of law requires comparative study of national legal systems representative of the whole international community.[19] Legislation regulating international commercial rules takes at least two different forms; that of international law, which emerges through inter-state negotiation, in such forms as bilateral treaties, and uniform international law rules, which provide a common textual basis for application in many states, such as the Vienna Convention (CISG) and UPICC. Since CISG deals only with contracts for the international sale of goods and UPICC's scope is much wider, they do not overlap except in sales contracts.[20]

The other version of uniform law is a result of a multi-state codification of a single and unique commercial law. The Vienna Convention – the United Nations Convention on Contracts for the International Sale of Goods, or CISG (Vienna, 1980) --contains a set of substantive provisions relating to the sale of goods. One observer has called it "the most significant piece of substantive contract legislation in effect at the international level."[21] As of March 2016, the 84 country signatories account for over 90 per cent of the world's trade in goods.[22]

One can legitimately describe rules in an international covenant as part of transnational commercial law, but not as part of the lex mercatoria, for the document enshrining them operates only by the will

---

approach accords to the list method and the adjudicatory method accord to the functional approach.

19.Tarcisio GAZZINI, « General Principles of Law in the Field of Foreign Investment », (2009) 10*J. World Invest. Trade* 103-119., p.107

20.*Id.*

21.Leon E TRAKMAN, « A Plural Account of the Transnational Law Merchant », (2011) 3 *Transnatl. Leg. Theory* 309-345.,p.330

22.Ralph H. Folsom and Michael Wallace GORDON, *International Business Transactions*, Second, United States, West Academic Publishing, 2016., p.39

of participating states.[23] The CISG Convention aims to establish a uniform, statutory international law of sales, thereby maximizing predictability in international commercial dealings and possibly supplying a substantive international law of contracts.[24]

The most notable instance of the third version comes from the Institut international pour l'unification du droit privé (UNIDROIT) – namely, its Principles of International Commercial Contracts (UPICC). This document serves many purposes; chief among them, it provides a contractual juridical framework for the parties, forms a juridical reference for interpretation, and serves as a model for national and international legislators.[25] UPICC is applicable as the law governing a contract when either the parties or the court itself have chosen it.[26]

The CISG and the PICC, working together, have been remarkably successful in addressing the needs of commercial players in international commerce. Taken together, the CISG and the PICC already provide a substantial and sufficient modern framework for the harmonization of international sales and contract law through a combination of hard law and soft law.[27]

23.Roy GOODE, « usage and its reception in transnational commercial law », (1997) 46 *Int. Comp. Law Q.* 1-36.p.2

24.Thomas E. CARBONNEAU et Marc S. FIRESTONE, « Transnational Law-making: Assessing the impact of the Vinenna Convention and the Viability of Arbitral Adjudication », (1987) 1 *J. Int. Dispute Resolut.* 51-80.

25.*UNIDROIT principles of international commercial contracts 2010*, International Institute for the Unification of Private Law, Rome, 2010, en ligne : <https://www.unidroit.org/english/principles/contracts/principles2010/integralversionprinciples2010-e.pdf> Preamble.

26.E. S. DARANKOUM, préc., note 9., p.427

27.Michael J. DENNIS, « Modernizing and harmonizing international contract law: the CISG and the UNIDROIT Principles continue to provide the best way forward », (2014) 19-1 *Unif. Law Rev.* 114-151.p.116

The codification of the *lex mecatoria,* as incorporated into uniform principles such as the UNIDROIT commercial contract principles, can therefore be regarded as responding to the demand believed to exist amongst the business community working in this globalised environment[28]. The text of the preamble of UPICC relates essentially to the application of the UPICC in the field of contract, to their use in interpreting or supplementing domestic law, or as a model for national and international legislators. The UPICC may be applicable in arbitral proceedings by choice of the parties or in state court litigation where the applicable conflict of laws rules respect the choice of the "rules of law" and the parties have chosen the UPICC[29]. According to preamble, even they may be applied in arbitration when the parties have not chosen any law to govern their contract. They may be used to interpret or supplement international uniform law instruments. They may be used to interpret or supplement domestic law[30]. They may serve as a model for national and international legislators. principles may be used not only to interpret and supplement even pre-existing international instruments, but also to fill gaps in individual provisions is an expression of and in conformity with the general principles underlying the CISG[31]. However, the parties to an international sales contract governed by the CISG may wish to stipulate either in their contract or after the commencement of a court or arbitral proceedings

---

28.Ross CRANSTON, « Theorizing Transnational Commercial Law », (2007) 42-7 *Tex. Int. Law J.* 597-617.p.605

29.Pascal HACHEM, « The CISG and Statute of Limitation », dans Ingeborg SCHWENZER (dir.), *35 years CISG and beyond*, 39, coll. international commerce and arbitration, The Hague, Elven international publishing, 2016 à la page 156.

30.Michael J. BONELL, « The law governing international commercial contracts and the actual role of the UNIDROIT Principles », (2018) 23-2 *Unif. Law Rev.* 15-41, 19.

31.Sleg EISELEN, « Unresolved damages issues of the CISG: a comparative analysis », (2005) 38-1 *Comp. Int. Law J. South. Afr.* 32-46.p.35

that the CISG should be interpreted or supplemented by the UNIDROIT Principles' in order to 'ensure that judges or arbitrators, when faced with ambiguities or veritable gaps in the CISG, will primarily resort to the UNIDROIT Principles to settle the issues and turn to domestic law only as a last resort[32].

This approach, generally, based on the comparative study of the civilized nations'legal norms. This approach isolates and elaborates principles and rules common to most existing legal systems, applying the common core of solutions to problems of contract law globally to meet the needs of international trade relations, including those between developed and less developed countries.[33] Therefore, values, pragmatic considerations, and ethical views provide perspectives in light of which meaningful similarities and differences between societies can be identified and their effects upon each society's legal order assessed and compared[34]. A positive effect of codification appears to be increased legitimacy of the lex mercatoria because it creates a set of rules that can be more or less uniformly followed on global basis, helping to address concerns of vagueness and uncertainty.[35]As professor Goode submits, the codification of legal rules is an effective vehicle to exercise the predictability which constitutes one of the principles of commerce[36]. One excellent example of the latter is the UNIDROITPrinciples, which

32.M. J. DENNIS, préc., note 27.p.132

33.Michael Joashim BONELL, *An International Restatement of Contract Law: the UNIDROIT Principles of International Commercial Contracts*, Second, New York, Transnational Publishers, Inc., 1997.

34.Arthur T. VON MEHREN, « The Rise of Transnational Legal Practice and the Task of Comparative Law », (2001) 75-5 *Tulane Law Rev.* 1215-1224.p.1223

35.Vanessa M JOHNSON, « Codification of the lex mercatoria: friend or foe? », (2015) 21-2 *Law Bus. Rev. Am.* 150-166.p.161

36.Roy GOODE, « The Codification of Commercial Law », (1988) 14 *Monash Univ. Law Rev.* 135-157.p.148

are a coherentcode of contract law affording precise and detailed rules[37].

Second, the adjudicatory approach elaborates transnational commercial law through the decisions of international arbitral tribunals.[38] It refines and consolidates the jurisprudence of international tribunals in the light of how their judgments interpret the principles of law.[39] A major source for unifying general principle is analysis of the arbitration awards that derive from general principles of law. Redfern observes that the principles of international law are not the whole corpus of law, but only certain specific rules of law that are likely to be relevant in any given dispute.[40]The United Nations Commission on International Trade Law (UNCITRAL) rules of arbitration, outlined the general principles of trade law, allowing use of them as substantive law when the disputing parties so chose.[41] Codified precedents of judges' rulings, show how they interpret these general principles from transnational instruments to create a normative set of rules. In fact, the adjudicatory approach follows the common law's principle of *stare decisis* (precedent rules) although such precedent is not of binding effects in arbitration. It is common knowledge that international arbitration lacks a doctrine of precedent, at least as it is formulated in the common-law system[42].

37.G. CUNIBERTI, préc., note 7.p.422

38.SALEHA HEDARALY, *Under the Infuence? The Use of ICC Arbitral Decisions in Canadian Law*, Montreal les Editions Themis 2015 p.7

39.*Id.*

40.N. BLACKABY et C. PARTASIDIES, préc., note 8., p.205

41 .Article 35 UNCITRAL Model Law 2010 states: "1. The arbitral tribunal shall apply the rules of law designated by the parties as applicable to the substance of the dispute." *UNCITRAL model law on international commercial Arbitration*, revised 2010, en ligne : <http://www.uncitral.org/uncitral/en/uncitral_texts/arbitration/2010Arbitration_rules.html>.consulté le 3 fevrier 2017

42.G. KAUFMANN-KOHLER, préc., note 4.p.357

The arbitral tribunal refers to earlier published decisions to render a judgment, creating a certain predictability in the arbitral process. The adjudicatory approach helps to harmonize versions of lex mercatoria from different sources, such as international instruments and trade usages. Thus, these tribunals play a key role in elaborating transnational principles. As Drahozal submits, International commercial arbitration—as the source of the "new Law Merchant" or *lex mercatoria*—also is identified as an example of a private legal system[43].Legislative and adjudicatory approaches to lex mercatoria are not mutually exclusive. The legislative method often applies concepts from arbitral case law, and the adjudicatory system often harnesses international written instruments to support its reasoning. Lando observes: "The law merchant is still a diffuse and fragmented body of law. It will grow with the growth of uniform laws, international trade customs and usages, and with the increasing number of reported awards."[44] Gaillard proposes approaching these principles as a method of decision-making rather than a list and notes their continuous evolution, so this thesis makes no attempt to identify the general principles of law, nor would that effort advance its arguments.[45]

International arbitration consists of two distinct disciplines: international commercial arbitration and investment arbitration, [46] which routinely overlap and are increasingly converging. They certainly advance similar objectives --globalization, economic integration, trade

---

43.Christopher R. DRAHOZAL, « Private Ordering and International Commercial Arbitration », (2009) 113-4 *Penn State Law Rev.* 1031-1050.p.1036

44.O. LANDO, préc., note 16.p.756

45.E. GAILLARD, «Use of General principles of International Law in International Long-Term Contracts», (1999) 27 *Int'l Business Law, 214-224, p.219*

46.N. BLACKABY et C. PARTASIDIES, préc., note 8.

promotion, and investment protection.[47] It is easy to confuse the two, and some commentators suggest that they may be the same. Is investment arbitration just a form of private commercial arbitration? Or, to put it another way, are investment disputes the same as, or just another form of, private commercial dispute?[48]

The response is important: if they are similar or the same, sources of law such as lex mercatoria and UPICC might well be applicable to both. However, it seems clear that they differ in origins, the nature of their proceedings, and the logic underlying them.

Commentators have responded to these issues in various ways. Hugo Perezcano, for example, has drawn a line between these two contexts of arbitration:[49]"While private commercial arbitration is an alternative means of dispute resolution in which parties seek to escape the judicial system where there are always rigidity, complexities and delays, in investment arbitration there may be no alternative. It may be the only means of resolving certain disputes. There are different criteria and different consequences. They share many commonalities, as well, but if we take a look at the question of remedies, under investment protection agreements in general the remedies available are either monetary compensation or restitution or a combination of both, at investment protection agreements, on the other hand, what is the usual suspect in investment claims is expropriation."

Gary Born writes:"Despite similarities, investment arbitration has characteristics that distinguish it from international commercial arbitration. That is particularly true of arbitrations conducted under the

---

47.Roger P. ALFORD, « The Convergence of International Trade and Investment Arbitration », (2013) 12 *St. Clara J. Int. Law* 36-63.

48.Hugo PEREZCANO, Philippe PINSOLLE et Thomas WALDE, « Damages in Investment Arbitration. Are the Standards different from commercial arbitration? The need for consistency », (2005) 39-6 *J. World Invest. Trade.*39-57.

49.*Id.*

ICSID, *InternationalCentre for Settlement of Investment Disputes*, 1965, but is also generally true of arbitrations under Bilateral Investment Treaties (BITs), NAFTA, and other treaty regimes.[50]

It holds particularly true in the fastest-growing area of international law: international investment law. Indeed, investment treaties have surged from less than 400 in number in 1989 to well over 2,900 bilateral, regional, and sectoral treaties today.[51] Some observers propose that, because investor-state arbitration calls on provisions of investment treaties and public international law, it applies principles relating to damages and remedies differently from private commercial arbitration. Some present UPICC as a set of principles of contract law, optimized for commercial arrangements between private parties. While they do envisage UPICC's possible use in investor-state contracts,[52] its drafters did not design it to regulate disputes about the exercise of sovereign powers, or disputes where the parties sit in an unequal private-versus-public relationship, as in the typical investment-treaty dispute. These differences between the two types of investment and commercial arbitration—one based on a contract and the other on a treaty—have a bearing on the choice of the arbitrators appointed to settle the relevant dispute. Arbitrators dealing with investment contracts are more frequently from a commercial arbitration background, while those dealing with investment treaty arbitration usually have public international law experience. The legal background and practical

50.Gary B. BORN, *International Arbitration: Law and Practice*, Second, Wolter Kluwers, 2016.,p.423

51.Charles N. BROWER et Stephan W. SCHILL, « Is Arbitration a Threat or a Boon to the Legitimacy of International Investment Law? », (2009) 9 *Chic. J. Int. Law* 471-498., G. B. BORN, préc., note 50. professor Gary B. Born has mentioned the number of the BITs as 2,900 in year 2016.

52.Jarrod HEPBURN, « The UNIDROIT Principles of International Commercial Contracts and Investment Treaty Arbitration: A Limited Relationship », (2015) 64-4 *Int. Comp. Law Q.* 905-933. p.929

experience of individual members of an arbitral tribunal may have a bearing on the decision of whether to apply the UPICC[53]. This fact may have somewhat facilitated the process of adaptation of private law (or more specifically contract law) provisions into the ambit of public international law in this particular case (of treaty claim)[54]. For decades, there has been endless debate over whether transnational law does really exist, and whether this general principle, which some see as a newlex mercatoria, can serve as the applicable law in international investment law. Few bilateral investment treaties contain a clause on the applicable law. When they do, they frequently indicate international law, normally in combination with domestic law, with phrases such as "principles," "rules and principles," or "generally recognized rules and principles" of international law.[55]The relationship between 'principles of international law' and 'general principles of law recognized by civilized nations' is somewhat murky. "It is clear that, the former notion includes the rules of international law derived from custom or treaty, while the latter category of principles is derived from domestic legal systems. However, it is submitted that the principles of the second category can gradually come to be recognized as the principles of the former category."[56]Depending on the claim, these obligations can arise under public international law, national law, or under both international and national law simultaneously. In fact, investment arbitration, thus, has much in common with commercial arbitration, but it has an additional

53.Piero BERNARDINI, « UNIDROIT Principles and international investment arbitration », (2014) 19-4 *Unif. Law Rev.* 561–569.p.564

54.Andrea Marco STEINGRUBER, « El Paso v Argentine Republic: UNIDROIT Principles of International Commercial Contracts as a reflection of 'general principles of law recognized by civilized nations' in the context of an investment treaty claim », (2013) 18-3-4 *Unif. Law Rev.* 509–531.

55.T. GAZZINI, préc., note 19., p.112

56.Sergey RIPINSKY, *Damages in International Investment Law*, London, British Institute of International and Comparative Law, 2008., p.44

public international law dimension[57].

Through reliance on general principles, international tribunals have recognized the existence of the number of the international rules relevant to investment disputes[58]. In 1927, the now-defunct Permanent Court of International Justice (PCIJ) in The Hague confirmed the principle of reparation in its judgment in the *Chorzow Factory* case: "It is a principle of international law, and even a general conception of law, that any breach of an engagement involves an obligation to make reparation."[59] Investment arbitral tribunals have frequently applied general principles of law, such as good faith, *res judicatas*, *kompetenz-kompetenz*, claimant's burden of proof, and unjust enrichment.[60] The reference to international law in state contracts surely refers to general principles of law, which seem *ipso facto* to be applicable law

to these contracts.[61]. Clearly general principles have helped shape rules in protecting foreign investment and featured prominently in arbitrations between states and foreign nationals.[62]

57.Giuditta CORDERO-MOSS et Daniel BEHNY, « The relevance of the UNIDROIT Principles in investment arbitration », (2014) 19-4 *Unif. Law Rev.* 570-608.p.572

58.Christopher F. DUGAN, Don WALLACE, Noah RUBINS et Borzu SABAHI, *Investor-State Arbitration*, United States, Oxford University Press, 2008, p. 216.

59.*Chorzow Factory case,(Germany v. Poland) Merits*, [1928] 17 Series A (Permanent Court of International Justice).at 47-48

60. In *Sea-Land Service, Inc. v. the Islamic Republic of Iran*, [1984] 6 _IUSCTR_ 149 (Iran_U"S. Claims Tribunal).p. 168, the Tribunal held that: "the concept of unjust enrichment had its origins in Roman law, it is codified or judicially recognized in the great majority of the municipal legal systems of the world, and is widely accepted as having been assimilated into the category of general principles of law available to be applied by international tribunals."

61.T. GAZZINI, préc., note 19. P.113

62.*Id.*

The borders between principles that apply in commercial disputes and those for investment disputes are fading. For example, the principle of mitigation in transnational instruments appears in arbitrations to limit the damage and impose a duty to damage against the state. The duty to mitigate is a principle of contract law in CISG and UPICC. The International Court of Justice (ICJ) in The Hague used it in an inter-state dispute, referring in the *Gabcikovo-Nagymaros Project* case[63] to "a principle that an injured state which has failed to take the necessary measures to limit the damage sustained would not be entitled to claim compensation for that damage which could have been avoided." Article 38 of the Statute of the International Court of Justice (hereafter ICJ Statute, chapter XIV of the United Nations Charter, 1945)[64] sets out the sources of the rules that the court should apply in deciding disputes in accordance with international law. These sources are, broadly speaking, treaty, custom, general principles of law, and judicial decisions and teachings of highly qualified publicists. Being listed under Article 38(1) of the ICJ Statute as a third source of international law after

---

63.*Gabčikovo-Nagymaros Project, Hungary v Slovakia, Judgment, Merits, ICJ GL No 92, [1997] ICJ Rep 7, [1997] ICJ Rep 88, (1998) 37 ILM 162, ICGJ 66 (ICJ 1997), 25th September 1997, International Court of Justice [ICJ]*

64.Article 38 of statute of International Court of Justice states: "1. The Court, whose function is to decide in accordance with international law such disputes as are submitted to it, shall apply:a. international conventions, whether general or particular, establishing rules expressly recognized by the contesting states; b. international custom, as evidence of a general practice accepted as law;c. the general principles of law recognized by civilized nations; d. subject to the provisions of Article 59, judicial decisions and the teachings of the most highly qualified publicists of the various nations, as subsidiary means for the determination of rules of law. 2. This provision shall not prejudice the power of the Court to decide a case *ex aequo et bono*, if the parties agree thereto." *Statute of international court of justice*, 1945, 3 Bevans 1179, 59 Stat 1055, TS No 993, 3 Bevans 1179,59 Stat1055,TS, No.993, enligne: <http://legal.un.org/ avl/pdf/ha/sicj/icj _statute_e pdf>. accessed 3 May 2017 treaties and customary international law, general principles become applicable in the absence of conventional rules or of rules of customary international law. The motivation for adding 'general principles of law' was the concern over possible 'incompleteness of the other two sources for deciding all cases which would be submitted for decision to the Court[65]. In another investor-state case, we see an ICSID arbitration states: "A duty to mitigate loss is one of the general principles of law which are part of international law."[66] These examples show the mitigation rule to be part of the general principles of law, which count among the rules of international law applicable in disputes.

As with any arbitral process, ICSID arbitration recognizes the principle of party autonomy at all stages of the procedure. The issue of the applicable law in ICSID arbitration follows therefore the general principle recognizing the parties' freedom to select the substantive rules applicable to the merits of the dispute[67]. The first sentence of Article 42(1) of the ICSID Convention refers to 'rules of law' rather than to systems of law. It is generally accepted that the parties are not restricted to agree on a single system of law but, rather, are free to combine, to select, and to exclude rules or sets of rules of different origin[68]. According to article 42 of the ICSID Convention:

"(1) The Tribunal shall decide a dispute in accordance with such rules of law as may be agreed by the parties. In the absence of such agreement, the Tribunal shall apply the law of the Contracting State party to the dispute [including its rules on the conflict of laws] and such rules of international law as may be applicable."

65.Piero BERNARDINI, « Private law and general principles of public international law », (2016) 21-2-3 *Unif. Law Rev.* 184-196.p.186

66.*Middle East Cement Co v Arab Republic of Egypt, ARB/99/6,* [2002] 7 ICSID Reports 174 (ICSID).

67.A. M. STEINGRUBER, préc., note 54.p.513

68.G. CORDERO-MOSS et D. BEHNY, préc., note 57.p.581

In line with this approach, the parties would be free to choose the Principles as the "rules of law" according to which the arbitrators would decide the dispute, with the result that the Principles would apply to the exclusion of any particular national law, subject only to the application of those rules of domestic law which are mandatory irrespective of which law governs the contract. In disputes falling under the ICSID Convention, the Principles might even be applicable to the exclusion of any domestic rule of law[69]. However, the application of the UPICC to investment contracts, as a widely accepted codification of transnational law, may be preferred due to the resistance of foreign parties to subject the contract to the law of the host State (or of the public entity party to the contract) out of fear that such law may be amended in the future to the detriment, of its interests and expectations (a fear that has been called 'ale'a de la souverainete'')[70].

Despite this presence in other fields of law, general principles of law appear seldom in public international law, just occasionally in the decisions of international courts and tribunals.[71]Investment treaties typically do not specify secondary rules, such as the rules that govern the consequences of a breach of treaty and the compensation owing. Tribunals have acknowledged that the content of these secondary rules must come from one of the other sources of international law -- customary international law or general principles of law. This all suggests that UPICC is not a useful source for 'primary rule' general principles of law to apply in an investment-treaty dispute.[72] If UPICC encapsulates

69.Fabrizio MARRELLA, « Choice of Law in Third-Millennium Arbitrations: The Relevance of the UNIDROIT Principles of International Commercial Contracts », (2003) 36-4 *Vanderbilt J. Transnatl. Law* 1138-1188.p.1145

70.P. BERNARDINI, préc., note 53.p.563

71.J. HEPBURN, préc., note 52. P.917

72. The rules on State responsibility may be described as "secondary rules, whereas the law relating to the content and the duration of substantive State obligations is determined by primary rules contained in a multitude of different

general principles of law, then tribunals could validly refer to its principles to fill the treaty or customary gap in specification of secondary rules.[73]Public international law is one possible source for general principles and lex mercatoria. Lord Mustill, who has written incisively and critically about lex mercatoria, refers to Lando's work and finds sources of lex mercatoria in, among others, public international law, uniform laws, general principles of law, rules of international organizations, international customs and usages, standard-form contracts, and reporting of arbitral awards.[74]

Relations between UPICC and international investment law have already received serious academic attention.[75] Professor Bonell submits that with respect to international investment contracts in general, there is no internationally uniform legislation comparable to the CISG. The legal sources are, apart from the domestic law of the host State and the bilateral investment treaties ("BITs"), the individual investment contracts which by their very nature focus on topics related to the particular investment, while neglecting matters of general contract law. Hence the need to identify the legal source for such general contract law[76]. An analysis of the growing body of investment jurisprudence suggests much more use of UPICC than scholars first assumed, although it's not common in investment arbitration, probably because contract

---

instruments and in customary law. James CRAWFORD, « The ILC's Articles on responsibility of states for internationally wrongful acts: Retrospect », (2002) 96-4 *Am. J. Int. Law* 874-890. p.883

73.J. HEPBURN, préc., note 52.P.916

74.Michael MUSTILL, « The New Lex Mercatoria: the First Twenty-Five Years », (1988) 4 *arbitration international* 86.republished in http://www.trans-lex.org/126900

75.J. HEPBURN, préc., note 52. P.906

76.Michael Joachim BONELL, « International Investment Contracts and General Contract Law: a Place for the UNIDROIT Principles of International Commercial Contracts », (2012) 17-1-2 *Unif. Law Rev.* 141–159.p.141

arbitration figures little in that field[77] for which we would blame underestimation of the relevance to it of general principles of law. But if these principles are clearly useful for investment arbitration, surely their role will expand.

The UPICC express principles of contract law, and their applicability may be relevant in two situations: (i) where the UPICC have been chosen as the applicable contract law and (ii) where the UPICC are considered as proof of general principles that are part of international law according to Article 38(1)(c) of the ICJ Statute and they are used to corroborate international law or national law. It is also necessary to examine the extent to which the UPICC may be assimilated to 'rules of law' that govern the dispute, may be applied as a source of international law, as a corroboration of international law, as a corroboration of national law, or as a correction of national law. The comprehensive set of investment arbitration cases referencing the UPICC show that in some cases, they have been used as 'rules of law' applicable to the dispute, as a source of international law or as a corroboration of international law. In investment arbitration case law, there are couple of examples of awards that make reference to the UPICC as an expression of generally recognized principles. There is some cases applying the UPICC directly as a source of international law, and some case law showing the use of the UPICC as corroboration in this context. Generally speaking, application of UPICC in investment arbitration rather than explicit reference to it as substantive law could prove invaluable when parties expressly or implicitly do that, for example, through references to general principles of law, lex mercatoria, or usages. This occurred in the *Lemire v. Ukraine* case,[78] in which an

77.August REINISCH, « The relevance of the UNIDROIT Principles of International Commercial Contracts in international investment arbitration », (2014) 19 *Unif. Law Rev.* 609-622.p.622

78.*Cf Joseph Charles Lemire v Ukraine, ARB/06/18,* [2000] 6 _ICSID Reports_ 59 (ICSID).

ICSID tribunal cited the UPICC preamble, stating that a reference to general principles of law or to lex mercatoria may lead to UPICC's application. The *Lemire* tribunal explicitly stressed this possibility as a negative choice of law, where the parties cannot agree on a specific national law:

"When negotiating the Settlement Agreement, the parties evidently gave thought to the issue of applicable law, and were apparently unable to reach an agreement to apply either Ukrainian or US law. Given the parties' implied negative choice of any municipal legal system, the Tribunal finds that the most appropriate decision is to submit the Settlement Agreement to the rules of international law, and within these, to have particular regard to the UNIDROIT Principles."

Another recent investment award that prominently invoked UPICC and relied on it as supporting argument is the recent *Al-Kharafi v. Libya* case.[79].The tribunal extensively addressed article 7.4.2 of UPICC to support its reasoning that Libyan law entitled the claimant to full compensation, including lost profits. It then noted that UPICC's article 7.4.3(3) gave it broad discretion to determine the actual amount of damages. As commentators have suggested, this kind of supplemental or confirmatory use of UPICC may help tribunals to legitimize their interpretations of and conclusions about national law.[80]The El Paso Arbitral Tribunal sought to find confirmation that a general principle of law recognized by civilized nations on the preclusion of wrongfulness in certain situations exists by relying on the UPICC. The El Paso Tribunal observed that the fact:

"That there is a general principle on the preclusion of wrongfulness in certain situations can hardly be doubted, as is confirmed by the UNIDROIT Principles on International Commercial Contracts,

79.*Mohamed Abdulmohsen Al-Kharafi & Sons Co v Libya*, 2013 Cairo Regional Center for International Commercial Arbitration, en ligne : <https://www.italaw.com/sites/default/files/case-documents/italaw 1554.pdf>.

80.J. HEPBURN, préc., note 52.p.909

a sort of international restatement of the law of contracts reflecting rules and principles applied by the majority of national legal systems.[81]"

Indeed, the Tribunal adapted provisions pertaining to the realm of private law, and more specifically to contract law (that is, the provisions of the UPICC), by considering them suitable for application in the field of investment law—a field of international law[82].In investment law, such a soft-law instrument could provide a contemporary view of the emerging, in several areas settled jurisprudence of international investment law.[83]The recognized sources in article 38 of the ICJ Statute interact with diverse soft-law instruments in various manners. In fact, the interaction between binding legal rules and non-binding (but influential) norms enriches investment law and allows legal decision-makers resorting to soft-law instruments to clarify open-textured terms in treaties or customary law. Legal institutes have been attempting to codify soft law in investment law.[84]The diminishing role of general principles of law in investment law relates to their vagueness. These concerns and the need for certainty and predictability in international investment relations lead to a move away from this less

---

81.*El Paso Energy International Company v Argentine Republic*, 2011 Icsid. *ARB/03/15. 31 October2011. Para 623*

82.A. M. STEINGRUBER, préc., note 54.p.524

83.Andrea K. BJORKLUND et August REINSCH, « introduction: the ILA study group on the role of soft law instruments in international investment law », dans andrea K. BJORKLUND et August REINISCH (dir.), *International Investment Law and Soft Law*, United Kingdom, Edward Elgar, 2012, p. 1-9.

84.*Id.*p.1, the ILA Study Group on the Role of Soft Law Instruments in International Investment Law was established by the ILA Executive Council in November 2008, its mandate was 'to study the development of soft law instruments in international investment law and the feasibility of a "codification" of the present state of this field of international economic law'. It had concluded its work with the publication of the Oxford Handbook on International Investment Law ,2008, which addressed major issues of both substantive and procedural investment law.

certain source of law.[85]Whereas general principles are grounded by their nature on the internal legal system of States, two being the conditions for their application as general principles of international law. First, they must exist and be uniformly applied in the great majority of States; second, they must be felt as obligatory or necessary also from the point of view of international law, meaning that they must be felt to pursue values and impose conduct that States also consider has to be pursued and imposed, or at least necessary, at the international level[86]. It is Worth noting that rules of national contract law do not necessarily have the ability of being elevated to the level of general principles of public international law, at least not the specific technical aspects of the rules, (for example, their scope of application, the modalities of their exercise, and the specific legal effects[87] According to professor Christoph Schreuer, it is possible for parties to completely internationalize an investment contract 'by referring exclusively to international law, to general principles of law or to a set of usages customarily governing like transactions.' Therefore, the simple circumstance that a rule is contained in the PICC is not sufficient proof that it is a general principle recognized in most legal systems. It is therefore necessary to distinguish the rules that express generally recognized principles from the rules that do not. It might be reasonable to conclude that some (but not all) of the principles established in the UPICC would qualify as general principles of law that could be applied as a source of international law in investment arbitration, provided that they are adapted to become suitable for application on the level of public international law. In this context, Schreuer states: "General principles of law are not an expression of general feelings of justice or equity but are part of the body of

---

85.Moshe HIRSCH, « sources of international investment law », dans Andrea K. BJORKLUND et August REINISCH (dir.), *international investment law and soft law*, United Kingdom, Edward Elgar, 2012.p.28

86.P. BERNARDINI, préc., note 65.p.187

87.G. CORDERO-MOSS et D. BEHNY, préc., note 57.p.586

international law which, in a particular case, must be proven and not presumed. This proof must be furnished on the basis of rigorous examination, if not all systems of law at least the most important major representative systems[88]." Where international law is applied directly, to the extent that the UPICC may be used as proof of the existence of general principles, they may become applicable as international law, provided that they are suitable for application as international law[89]. Actually, general principles of law could help overcome the fictions between the public international law framework and the private law dispute settlement if those engaged in investor-state arbitrations do not only consider general principles of law, but recognize the potential of general principles of public law to reshape investment arbitration[90].Regardless of the interaction between UPICC and domestic law as the confirmatory or interpretive role of principles, or the possibility of directly choosing principles in arbitrating treaty disputes, this study tries to examine the capability of the general principles of law, in particular UPICC, for being the substantive law in international investment arbitration. The fact that international law lacks a central law-making body has given international tribunals a central role in establishing international legal principles, defining their scope and content, and developing new concepts.[91]

What then of the precedential value of previous decisions by investment tribunals? Article 59 of the ICJ Statute, as well as article 1136 of the North American Free Trade Agreement (NAFTA), clearly rejects

---

88.Christoph H. SCHREUER, *The ICSID Convention: A Commentary*, Second, New York, Cambridge University Press, 2009.p.610

89.G. CORDERO-MOSS et D. BEHNY, préc., note 57.p.607

90.Stephan W. SCHILL, « General Principles of Law and International Investment Law », dans Tarcisio GAZZINI et Eric BRABANDERE (dir.), *International Investment Law, the Sources of Rights and Obligations*, USA, Martinus Nijhoff Publishers, 2012.133-181, p.136

91.S. RIPINSKY, préc., note 56.,p.46

the doctrine of precedent in international law.[92] Although these texts consider "judicial decisions" as only a "subsidiary" source of public international law, almost all investment awards include numerous references to prior decisions of investment tribunals. Notwithstanding tribunals' statements rejecting precedent, investment tribunals are likely to follow the accretion of rulings on the same subject matter (in similar circumstances) and to develop *jurisprudence constante* (the persuasive role of earlier decisions) to enhance stability and predictability in this sphere. The central issue is that, the investment tribunal decisions are themselves a source of applicable law that can be persuasive but nonbinding[93]. On the other hand, the practice of investment tribunals affects the evolution of international law in a number of ways. Even, it may be more appropriate to speak of the influence of tribunal practice on international law. One area is the drafting of treaties. The more recent treaties in the field of investment protection display a number of features that are clearly in reaction to tribunal practice. This influence of judicial practice on the development of treaty law is actually quite

92. Article 59 of the ICJ Statute states: "The decision of the Court has no binding force except between the parties and in respect of that the disputing parties and in respect of the particular case." *statute of international court of justice*, 1945, en ligne :
<http://legal.un.org/avl/pdf/ha/sicj/icj_statute_e.pdf>.Prec note,64. Also article 1136 of NAFTA states: "1. An award made by a Tribunal shall have no binding force except between the disputing parties and in respect of the particular case" *North America Free Trade Agreement (NAFTA)*, 1994, R.T. Can. n.2en ligne :
<http://www.international.gc.ca/trade-agreements-accords-commerciaux/agr-acc/nafta-alena/text-texte/11.aspx?lang=eng>. *accessed 2 February 2015.*,

93.C. F. DUGAN, D. WALLACE, N. RUBINS et B. SABAHI, préc., note 58, p. 217.

complex. On some points, the treaty drafters take guidance from tribunal practice[94].

Respecting the principle of confidentiality in international arbitration, the tribunals do not publish their arbitral awards and keep them secret even from members of the trade. The reporting of arbitral awards has been a crucial element in the development of the law merchant.[95] For the first time in the practice of international arbitration, a tribunal --the Iran_United States Claims Tribunal –must publish its decisions, revealing a type of material never before available in such volume and variability.[96] So far, 38 volumes have appeared and are widely available in most universities.[97] After large-scale nationalization in Iran following the Islamic Revolution of 1979, the Iran-U.S. Claims Tribunal emerged in 1981 to settle nearly four thousand claims that American companies laid against Iran, relating mostly to expropriation and contracts. As the statistics on the tribunal's official website reveal, the tribunal has finalized 3,936 cases in investor-state claims and rendered 881 awards, partial awards, decisions, and awards on agreed terms. This constituted the largest case load ever for international arbitration in investor-state disputes. Lilich has described it as the most

---

94.Christoph SCHREUER, « The Development of International Law by ICSID Tribunals », (2016) 31-3 *ICSID Rev.* 728–739.p.737

95.O. LANDO, préc., note 16., G. CUNIBERTI, préc., note 7.p.396

96.AIDA AVANESSIAN, *Iran-United States Claims Tribunal in Action* Great Bretain Martinus Nijhoff, 1993 , p.6

97 .Article 32 of the Tribunal Rules of Procedure provides that: "5) All awards and other decisions shall be made available to the public."FULL TRIBUNAL OF IRAN_UNITED STATES CLAIMS, *tribunal rules of procedure*, 3 mai 1983, enligne :<http://www.iusct.net/General%20Documents/5TRIBUNAL%20RULES%20OF%20PROCEDURE.pdf.Since, 1983 the *GrotiousPublications* of the University of Cambridge began to publish a collection entitled Iran-United States Claims Tribunal Reports (IUSCTR) respecting the rule set out in the constituting act of the Tribunal.

notable achievement in the law on international claims in the second half of the 20th century. The tribunal has handed down a number of significant awards involving compensation and valuation issues.[98]

The broad formulation of article V of the tribunal's Claim Settlement Declaration (Algiers Accords, 1981) –its constitutive instrument --has permitted it to search out authority pretty much where the tribunal applies general principles of law in its judgments. Berger points out the tribunal's role in the emergence of general principles: "In spite of the particular political situation which has surrounded the decision-making of this Tribunal, these awards continue a most valuable quarry for the development and practical application of general principles of law."[99]

The tribunal routinely applies general principles of transnational law, which it has greatly helped to develop because the judges tend to agree on this. However, the tribunal did not apply UPICC directly in its arguments[100] till 2014, when it finally appeared in a final award issued in an interstate claim[101]. In this award to determine the interest rate, in proposing the prime bank lending rate in the United States as the rate of interes applicable in the investment dispute, the Tribunal was mindful of Article 7.4.9 (2) of the UNIDROIT Principles 2010, when held:

98.Richard B. LILLICH, *the Valuation of Nationalized Property in International law*, IV, United States, University Press of Virgiana, 1987.p.xii

99.Klaus Peter BERGER, *The Creeping Codification of the Next Lex Mercatoria*, Second, Great Bretain, Wolters Kluwer, 2010.p.86

100.Charles N. BROWER et Jeremy K. SHARPE, « The Creeping Codification of Transnational Commercial Law:An Arbitrator's Perspective », (2004) 45-1 *Va. J. Int. LAW* 199-220.p.211

101.*Iran v United States, A15, [2014] Award No. 602-A15(IV)/A24-FT published on the tribunal official website en ligne: <http://www.iusct.net/General%20Documents/AWARD/4AJoint%20Separate%20Opinion%20IR%20Members%2001%2007%202014%20(Final).pdf>*.15.para.4

"288. Accordingly, having considered all relevant circumstances and the submissions made, in the present Cases, the Tribunal deems it fair and reasonable to award Iran simple prejudgment interest on all amounts awarded to Iran .... In selecting the prime bank lending rate in the United States as the rate of interest applicable in these cases, the Tribunal was also mindful of Article 7.4.9 (2) of the UNIDROIT Principles 2010, which provides: The rate of interest shall be......."

This stipulation in tribunal language denotes the tendency of this tribunal to invoking the rules of UPICC as the rules of international law which could be applied independently. The application of UPICC by Iran_U.S. Claims Tribunal supports this statement that, disputes arising out of bilateral or multilateral investment treaties may also prove fertile ground for the application of the UNIDROIT Principles, especially considering the explicit role given to general principles of international law in the resolution of disputes arising under those treaties[102].This study chose compensation to examine from the long list of general principles of law that the tribunal has considered. I had two major reasons for selecting compensation respecting its great value as a remedy and its crucial role in expropriation and commercial disputes.

First, the right to claim damages is the single most valuable remedy available under CISG[103]and UPICC. Indeed, of all the articles in the CISG, those on damages and payment of interest generate the most litigation and comment. The lack of uniform rules in this area is particularly problematic.[104] The judges' varying approaches mean that parties in similar situations may receive significantly different results. With damages under customary international law, the very general

---

102.C. N. BROWER et J. K. SHARPE, préc., note 100.p.212

103.Bruno ZELLER, *Damages under the CISG*, Second, New York, Oxford University Press, 2008.p.66

104.John Y. GOTANDA, « Awarding Damages Under the United Nations Convention on the International Sale of Goods: A Matter of Interpretation », (2006) 37 *Goergetown J. Int. Law*.95-140.p.130

international rules on compensation introduce subjectivity and discretion to application of the legal principles. These factors significantly impede emergence of a uniform and consistent jurisprudence.[105] The CISG remedy of damages has given rise to a number of problems that are either unresolved or that judges and arbitrators have dealt with in a non-uniform manner.[106] However, any arbitration process could result in the award of damages, which the arbitrator must decide.

Second, compensation plays a leading role in the tribunal's practice vis-à-vis expropriation and commercial disputes. Due to the relatively small number of cases, the trend of law concerning the calculation of damages under investor-State arbitration is sometimes not clear enough to be established as a strong precedent[107].

In expropriation, the standards of compensation and the valuation method are somewhat clear now because of arbitral awards by various 20th-century authorities on nationalization and the jurisprudence particularly of the Iran-U.S. Claims Tribunal.[108] This study has two major objectives: first, to understand how international arbitration interprets and applies the general principle of compensation, and, second, to evaluate the efficiency and effectiveness of the UNIDROIT Principles of International Commercial Contracts (UPICC), particularly its damage rules, in investor-state arbitrations. Indeed, proper evaluation of any legal mechanism requires examination of its

---

105.Sergey RIPINSKY, « Assessing Damages in Investment Disputes: Practice in Search of Perfect », (2009) 10 *J. World Invest. Trade*.P.5

106.Djakhongir SAIDOV, « Damages: The Need for Uniformity », (2006) 26-7 *J. Law Commer.* 393-403.,p.393

107.Alex LO, « Determining Damages in ICSID Arbitration: A Problem of Uncertainty », (2013) 6-1 *Contemp. Asia Arbitr. J.* 75-105.p.80

108.Tamada DAI, « Assessing Damages in Non-Expropriation Cases Before International Investment Arbitration », (2009) 52 *Jpn. Yearb. Int. Law*.309-334., P.309

actual application. We can best assess the general-principles method by exploring its use in arbitral practice.[109]

General principles of law are so broad as to be of little practical utility except to give comfort to an arbitrator or respectability to his or her award. For instance, the principle *pacta sunt servanda* (agreements must honoured) is gospel everywhere, but what we need to know is the circumstances in which a party may *not* perform. The principle of *rebus sic stantibus* (things thus standing) is fine as a general principle, but too vague to be of much practical use.[110] Compensation, like all such principles, is easy to state but much more difficult to apply to the facts of a particular case. What many people may not realize, however, is how much the decisions and precedents of the Iran-U.S. Claims Tribunal have helped to forge the internationally accepted principles of commercial law, or lex mercatoria. Until relatively recently, a pattern of repetitive behaviour among merchants was not sufficient to give an international trade usage normative force. There had to be general acceptance that they acted that way from a sense of legally binding obligation, not from mere courtesy, convenience, or expediency.[111] The correct way to establish this transformation is to study arbitration awards to see whether such conduct had become a binding rule in arbitration. Obviously, any attempt to justify application of the general principles requires examination of their efficiency in investment arbitration. Investment arbitration deals principally with expropriation matters, which are part of international law and have no relationship with UPICC and the principles of contract law.

Generally, the lack of certainty and predictability of legal rules has limited the applicability of the lex mercatoria in international arbitration. In any event, assessments of certainty and clarity can be

---

109.E. GAILLARD, préc., note 45, p.221

110.R. GOODE, préc., note 23.p.18

111.*Id.*

somewhat subjective and are often unrealizable illusions in a rapidly changing world.[112] None the less, in international commercial disputes, predictability is a central component of the applicable law. Christopher Drahozal, in his article published in 2005, concluded that the data on the contractual practices of international merchants suggests that lex mercatoria has simply lost practical significance, if it ever had any[113].Again, he states, In the overwhelming number of cases, parties to international arbitration agreements reject the option of having their dispute resolved under privately developed commercial rules, the so-called new law merchant or lex mercatoria. Instead, they choose to have their dispute resolved under publicly created laws[114].

This study attempts to probe the doctrine of lex mercatoria has significance and it remains very much alive, and applicable in international dispute resolution. to resort to lex mercatoria in cases where the parties have remained silent on the law governing their contract, and significantly shows that arbitrators regularly resort to the contents of lex mercatoria as the general principles of law. The UNIDROIT Principles do not provide any express definition, but the assumption is that the concept of "commercial" contracts should be understood in the broadest possible sense, so as to include not only trade transactions for the supply or exchange of goods or services, but also other types of economic transactions, such as investment and/or concession agreements, contracts for professional services, etc[115]. The rules of the PICC do not expressly refer to procurement contracts or

---

112.JH DALHUISEN, « legal order and their manifestation: the operation of the international commercial and financial legal order and its lex mercatoria », (2006) 24 *berkeley journal of international law* 129-191.p.154

113.Christopher R. DRAHOZAL, « Contracting out of National Law: An Empirical Look at the New Law Merchant », (2005) 80-2 *Notre Dame Law REeview* 523-552.p.551

114.C. R. DRAHOZAL, préc., note 43.p.1033

115.F. MARRELLA, préc., note 69.p.1144

States as parties to a contract, and the comment on the preamble also does not mention the problem. True, it is assumed that contracts subject to investment arbitration under the International Centre for Settlement of Investment Disputes (ICSID) may be governed by the UPICC[116]. This study will assess to what extent the UPICC have been or may be used as 'rules of law' that govern the dispute, as a source of international law, as corroboration of international law. The method of this study consists of refining and determining the jurisprudence of the Iran-U.S. Claims Tribunal on compensation and comparing it with the compensation rules in UPICC and CISG. It is not the purpose of this study to survey the law of damage in international arbitration. Instead the focus will be on the exploration of some central aspects of the law of damages as discussed in the practice of Iran-U.S. claims tribunal.

Therefore, the method of this current study consists of comparative study of the practice of the Iran_United States Claims Tribunal, where the complaint has been awarded either compensation or damages, and the rules of such transnational instruments as the United Nations Convention on Contracts for the International Sale of Goods (Vienna, 1980), or CISG, and the UNIDROIT Principles of International Commercial Contracts (2010), or UPICC, which have helped to make more certain and predictable law for international arbitral tribunals to apply. In this regard the study applied a functionalist comparative method in this part[117]. Because the awards of the Iran_U.S.

116.Oliver REMIEN, « Public law and public policy in international commercial contracts and the UNIDROIT Principles of International Commercial Contracts 2010: a brief outline », (2013) 18-2 *Unif. Law Rev.* 262-280.p.266

117.Ralf MICHAELS, « The Functional Method of Comparative Law », (2005) paper 26 *Duke Law Sch. Fac. Scholarsh. Ser.* 1-47, 37., the author emphesisis on" the ability of this method to reveal which of different laws is the best, regardless of doctrinal constructions, and second, its ability to guide the process of writing an optimal uniform law that overcomes and transcends the doctrinal peculiarities of local legal systems."

Claims Tribunal fall within investment arbitration and obviously relate to international law, this study also considers the relevant articles in International Law Commission (ILC) Draft Articles on the Responsibility of States for Intentionally Wrongful Acts (2001).[118] This last set of rules serves as a major resource on international law of compensation. As Sergey Ripinsky observes, it offers the best guidance on the international law of compensation in investor-state disputes.[119] When there is a "legal vacuum" of authority on an issue, courts and arbitral panels will turn to whatever is available. In that situation, the ILC document is extremely influential, perhaps even more than any treaty.[120] In addition, the study will take into account World Bank Guidelines on the Treatment of Foreign Direct Investment (1992), to compare its provisions with the contents of the tribunal's decisions. This non-binding document outlines useful parameters in the admission and treatment of private foreign investment in the territories of World Bank member countries.[121] These instruments –ILC Draft Articles, and World Bank Guidelines; fulfil three major functions in investment jurisprudence: they can help interpret ambiguous provisions in international treaties, fill gaps in existing international investment law, and support legal findings arising from other sources of investment law, such as treaty or customary law. Therefore, this study employs these

---

118.*International Law Commission, Draft articles on Responsibility of States for Internationally Wrongful Acts*, 10 novembre 2001, en ligne : <http://legal.un.org/ilc/texts/instruments/english/commentaries/9_6_2001.pdf> (consulté le 8 janvier 2018).

119.S. RIPINSKY, préc., note 56., P 43

120.DavidD. CARON, « The ILC Articles on State Responsibility: The Paradoxical Relationship Between Form and Authority », (2002) 96 *Am. J. Int. Law*. 857-873, P.857

121.*world Bank Guideline on the Treatment of Foreign Direct Investment*, 1992, volume 2, en ligne : <http://documents.worldbank.org/curated/pt/955221468766167766/pdf/multi-page.pdf>.accessed 3 May 2017 instruments to analyse and/or support the tribunal's position in awarding compensation.

This study consists of six chapters, five of which examine the subject matters of damage in the tribunal's practice. Chapter one examines the genesis and the legal structure of the Iran-United States Claims Tribunal. Chapter two identifies the main approaches to standard of compensation, in order to reveal how many concepts of compensation can be at play in arbitration. This analysis is important because of the ambiguity and uncertainty surrounding the duty to full compensation. Chapter three reviews the factors that limit awards of compensation, because limiting damages reduces the liability in damages. This analysis relates limiting damages to the general measure of damages. Generally, the tribunal recognizes the legal concepts of causation, foreseeability, certainty, and mitigation as the criteria for measuring damage. Chapter four examines the general concepts of *damnum emergens*, or suffered loss, and *lucrum cessans*, or damages arising and profits lost, in the tribunal's jurisprudence. Actually, these concepts appear widely in many systems of civil law, which frequently apply them to determine heads of damages potentially available for breach of contract and tort claims and to isolate remedies for wrongful acts. We also seek to ascertain which heads of damages the tribunal treats as compensable. Chapter five reviews the tribunal's methods of valuation of damage, particularly assessment of expropriated assets. Although the valuation methods are a kind of accounting, the tribunal argued that they were crucial to assessing the recoverability of lost profits, lost revenue, and future prospects. Chapter six considers the subject matter of interest on damage in the tribunal's practice. The tribunal has wrestled with the problematic issue of its authority to award interest and the complicated, related issues of the rate of interest, the accrual period, and the form of interest. The Conclusion presents a general assessment of the theory of this study and draws several conclusions in the light of the issues it examined.

Chapter One

The Iran-United States Claims Tribunal

1.1 General

In the period from 1955 to 1978, commercial and economic cooperation between Iran and United States grew rapidly. After the two nations signed the Treaty of Amity, Economic Relations, and Consular Rights in 1955[122], complex business relationships developed, leading to the investment of billions of dollars in Iran. By the time of the Iranian Revolution in 1979, U.S. economic interests in Iran were both significant and conspicuous. American military sales to Iran peaked in 1977 at nearly $6 billion, and U.S. oil companies owned 40 per cent of the multinational consortium that controlled the purchase of Iranian oil. A bilateral agreement of 1976 predicted that non-oil and non-military trade between the two countries would reach $15 billion by 1981.[123]

Economic relations were strongest in military equipment and investment in oil industries.[124]The framework consisted usually of state contracts or investment agreements between U.S. companies, the Iranian government, its agencies, or state-owned companies acting on its behalf,

---

122.*Treaty of Amity, Economic Relations, and Consular Rights. Signed at Tehran, on 15 August 1955, between Iran and United States,Treaty Series, Volume 284, 1957,1958, Secretariat of the United Nations*, en ligne : <https://treaties.un.org/doc/Publication/UNTS/Volume%20284/v284.pdf>.consulté le 3 fevrier 2017

123.Kate GILLESPIE, « U.S. corporations and Iran at the Hague », (1990) 44-1 *Middle East J.* 18-36.

124.Charles N. BROWER et Jason D. BRUESCHKE, *The Iran - United States Claims Tribunal*, the Hauge, Martinus Nijhoff Publications, 1998.p.4

and foreign investors, usually multinational companies, and most related to oil, mining, or other industries in Iran. Beginning in 1977 civil unrest increased in Iran, and oil, gas, and most sectors of other industries went on strike. This civil unrest eventually entailed led to a revolution that overthrow the monarchy, and a new government came to power in February 1979. This period saw mass demonstrations, political disturbances, and strikes and riots. Strikes disrupted key industries, including oil production and processing and banking,

Naturally, it became difficult for U.S. companies to operate normally and to carry out routine business transactions. Therefore, many American businesses evacuated the dependents of their employees. However, when the situation continued to deteriorate, the bulk of U.S. operations withdrew most or all of their employees in December 1978 and January 1979. In fact, by late December 1978, most had suspended activities in Iran, and many employees returned to the United States.[125]

The new government initiated steps to bring the economy more under its control. In June 1979 it embarked on a systematic program of nationalization. The governing revolutionary council took over banks on 7 June 1979 and insurance companies on 25 June. In addition, it seized all metal production, ship building, and the automotive and aircraft industries. The new constitution of July 1982 grants the state ownership of and exclusive right to administer all the major mines and industries. According to its principle 44:

"The economy of the Islamic Republic of Iran is to consist of three sectors: First, the state sector is to include all large-scale and mother industries, foreign trade, major minerals, banking, insurance, power generation, dams and large-scale irrigation networks, radio and television, post, telegraph and telephone services, aviation, shipping,

---

125.George H. ALDRICH, *The Jurisprudence of the Iran-United States Claims Tribunal*, New York, Oxford University Press, 1996.also,C. N. BROWER et J. D. BRUESCHKE, préc., note 124.p.4

roads, railroads and the like; all these will be publicly owned and administered by the State.,"[126]

One event in this era crystallized the estrangement between Iran and the United States and brought it to a head. The Islamic revolution was characterized by strong anti-American rhetoric. Iranian students occupied the U.S. embassy in Tehran in November 1979 and took the staff as hostages. Although strikes and unrest had halted many American firms' commercial projects since 1977, the hostage crisis ended all political and economic cooperation between these two states.

Because of the vast and costly business disruptions and the scale of private claims brought by U.S. corporations, the Iranian judiciary refused to adjudicate the claims or to recognize their government as a party to thousands of contracts. It is a general principle that a simple breach of contract by a state does not create international responsibility for it unless there has been a denial of justice. A denial of justice will arise if the alien is unable to gain access to the courts or if the judicial system operates so as to preclude a legitimate settlement of the claim.[127]

Various of the parties involved soon began to feel the need to set up some sort of central body to address all these claims. On January 19, 1981, an arbitral tribunal to resolve the claims between the two states and their nationals is established by the signed accord between Iran and United States. It is still operating over 35 years later –the longest-lasting such body ever. International jurists seem to agree that the tribunal's cases and awards offer a rich new avenue to examine international commercial arbitration. This chapter briefly reviews the tribunal's structure, the relevant law, and the decisions' contribution to international arbitration practice.

---

126 .The *constitution act of the Islamic Republic of Iran*, 1982, en ligne : <https://www.constituteproject.org/constitution/Iran_1989.pdf?lang=en>.consulté le 6 fevrier 2017

127.Wayne MAPP, *The Iran-United States Claims Tribunal, The first ten years*, Manchester, Manchester University Press, 1993.p.115

1.2 The Algiers Accords (1981)

After three years' negotiation and with mediation by the republic of Algeria, the U.S. and Iranian governments signed the Iran-United States Accord on 19 January 1981, which set up the Iran-United States Claims Tribunal to settle all private and public disputes have been raised after revolution between these two states. One could call it the biggest financial deal in history to that time.[128] In simple terms, Iran agreed to release the U.S. hostages, while the United States promised to effect the return of Iranian assets and dismiss litigation against Iran in American courts.[129] Some authors believe that based on the nature of the Algier Accord that advance a resolution system to decide on the investment claims, this accord could be regarded as a retroactive BIT. Caron submits that the Claims Settlement Declaration should be treated as a 'retrospective-bilateral investment treaty-BIT'. The supposed similarities between the Declaration and BITs are based on analogies of form rather than application of substantive principles[130].

The Algerian government issued two declarations to which Tehran and Washington adhered. First, the General Declaration provided for the release of the hostages in return for U.S. undertakings to nullify attachments of Iranian capital in U.S banks and cease litigation against Iran in its courts. Second, the Claims Settlement Declaration established the Iran-United States Claims Tribunal to resolve various

---

128.C. N. BROWER et J. D. BRUESCHKE, préc., note 124.p.6

129.*Declaration of the government of the democratic and popular republic of Algeria*, _IUSCTR_ Vol.1 (1981).Article.6

130.David D. CARON, « The Iran_U.S. Claim Tribunal and Investment: Arbitration: Understanding the Claims Settlement Declaration as a Retroactive BIT », dans Christopher R. DRAHOZAL et Christopher S. GIBSON (dir.), *The Iran_U.S. Claim Tribunal at 25, the cases everyone needs to know for investor-state & international arbitration*, United States, Oxford University Press, 2007.375-385, p.383

claims resulting from Iranian expropriations and breach of commercial contracts. The next day, 20 January 1981, the New York Federal Reserve Bank and overseas branches of U.S. banks transferred eight billion dollars to an escrow account, and Iran released the hostages.[131]

The new claims tribunal would hear and adjudicate claims by U.S. nationals against Iran and also certain claims by Iranian nationals against Washington and between the two governments[132]. Accordingly, the United States also waived its right to proceed further against Iran before the International Court of Justice in The Hague. The claims tribunal would settle the related claims of Iran and the United States through binding third-party arbitration: "Claims referred to the arbitration Tribunal shall, as of the date filing of such claims with the Tribunal, be considered excluded from the jurisdiction of the Courts of Iran, or of the United States, or of any other Court.[133]"

1.3 Genesis of the Iran-U. S. Claims Tribunal

Article 1 of the Claims Settlement Declaration[134] provided nine months for filing claims with the tribunal, until 19 October 1981. All claims had to be filed with the tribunal by 19 January 1982. Applicants filed approximately 3,816 claims before the deadline. These included

131.C. N. BROWER et J. D. BRUESCHKE, préc., note 124.p.7

132.Robert B. VON MEHREN, « The Iran-U.S. arbitral tribinal », (1983) 31-3 *Am. J. Comp. Law* 713-730.p.715

133.ALGIERS ACCORDS, *Claims Settlement Declaration*, préc., note 129. article.VII

134 .Id. Article I of Claims Settlement Declaration states: "Iran and the United States will promote the settlement of the claims described in Article II by the parties directly concerned. Any such claims not settled within six months from the date of entry into force of this Agreement shall be submitted to binding third-party arbitration in accordance with the terms of this Agreement. The aforementioned six months' period may be extended once by three months at the request of either party." préc., note 129

965 'large' B cases ($250,000 or more) and 2,782 'small' B claims (less than $250,000), and 69 'B' cases (disputes directly between the two governments) In addition, 24 A cases --disputes about interpretation of or compliance with the accords, have been filed.

There seems to be no precise count of the total of the claims brought before the tribunal, but Westberg writes: "The total dollar value of all claims has been estimated to be as high as $60 billion."[135]However, a communiqué of May 9, 2016[136]on the tribunal's official website reveals that it had finalized 3,936 cases and rendered 881 awards, partial awards, decisions, and awards on agreed terms.

The lump-sum settlement –an Award on Agreed Terms from the tribunal on June 22, 1990 --provided for the "full, final and definitive settlement" of certain small claims against Iran, pending before the tribunal in return for Iran's paying a comprehensive lump-sum amount of $105 million. The U.S. Department of Justice's Foreign Claims Settelment Commission (FCSC) adjudicated the Iran claims program from June 1990 to February 1995. Of the roughly 3,100 claims the FCSC received, it issued 1,066 awards to 1,075 claimants, totalling $41,570,936.31 in principal and $44,984,859.31 in interest. It dismissed 578 claims, either at the request of the claimants or because it could not locate the claimants. It denied the remaining 1,422 claims.[137]

Obviously, the tribunal's task was daunting Lillich states: "In recent history no arbitral tribunal has faced the enormous task now

---

135. 1983-1984 Tribunal annual report recited in John A. WESTBERG, *International Transactions and Claims involving Government Practice, Case Law of The Iran -United States Claims Tribunal*, Washington, D.C., International Law Institute, 1991.p.12

136.*Communique regarding the work of the Tribunal*, 16/1, 2016, en ligne : <https://www.iusct.net/Pages/Public/A-News.aspx>.consulte 2 fevrier 2017

137.Richard B. Lillich and David J. BEDERMAN, « Jurisprudence of the Foreign Claims Settelment Commission: Iran Claims », (1997) 91-3 *Am. J. Int. Law*.p.436

before the Tribunal."[138]The disputes arose out of Iran's cancellation of its own state contracts, which brought to the fore the complexities of disputes over long-term contracts. Generally, these claims arose because of Iranian expropriation of American assets in Iran and that country's breach of commercial contracts between American nationals and its own government entities, including contracts for sales, construction, and BOT (build-operate-transfer). "There are other important international and commercial issues that have faced the Tribunal. These include whether and when a nationalization or expropriation had occurred, and if it had, the standard of compensation; the validity and effect of monetary exchange controls; the application of the doctrine of force majeure; the effect of exchange rates; the ascertainment of damage remedies; the effect of forum selection clauses; and which laws to apply to a transaction."[139]

1.4 The Tribunal's Structure

The tribunal consists of nine members: Iran and the United States each appoint three; those six people name the other three, who come from third countries. The nine members sit in three separate chambers, each consisting of an American, an Iranian, and a third-country member, to hear and decide the claims. The nine sit together as a full tribunal to decide questions of interpretation of the accords and of basic legal issues common to a number of claims.[140]

138.Richard B. LILICH, *The Iran-United States Claims Tribunal, 1981-1983*, United States, the University Press of Virginia, 1984.p.87

139.Nagla NASSER, *sanctity of contracts revisited*, Netherlands, Kluwer publishers, 1995.p.187

140.J. A. WESTBERG, préc., note 135.p.5, Article III of the 'Claims Settlement Declaration' states: "The Tribunal shall consist of nine members or such larger multiple of three as Iran and the United States may agree are necessary to conduct its business expeditiously. Within ninety days after the entry into force of this Agreement, each government shall appoint one-third of the members.

The Iranian and American members met for the first time at the Peace Palace in The Hague on May 18, 1981[141]. On October 19, 1981, the tribunal's Swedish president, Gunnar Lagergren divided the tribunal's members into three chambers and directed that they should hear all cases. The deadline for filing virtually all claims other than interpretive disputes was January19, 1982.[142] The Claims Settlement Declaration (Algiers Accords) has provided practical machinery for enforcing the tribunal's awards. Following its agreement with the United States in 1981, Iran deposited $1 billion in a third-party escrow account. This 'special security' account was held in escrow by the Central Bank of Algeria, along with a subsidiary of the Central Bank of the Netherlands, and was available to pay awards the tribunal made to U.S. claimants. Iran agreed to replenish this account as necessary to maintain a minimum balance of $500 million[143].

1.5 The Tribunal's Jurisdiction

Generally, the Algiers Accords of 1981 clearly laid out the tribunal's jurisdiction. Article II of the Claims Settlement Declaration states:

"The tribunal is established for the purpose of deciding claims of nationals of the United States against Iran and claims of nationals of Iran against the United States, and any counterclaim which arises out of

---

Within thirty days after their appointment, the members so appointed shall by mutual agreement select the remaining third of the members and appoint one of the remaining third President of the Tribunal. Claims may be decided by the full Tribunal or by a panel of three members of the Tribunal as the President shall determine. Each such panel shall be composed by the President and shall consist of one member appointed by each of the three methods set forth above." ALGIERS ACCORDS, *Claims Settlement Declaration*, 19 janvier 1981.

141.G. H. ALDRICH, préc., note 125., p.6

142.*Claims Settlement Declaration*, préc., note 129., article III

143.R. B. VON MEHREN, préc., note 132.p.720

the same contract, and also over official claims of the United States and Iran against each other arising out of contractual arrangements between them. The Tribunal's principal subject matter jurisdiction covers claims arising out of "debt, contracts (including transactions which are the subject of letter of credit or bank guarantees), expropriation or other measures affecting property rights."

The tribunal's jurisdiction regarding dispute parties *(*ratione personae*)* is dealt with in claims of the Unites States nationals against the Government of Iran and the Claims of two States against each other [144]. In the tribunal's first interpretive case, *Iran v. The United States, Case A/2,*[145] the judges determined that they had no jurisdiction to hear claims by Iranian government entities against U.S. nationals, even though Iran could make a counter-claim against any U.S. national that made a claim against Iran. As a result, Iran withdrew 1,330 claims from the tribunal. Generally, regarding the subject matter Jurisdiction (ratione materii), claims that fall within the tribunal's jurisdiction relate to one of three categories claims arising out of debt, out of contract, and/or out of expropriation.[146]The most crucial issue that raised the controversies in setting up the tribunal was the matter of applicable law. The applicable law in the tribunal as the substantive law governing disputes constitutes a unique feature of the tribunal. This matter is examined in next paragraphs.

144.C. N. BROWER et J. D. BRUESCHKE, préc., note 124.P.26

145.*Iran v United states, Case A/2,* [1982] 1 -IUSCTR- 102 (Iran_U.S. Claims Tribunal).

146 .Article II of Claim Settlement Declaration states: "2. The Tribunal shall also have jurisdiction over official claims of the United States and Iran against each other arising out of contractual arrangements between them for the purchase and sale of goods and services."*Claims Settlement Declaration*, préc., note 129.

1.6 The Applicable Law

The characteristic that most distinguishes the tribunal from any other international arbitral tribunal is its great discretion in being able to apply the general principles of law. During negotiations leading to the Algiers Accords, the Iranians understandably opposed the application of U.S. law or any other national law except that of Iran, and the Americans rejected Iranian law because of uncertainty over what that law might be. Yet both sides apparently agreed quickly to the following language in article V[147]: "The Tribunal shall decide all cases on the basis of respect for law, applying such choice of law rules and principles of commercial and international law as the Tribunal determines to be applicable, taking into account relevant usages of the trade, contract provisions and changed circumstances."

In fact, the selection of such a neutral system is at the dispute resolution stage as opposed to the contracting stage. In either event, the reason for the selection of such a system of law is usually a desire to insulate such a dispute resolution process from the vagaries of an otherwise possibly applicable municipal system of law considered potentially capable of jeopardising interests under the dispute. This attempt at the "internationalisation" or "de-localisation" of the applicable law has especially been noticeable in the past in state contracts[148].

Also, article 33 of the tribunal's 'Rules of Procedure' gives it wide leeway to refer to principles of commercial and international law and the usages of the trade applicable to the transaction: "1)The arbitral tribunal shall decide all cases on the basis of respect for law, applying such choice of law rules and principles of commercial and international law as the arbitral tribunal determines to be applicable, taking into

147.J. A. WESTBERG, préc., note 135.p.65

148.Gbenga BAMODOU, « Exploring the Interrelationship of Transnational Commercial Law, "The New Lex Mercatoria" and International Commercial Arbitration », (1998) 10-7 *Afr. J. Int. Comp. Law* 31-59.p.50

account relevant usages of the trade, contract provisions and changed circumstances."[149]

By using the wording "on the basis of respect for law" rather than "according to law," article V allows the tribunal maximum freedom in its choice of substantive law. This language ensured that the judges, though not bound to apply any specific national law, have to refer to established legal rules and principles.[150] Article V does not limit them to international law; they may also invoke principles of commercial law, choice of law rules, and contract provisions in determining claims. Chamber I interpreted article V regarding applicable law as follows:[151] "This tribunal may often find it necessary to interpret and apply treaties, customary international law, general principles of law and national laws." However, article 32 of the 'Rules of the Tribunal' states that "each award must state the reasons upon which the award is based."

The tribunal has often relied on Iranian, American, or a third country's national law, or on public international law, and refers to general principles of law. This diversity in applicable laws offers the judges wide discretion in applying legal rules. They have emphasized their freedom of choice:

"The Tribunal finds that according to Article V of the Claims Settlement Declaration, the Tribunal is not required to apply any particular national or international legal system. On the contrary, the Tribunal is vested with extensive freedom in determining the applicable law in each case."[152]

Reliance on 'general principles' may prove particularly attractive in the increasing number of commercial disputes between

---

149.TRIBUNAL RULES OF PROCEDURE, prec. note 97, art.33,

150.A. AVANESSIAN, préc., note 96. p.241

151.*CMI International, Inc, the Islamic Republic of Iran*, [1983] case no.245, 4 _IUSCTR_ 263 (Iran_U.S. Claims Tribunal).p.266

152.*Anaconda-Iran, Inc. v. the Islamic Republic of Iran*, [1986] case no.167, 13 -IUSCTR- 199 (Iran_U.S. Claims Tribunal). P.232

parties from different legal, social, and economic cultures.[153] The tribunal has rarely decided on the basis of just one set of national rules, even in cases where the parties might arguably have agreed on them as the rule of decision.[154] Typically, the judges have not articulated the rules or principles they used to determine the law they applied. Instead, they have used their discretion to draw from three recurring sources: contract law, general principles of law, and public international law, especially contract law.[155] Mouri correctly notes: "The Tribunal assumption (in case no. 18) seems to be that national law and general principles of law would apply only where a private party is a claimant. No case involving individuals can be decided by mere reference to public international law. On the other hand, application by a tribunal of general principles of law or the municipal law of a given country will not deprive it of its international (inter-state) character.[156] We next examine the law sources that the tribunal seems to have used in its judgments.

1.6.1 Disputes Arising out of Expropriation

Claims arising out of Iranian expropriation or nationalization of foreign investors' property represent the largest group of the tribunal's non-contractual claims. The judges referred all the related matters to the principles of international law. An analysis of these judgments shows that the tribunal avoided making reference to or applying any national law.

153.Grant HANESSIAN, « General principles of law in Iran-U.S. claims tribunal », (1989) 27 *Colum J. Transnatl. Law* 309-352.p. 344

154.John R. CROOK, « Applicable Law in International Arbitration: The Iran-U.S. Claims TRribunal Experience », (1989) 83 *Am. J. Int. Law* 278-311.p.278

155.*Id.*

156.Allahyar MOURI, *The International Law of Expropriation as Reflected in the Work of the Iran-U.S. Claims Tribunal*, The Netherland, martinus Nijhoff, 1994.p 47

1.6.1.1 International law

In regard to expropriation claims, the tribunal readily applied international law. In the *Phillips Petroleum Company* case,[157] the majority stated:

"76. As the tribunal has held in a number of cases, expropriation by or attributable to a State of the property of an alien gives rise under international law to liability for compensation, and this is so whether the expropriation is formal or de facto and whether the property is tangible, such as real estate or a factory, or intangible, such as the contract rights involved in the present Case."

Therefore, because of article V and the tribunal's international nature, public international law governs s any issue of state responsibility, such as expropriation or unjust enrichment.

1.6.1.2 Treaty of Amity

The governing law vis-à-vis expropriation must also factor in the Treaty of Amity (1955) between Iran and United States. This agreement contains extensive provisions about the state's responsibility to support and compensate American investors. In a typical investor-state dispute, a tribunal would first examine the relevant investment treaty.[158] After the Islamic Revolution, neither signatory repudiated the 1955 treaty, which thus remained in force. When the tribunal started work, there was some debate about how it should interpret and apply treaty provisions. One Iranian judge submitted that the Claims Settlement Declaration did not give the tribunal authority to interpret the treaty. The tribunal's Judge Brower correctly noted, "However, the Tribunal has the authority to

157.*Phillips Petroleum Company v. the Islamic Republic of Iran and NIOC*, [1989] case no.39, 21 -IUSCTR- 22 (Iran_U.S. Claims Tribunal).para.76, p.106

158.S. RIPINSKY, préc., note 56., p.48

interpret the Treaty particularly because, the Treaty of Amity is part of the corpus of international law between the United States and Iran."[159] Finally, in the *INA Corporation* case,[160] the tribunal based its discussion about compensation on articles of the treaty. at:

"For the purpose of this case we are in the presence of a lex specialis, in the form of the Treaty of Amity, which in principle prevails over general rules. The continued validity and effect of the Treaty have not been contested by the Respondent in any of the written pleadings in this case. The Tribunal must therefore assume that for the purpose of the present case the Treaty remains binding as it is drafted."

In many claims, the tribunal has referred to the treaty's rules, particularly those that relate to state responsibility, the unlawfulness of states' acts, or the standard of compensation. In *Amoco International Finance,*[161]for determining what international law provided for states' acts, the award looked to the Treaty of Amity as a lex specialis and to customary international law as the lex generalis. In fact, the judges have treated the Treaty of Amity as the lex specialis to follow. Nevertheless, regarding expropriation, there is no indication that the tribunal sees treaty standards as differing from standards of customary international law. Rather, it has emphasized, for example, that the treaty does not alter the general rules of international law vis-à-vis the concept of a taking.[162]

159.*SEDCO, Inc. v. the Islamic Republic of Iran and National Iranian Oil Company,* [1986] case no.129, 10 -IUSCTR- 180 (Iran_U.S. Claims Tribunal).p.190

160.*INA Corporation v. the Islamic Republic of Iran,* [1985] case no.161, 8 -IUSCTR- 373 (Iran_U.S. Claims Tribunal).p.378

161.*Amoco International Finance Corp. v the Islamic Republic of Iran,* [1987] case no.56, 15 _IUSCTR_ 189 (Iran_U.S. Claims Tribunal).

162.Richard B. LILLICH et Daniel BARSTOW MAGRAW, *The Iran-United States Claims Tribunal: Its Contribution to the Law of State Responsability*, New York, Transnational Publishers, Inc., 1998. P.185, 187,

The tribunal advocated its argumentation in this regard in Amoco award satating:

"As a lex specialis in the relations between the two countries, the Treaty supersedes the lex generalis, namely customary international law. This does not mean, however, that the latter is irrelevant in the instant Case. On the contrary, the rules of customary international law may be useful in order to fill in possible lacunae of the Treaty, to ascertain the meaning of undefined terms in its text or, more generally, to aid interpretation and implementation of its provisions[163]."

1.6.2 Disputes Arising Out of Contractual Relation

Actually, most of the claims related to sale contracts and construction or consultancy contracts, as in the *Economy Forms Corp.* case.[164] Chamber I of the tribunal held that it would decide contract claims pursuant to the "proper law of the contract." It used a centre-of-gravity test to find that law. When facing such issues, the tribunal has usually applied general principles of commercial or public international law, but rarely national law.[165] As it wrote in *Mobil*,[166]"The Tribunal does not consider it appropriate that such an Agreement be governed by the law of one Party."

163.*Amoco International Finance Corp. v the Islamic Republic of Iran*, préc., note 161.para.112

164.*Economy Forms Corporation v the Islamic Republic of Iran*, [1983] case no.165, 3 _IUSCTR_ 42 (Iran_U.S. Claims Tribunal).para.42,47-8

165.J. R. CROOK, préc., note 154.,P.288

166.*Mobil Oil Iran, Inc. v. the Islamic Republic of Iran*, [1987] case no.7, 16 - IUSCTR- 3 (Iran_U.S. Claims Tribunal).p.28, para. 81, the claimant involved an extraordinary contract, the Sale and Purchase Agreement between a consortium of Western oil companies and Iran, which the Tribunal concluded was governed for most purposes by "the general principles of commercial and international law."

In *RJ Reynolds Tobacco Co.*,[167] the main element of a claim involved tobacco products that the respondent acknowledged had been delivered and not paid for. The tribunal had explicitly rejected parties' calls to refer to national law for aid in analysing simple transactions, but decided that the issues in this case did not require such an analysis and to resolve all questions by reference to the parties' practice and the contract's relevant provisions. In its first step, it attempted to find proper law of the contract. But this approach does not mean that the tribunal accepted the contract provisions as the sole source of the obligation, and it did not restrict itself to a particular national law. We next examine how the tribunal applied several law sources as general principles of law, comparative law, and lex mercatoria.

1.6.2.1 General Principles of Law

As a result of the abandonment of the traditional view that a contract that is not between states must be subject to some municipal law[168] and the gradual acceptance that tribunals may apply even public international law to contracts of private parties, principles of international law and general principles of law have now become quite applicable to so-called quasi-international disputes --namely, disputes between a state and a foreign national --in international adjudication. As Schreuer submits; the practice of ICSID tribunals on general principles of law may be illustrated by the following examples:[169] "good faith; prohibition of corruption; nobody can benefit from his or her own fraud (nemo auditurpropriamturpitudinemallegans); general principles of contract law including pacta sunt servanda, estoppel; unjust enrichment; full compensation of prejudice resulting from a failure to

167.*R.J ReynoldsTobacco Co. v the Islamic Republic of Iran, partial award*, [1984] case no.35, 7 _IUSCTR_ 181 (Iran-U.S. Claims Tribunal).para.181-190

168.N. BLACKABY et C. PARTASIDIES, préc., note 8. No.7-80

169.C. H. SCHREUER, préc., note 88. P.609

fulfil contractual obligations; the principle of compensation in case of nationalization; general principles of due process; the claimant bears the burden of proof; res judicata; prohibition of abuse of right; the duty to mitigate damage; no one can transfer a better title than he or she has (nemo plus iuristransferrepotestquam ipse habet);valuation of damages.

Therefore, general principles of law are particularly useful in cases that involve state actors, as in investment relationships. In awards in such cases that relate to claims arising out of measures affecting property rights, such as unjust enrichment, quasi-contracts, deprivation of property rights, or to secondary claims in expropriation, such as claim of interest, the tribunal applies the general principles of law in some cases it has applied general principles of law by specific reference; for example, in *General Dynamics*,[170] it states:

"The Tribunal concludes that payment for General Dynamics's services was not contingent on the Navy expressly approving the report. Even so, the fact remains that General Dynamics was obligated, under general principles of law, to perform its duties under the contract satisfactorily and with due diligence. The Tribunal is not satisfied that under the circumstances of the transaction the Navy would be liable for such costs pursuant to trade usage or general principles of commercial law."

The tribunal uses "general principles of law" to determine and apply norms common to Iran and the United States. Reliance on "general principles" may prove particularly attractive in the increasing number of commercial disputes between parties from different legal, social, and economic cultures.[171]

The tribunal's Chamber III, in *Anaconda-Iran, Inc.*,[172] stated:

170.*General Dynamics Corp. v the Islamic Republic of Iran*, [1984] case no.238, 5 -IUSCTR- 386 (Iran_U.S Claims Tribunal).p.394

171.G. HANESSIAN, préc., note 153.p.311

172.*Anaconda-Iran, Inc. v. the Islamic Republic of Iran*, préc., note 152.para, 232

"Article V of Claims Settlement Declaration creates a novel system of determining the applicable law. The Tribunal is not required to apply any particular national or international legal system. On the contrary, the Tribunal is vested with extensive freedom in determining the applicable law in each case."

In *Isaiah*,[173] it was argued than Iranian law must be applied to the dishonoured cheque that was the ground of the claim to the unjust enrichment took place in Iran, the Tribunal has indicated to general principle stating that: "The Tribunal is free to apply general principles of law in a case such as this, although there is no reason to believe the result would be different if only Iranian law were applied."

1.6.2.1.1 Sources of the Tribunal's General Principles of Law

Berger submits that there are two reasons that, despite the significance of general principles, justify the theory of transnational commercial law might not be based on them. First, these principles do not supply an applicable legal system, and, second, whereas they emanate from relevant domestic laws, they do not cover the specific commercial realities of international trade and commerce.[174] This assertion was considered by the tribunal, which expanded on it. The tribunal, in extracting general principles of law, has acted very conservatively. It has first compared the stems of the rule in different legal systems and reviewed the doctrine, commercial usages, and international arbitration practice and then has distilled reliable principles to apply proportionately to the circumstances of the case.

In what follows, I examine the chief method the tribunal used to reach the general principles of law.

173.*Isaiah Benjamin v. Bank Mellat*, [1983] case no.219, 2 _IUSCTR_ 232 (Iran_U.S. Claims Tribunal)., p. 237

174.K. P. BERGER, préc., note 99.p.202

1.6.2.1.1.1 Comparative Municipal Law

General principles of law therefore serve to transform domestic contract law into international commercial law. Once they have been ascertained, they prove influential in transnational commercial law, just as they do in domestic law. A central question when determining the existence of general principles is which legal orders to include in a comparative survey. When article 38(1) of the statute of the ICJ speaks of the general principles of law recognized by civilized nations, this statement is generally understood as meaning that a certain principle must exist in the principal legal orders of the world[175]. As the mission of the arbitrators in the Iran_U.S. Claims Tribunal was to base their decisions on the general principles, so they were aware that to distill the general principles, they should discuss the application of the given principles in the most civilized nations' legal systems. Obviously, when the arbitrators or the lawyers come from different legal systems or legal cultures, they are bearing their traditional concepts of law in their argumentations[176].whereas general principles are grounded by their nature on the internal legal system of States, two being the conditions for their application as general principles of international law. First, they must exist and be uniformly applied in the great majority of States; second, they must be felt as obligatory or necessary also from the point of view of international law, meaning that they must be felt to pursue values and impose conduct that States also consider has to be pursued and imposed, or at least necessary, at the international level[177].

The tribunal focuses on Iranian and U.S. national law, although it has consulted the laws of various nations, including major common- and civil-law countries. It attempts to support the legal principles with references from different legal systems. For example, in the *Shannon &*

175.S. W. SCHILL, préc., note 90.p.147

176.A. T. VON MEHREN, préc., note 34.p.1223

177.P. BERNARDINI, préc., note 65.p.187

Wilson, Inc.,award,[178] when it discussed the rights of third-party beneficiaries, it referred to;"Black's Law Dictionary p. 1327 (5th ed.). See also Article 196, Iranian Civil Code (M. Sabi trans. 1973); 4 A. Corbin, Contracts 1774 (1951)" In *Gould Marketing Inc.*,[179] while deliberating the termination of the contract as a result of frustration, cited English and French law: "For American law see Corbin on Contracts 1367 et (1962) 18 Willson law of contract set seq); for English law, Fibrosa Spolka Akcyjna v. Fairbairn L.C.B. Ltd., (1943) A.C. 32. A similar rule exists in civil law. For French law see Repertoire Dalloz, Droit Civil, Contrats et Conventions par Boyer 271,272." In both awards, the tribunal has referred to several legal systems and sources to interpret the principles of law as precisely as possible.

In fact, the arbitrators in these awards attempted to quantify the application of the given principles in major legal tradition, in order to distilling of the general principles. It is worth to note that the Tribunal has disregard any particular legal theories that advance by Iranian party as the rules of Sharia. Although, frequently Iranian party claimed that the award of interest is prohibited under the rules of Islamic law, but the tribunal did not recognised the specific Islamic rules, as the general principles of law, then, put these argumentations aside from the process of finding applicable law.

1.6.2.1.1.2 Lex Mercatoria

In the practice of the tribunal, 'general principles of law' also draw on the customs, usages, and practices of international commerce known as the lex mercatoria, or merchant law. The Iran--U.S. Claims

---

178.*Shannon & Wilson, Inc. v. Atomic Energy Org. of Iran,* [1985] 9 -IUSCTR- 397., P.401

179.*Gould Mktg., Inc. v. the Islamic Republic of Iran,* [1984] 6 -IUSCTR-272.p. 274

Tribunal frequently refers to principles of commercial law without clearly distinguishing them from principles of international law, such as the obligation to pay compensation.

The Iran-United States Claims Tribunal, by consistently applying principles of commercial law in deciding many of the commercial cases before it, has contributed significantly to the stabilization and development of a multitude of principles and rules of the lex mercatoria. Indeed, the development of a body of international commercial law has made a quantum advance due to the work of the Tribunal, and its jurisprudence in commercial cases represents considerable sources for those who are working on research and apply transnational commercial law, such as international arbitral tribunals and counsel engaged in international commercial arbitration. One author submits; "no less importantly, the Tribunal's experience has shown that an international arbitral tribunal can efficiently decide cases 'on the basis of respect for law' by applying general principles of commercial law rather than national law."[180]The tribunal has consciously tried to promote the development of such a lex mercatoria.[181] Frequently it has mentioned that the judging of a contractual dispute needs to invoke a particular law. It refused to consider and judge a contractual claim in terms of the wording of the contract. In the *Anaconda-Iran* case,[182] the claimant argued that, because the contract contains no provision subjecting it to any national law, the parties intended that no particular law govern the contract. Therefore, it asked the tribunal to apply only the self-executing terms of the contract under the doctrine of *pacta sunt servanda* and the usage of the trade. Chamber III disagreed and held that *pacta sunt servanda* is not

180.Maurizio BRUNETTI, « The Lex Mercatoria in Practice: The Experience of the Iran- United States Claims Tribunal », (2002) 18-3 *Arbitr. Int.* 355 et seq.

181.G. H. ALDRICH, préc., note 125. p.157

182.*Anaconda-Iran, Inc. v. the Islamic Republic of Iran*, préc., note 152. Para. 122-123-129-232-233 operative *in vacuo* but must refer to a particular system of law. As well, no contract could be self-sufficient and governable by no particular law. The judges concluded: "The Tribunal is required to take seriously into consideration the pertinent contractual choice of law rules, but is not obliged to apply those if it considers it has good reason not to do so" and finally decided against applying a national law and took "into consideration relevant usages of trade as well as relevant principles of commercial and international law."

In the *Mobil Oil Iran* case,[183] the claimant argued that the agreement created, by itself, a legal system governing the relationship of the parties and invoked the contract's article 29: "The rights and obligation of the parties shall be governed by and according to the provisions of this agreement." The judges rejected this argument. In its memorial, the respondent quoted Sausser-Hall's observation in the *Aramco* arbitration:

"It is obvious that no contract can exist in vacuo, i.e., without being based on a legal system. The conclusion of a contract is not left to the unfettered discretion of the parties. It is necessarily related to some positive law which gives legal effects to the reciprocal and concordant manifestation of intent made by the parties. The contract cannot even be conceived without a system of law under which it is created. Human can only create a contractual relationship if the applicable system of law has first recognized its power to do so.[184]"

In the *Oil Fields of Texas* case,[185] which related to the lease of equipment for petroleum exploration, the issue concerned the consequences of a de facto succession. The claimant sought payment

183.*Mobil Oil Iran, Inc. v. the Islamic Republic of Iran*, préc., note 166.*para, 75,81*

184.*Saudi Arabia v Arabian American Oil Company(Aramco), 1958, 27, I.L.R 117, 165*, 1958.

185.*Oil field of Texas, Inc. v the Islamic Republic of Iran*, [1982] case no.43, 1 _IUSCTR_ 347 (Iran_U.S. Claims Tribunal).

based on contractual obligations and compensation on the grounds of unjust enrichment and expropriation. As the parties did not agree on the applicable law, the claimant argued that the liability of the National Iranian Oil Company, as agent of the Government, was subject to commercial law, while the respondent argued for applying Iranian law. The judges reasoned that, since there is no well-developed body of law to cover the circumstances of the case, the applicable rules should come from general principles of law or the rules of international law. As a result, they decided that, after a de facto succession, the surviving entity must pay appropriate compensation.[186]

The tribunal has decided claims with specific reference to the usages of a particular trade. Such cases have involved issues in the more internationally regulated fields of trade[187]. In the *Carolina Brass, Inc.*, case,[188] which concerned carriage of goods, it decided according to the Hague Rules (1924), re "Bills of Lading, and Protocol of Signature" in commercial shipping:

"It need not decide whether the laws of Iran, the United States, India or the Netherlands should apply to this particular case in order to establish that the time limitation contained in Article three of The Hague Rules and paragraph 21 of the bill of lading is applicable in this case, since the law in each of these countries is similar, and all are in conformity with the wide spread practice reflected in The Hague Rules."

The tribunal's adjudication of private rights --and its elaboration of a body of law applicable to private-law disputes --in an

---

186. *Id.* The tribunal held: "The development of international law has always been a process of applying such stablished legal principles to circumstances not previously encountered."

187.Mohsen MOHEBI, *The International Law Character of the Iran-United States Claims Tribunal*, Boston, Kluwer Law International, 1999, p. 130.

188.*Carolina Brass Inc. v Arya Shipping Lines,* [1986] case no.10035 _IUSCTR_ 139 (Iran_U.S.Claims Tribunal).p.134

international forum that traditionally applied only public international law reveals non-state actors' increasing role in developing and enforcing international law.[189] Also, the tribunal's general-principles jurisprudence furthers the current trend towards 'denationalizing' private international arbitration.

1.6.2.1.1.3 Public International Law

The tribunal also has referred extensively to public international law in determining the nationality of claimants and in cases regarding deprivation of property interests. In such cases, it frequently refers simply to "general principles of international law" as the basis for its decision, leaving doubt as to whether it means customary international law of "general principles of law recognized by civilized nations." For example, in the *RJ ReynoldsTobacco Co.*, case,[190] it states, vis-à-vis possibly awarding compound interest: "There are few rules within the scope of the subject of damages in international law that are better settled than the one that compound interest is not allowable."

1.6.3 Procedural Law of the Iran-U.S. Claims Tribunal

Article III, section 2, of the Claims Settlement Declaration of 1981 prescribed the procedural rules for the Iran-U.S. Claims Tribunal (IUSCT) to follow: "Members of the Tribunal shall be appointed and the Tribunal shall conduct its business in accordance with the arbitration rules of the United Nations Commission on International Trade Law (UNCITRAL) except to the extent modified by the Parties or by the Tribunal to ensure that this Agreement can be carried out."

It is clear that the broad base and inherent elasticity of the

189.G. HANESSIAN, préc., note 153. P.317

190.*R.J ReynoldsTobacco Co. v the Islamic Republic of Iran, partial award*, préc., note 167.p.191

UNCITRAL Rules[191] have proved invaluable in laying a firm foundation for the development of these rules. Changes have accommodated the special needs of this unique arbitral body--the IUSCT-- as its work has proceeded.[192] With regard to its application of the UNCITRAL Rules, Judge Bellet states:[193] "One particularly beneficial opportunity proved by the Algiers negotiators was in fact, the occasion to apply the UNCITRAL Rules -- which only date from 1976 --on a large scale to a multi-case arbitral Tribunal. By enacting the UNCITRAL Rules, the United Nations had sought to establish a body of procedural rules embodying a compromise between common and civil law systems. It was to this compromise that the Iranian jurists and the American jurists agreed, and the Tribunal benefited considerably thereby." The UNCITRAL arbitration rules, as modified by the tribunal and adopted as "Tribunal Rules of Procedure" (May 3, 1983), apply to all proceedings before the tribunal.

1.7 The Nature of the Tribunal

The precise legal status of the Iran/US Claims Tribunal remains a subject of controversy even as its mandate draws to a close after more than twenty years of activity[194]. Writers have disagreed about the nature of the Iran-U.S. Claims Tribunal. Some regard it, because states created

---

191. UNCITRAL proposed the Arbitration Rules on 1976. Based on General Assembly Resolution No. 31/98 http://www.uncitral.org/pdf/english/texts/arbitration/arb-rules/arb-rules.pdf. Consulte, le 3 fevrier 2017

192.Karl Heinz BOCKSTIEGELT, « Applying the UNCITRAL Rules: The Experience of the Iran-United States Claims Tribunal », (1986) 4 *Int. TAX Bus. LAWYER*.266-271, p.266

193.*Amoco International Finance Corporation v. Islamic Republic of Iran*, [1985] 14 _IUSCTR_ 112 (Iran-U.S. Claims Tribunal).para. 179, p. 243.

194.Zachary DOUGLAS, « The hybrid foundations of investment treaty arbitration », (2003) 74 *Br. Year b. Int. Law* 151-289, 160.

it, as an inter-state mechanism belonging to public international law, while others, because of the multiplicity of its individual claims and its referring to private law, regard it as a private arbiter. Is it a private arbiter created to resolve private law disputes arising under different systems of law, and to hear private law claims against Iran and the United States? Is it an inter-state body charged with ruling on the respondent state's responsibility under public international law? Or is it performing both functions?

The founding Algiers Accords twice point to the tribunal's international character. Principle B of the General Declaration observes: "It was the purpose of both parties to terminate all litigation as between the government of each party and the nationals of the other and to bring about the settlement and determination of all such claims through binding arbitration." Article II, paragraph 1, of the Claims Settlement Declaration states:[195] "An international arbitral tribunal (the Iran-United States Claims Tribunal) is hereby established for the purpose of

195 .Article II(1) of the Claims Settlement Declaration states: "An international arbitral tribunal (the Iran-United States Claims Tribunal) is hereby established for the purpose of deciding claims of nationals of the United States against Iran and claims of nationals of Iran against the United States, and any counterclaim which arises out of the same contract, transaction or occurrence that constitutes the subject matter of that national's claim, if such claims and counterclaims are outstanding on the date of this Agreement, whether or not filed with any court, and arise out of debts, contracts (including transactions which are the subject of letters of credit or bank guarantees), expropriations or other measures affecting property rights, excluding claims described in Paragraph 11 of the Declaration of the Government of Algeria of January 19, 1981, and claims arising out of the actions of the United States in response to the conduct described in such paragraph, and excluding claims arising under a binding contract between the parties specifically providing that any disputes thereunder shall be within the sole jurisdiction of the competent Iranian courts, in response to the Majlis position."*Claims Settlement Declaration*, préc., note 129.

deciding claims of nationals of the United States against Iran and claims of nationals of Iran against the United States."

These two statements together not only show the body's international character but also clearly indicate the fusion of state and private party claims in one procedure, as it addresses both inter-governmental and private party-state claims. One of the tribunal's awards–in *Esphahanian*, involving dual nationality–outlines the body's dual purpose:

"While it was clearly an international tribunal established by treaty, and while some of its cases involved disputes between two governments and involved interpretation and application of public international law, most disputes (including all those brought by dual nationals) involved a private party on one side and a government or government-controlled entity on the other, and many involved primarily issues of municipal law and general principles of law. It stated that in such cases it was the rights of the claimant, not of his nation, which were to be determined by the Tribunal[196]."

According to Judge Brower of the tribunal, "Despite the apparent hesitancy, there can be little doubt that the Tribunal is an international institution established by two sovereign States and subject to public international law."[197] On this view the tribunal is a hybrid, which rules on both the respondent state's responsibility in international law and its liability in private law. The tribunal emerges in an international context but considers the private claims.

In fact, its practice represents a transnational legal process. As Harold Koh comments, the Tribunal is non-traditional, because it cannot be cabined within domestic law or international law as a traditional classification.The proceeding of the tribunal is dynamic not

196.*Esfahanian v Bank Tejarat,* [1983] case no.157, 2 -IUSCTR- 157 (Iran_U.S. Claims Tribunal).

197.C. N. BROWER et J. D. BRUESCHKE, préc., note 124.p.16

static, it resolved the disputes raised out of private business deals in theseveral different sources from private to public law. The tribunal is non-statist; the key actors in this process were not just nation-states but also the individuals and the monetary fund such as banks and enterprises. It is normative, this tribunal not only generated law such as international public law of dispute resolution, but generated new interpretations of these rules and internalized them into domestic law.[198]

In fact, its practice illustrates each of the features of transnational legal process that appeared above: the substantial role of 'general principles of law' in its judgments, emerging from varied sources of law, including "uniform laws" (such as the UNCITRAL instruments); codes of conduct of international organizations; customs and usages; municipal law; and the inevitable confluence of 'public' and 'private' sources of rights. These features substantially enhance the development of a new system of transnational commercial law.[199]

1.8 The Precedential Value of Tribunal Practice

Generally, the IUSCT's arbitration practice does not create a binding precedent for any other arbitration.[200] Judicial decisions in international law are not strictly a formal source of law, but may serve as evidence of the law. A coherent body of previous jurisprudence may well

---

198.Harold Hongju KOH, « Transnational Legal Process », (1996) 75 *Neb. Law Rev.* 181--207.p.185

199.G. HANESSIAN, préc., note 153.p.351

200. Article 1136 of the North American Free Trade Agreement (NAFTA)provides: "An award made by a Tribunal shall have no binding force except between the disputing parties and in respect of the particular case."*North America Free Trade Agreement (NAFTA)*, en ligne : <http://www.international.gc.ca/trade-agreements-accords-commerciaux/agr-acc/nafta-alena/text-texte/11.aspx?lang=eng>.

affect any given case.[201] As the introduction explained, international instruments, such as the Statute of the International Court of Justice, (ICJ) clearly state this point. What is clear is that under Article 59 of the ICJ Statute, the decisions of the ICJ have no "binding force except between the parties", therefore, There is no doctrine of *staredecisis* under international law. The same is true for international investment law. Thus, ICSID, Article 53(1) provides that "the award shall be binding *on the parties,*" and, therefore, not on *other* parties. But in view of the fact that investmenttribunals are increasingly relying on the decisions of other investment tribunalswhen settling disputes[202], the question of the binding nature of these awards hasbecome one of the most controversial questions currently being debated by scholars.

Article 38(1)(d) of the Statute of the International Court of Justice (ICJ Statute) refers to judicial decisions not as sources of international law but, rather, as subsidiary means for the determination of rules of law. Although, 'judicial decisions' are considered only a 'subsidiary' source of public international law, almost all investment awards include numerous references to prior decisions of investment tribunals. Even though investment tribunals see no precedents in their jurisprudence, they tend to follow the accretion of rulings on the same subject matter (in similar circumstances). Investment arbitrators also often infer customary rules from other investment tribunals' awards [203]The resulting *jurisprudence constante* (one identical solution for the same cases) enhances stability and predictability in this sphere.[204]. For the

---

201.James CRAWFORD, *Brownlie's Principles of Public International Law*, 8th éd., United Kingdom, Oxford University Press, 2012.p.37

202.Patrick DUMBERRY, « The Role and Relevance of Awards in the Formation, Identification and Evolution of Customary Rules in International Investment Law », (2016) 33-3 *J. Int. Arbitr.* 269-287.p272

203.A. K. BJORKLUND et A. REINSCH, préc., note 83.p.3

204.Yannick RADI, « Precedent, 'Jurisprudences Constantes' and Coherence in International Investment Arbitration », (2014) 1 *Belg. Rev. Arbitr.*1-19, p.8

predictability of investments and the credibility of the dispute resolution system, that rule cannot change from one proceeding to another. Hence, more consistency must be the goal. It is important to remember that the credibility of the entire dispute resolution system depends on consistency, because a dispute settlement process that produces unpredictable results will lose the confidence of the users in the long term and defeat its own purpose. These final points lead to the overall conclusion that 'arbitral precedent' is a necessity for certain types of disputes, if not only for the sake of the rule of law[205].

The tribunal's greatest impact is likely to flow from the many hundreds of contentious cases it has decided and the persuasive value of its jurisprudence beyond the specific cases that were at issue. The published decisions constitute an invaluable collection of materials and jurisprudence on issues of public international law, international commercial law, and the procedure of international arbitration. One author calls these awards an untouched gold mine for international courts and tribunals.[206]

The IUSCT is, in the aggregate value of its awards, the largest international arbitration project in modem legal history.[207] Its decisions on expropriation and compensation have received the widest attention and comment, which is hardly surprising. It is the first international arbitral body in years to confront a docket of substantial and generally well-argued expropriation cases.[208] Judge Mosk observed about its legal

205.G. KAUFMANN-KOHLER, préc., note 4.p.378

206.Peter MALANCZUK, « mixing legal cultures in international arbitration. the Iran_United States Claims Tribunal », dans Vijay K. BHATIA (dir.), *Legal Discourse across Cultures and Systems*, Hong Kong, Hong Kong University Press, 2008.,35-54, p.51

207.G. HANESSIAN, préc., note 153. p.310

208.J. R. CROOK, préc., note 154. P.300

assertions:[209] "These opinions should be of value to practitioners who advise on international transactions, to those who are involved in international Commercial litigation, and to those who will be involved in establishing dispute resolution mechanisms in the future." Judge Brower, after pointing out the role of trade usage in arbitration –as per article 13(5) of the Rules of Conciliation and Arbitration of the International Chamber of Commerce (1986)[210] and article V of the IUSCT's Claims Settlement Declaration -- concludes, "The fact that this 'global court' works, and works well, is proven by its consistent triumph over adversity."[211]

The tribunal's precedents are cited elsewhere virtually daily and have begun to appear as citations in decisions of other international tribunals. This is particularly so for its decisions on public international law. The tribunal has always relied on customary international law for its conclusions, and its awards have practical relevance to a wide variety of factual situation that arise under NAFTA. Thus, its jurisprudence on expropriation may be relevant for tribunals adjudicating NAFTA's

---

209.Richard M. MOSK, « Lessons From The Hague - An Update on the Iran-United States Claims Tribunal », (1987) 14-11 *Pepperdine Law Rev.* 819-826.p.825

210.Article 21 (2)of the Rules of Arbitration of the International Chamber of Commerce, providing that "In all cases the arbitrator shall take account of the provisions of the contract, if any between the parties and of any the relevant trade usages." INTERNATIONAL CHAMBER OF COMMERCE, *ICC Arbitration Rules*, amended 2017, en ligne : <https://cdn.iccwbo.org/content/uploads/sites/3/2017/01/ICC-2017-Arbitration-and-2014-Mediation-Rules-English-version.pdf>.

211.Charles N. BROWER, « The Global Court: The Internationalization of Commercial Adjudication and Arbitration », (1997) 26 *Baltim. Law Rev.*9-14, p.9

chapter 11, on investment.[212] In fact, the tribunal's jurisprudence can serve as a persuasive authority in investor--state arbitration, because it usually applies general principles of law. Thus, these decisions could be persuasive precedents for any investor--state arbitration with similar facts and decisional law: "Many of the decisions of the Tribunal contain valuable statements on the law of compensation and represent an important contribution on the subject."[213]

The commentators have noted the precedential value of awards in two areas: development of the arbitration rules an international law of expropriation.[214] Some notable awards receive frequent mention in decisions by the World Bank's International Centre for Settlement of Investment (ICSID). The international law of state responsibility for injury to foreign investors presents a number of unresolved problems. Because so many Iranian-government measures, both formal and informal, affected U.S. investors, the tribunal is unusually influential vis-à-vis development of the law in this area. Many lawyers have served in the tribunal and gained experience through its 3½ decades of operation. Nowadays these people may be working in other international investment arbitrations and may transfer their experience there. Sornarajah comments: "The personnel of arbitral tribunals are usually persons who have experience sitting on other tribunals which deal with investment issues. Thus, members of the Iran–U.S. Claims Tribunal now sit on ICSID tribunals and bring with them the experiences gained while on the earlier tribunal. This is an inevitable process. The impact of the takings cases decided by the Iran–US Claims Tribunal is beginning to be felt in this area, despite the fact that the wording of the treaty

---

212.Maurizio BRUNETTI, « The Iran-United States Claims Tribunal, NAFTA Chapter 1, and the Doctrine of Indirect Expropriation », (2001) 2-1 *Chic. J. Int. Law* 203-212., p.205

213.S. RIPINSKY, préc., note 56.p.16

214.R. M. MOSK, préc., note 209. P.825

creating the tribunal on takings was different."[215] The tribunal has rendered approximately 60 awards on compensable taking under international law, thereby addressing crucial issues, including the date of taking, attributability of an action to the state, the standard of compensation, and valuation methods.[216]

The tribunal has also ruled on many contractual claims. According to one author, these awards will long constitute the best source of case law for elaborating an international lex mercatoria.[217] The tribunal's role in interpreting and applying general principles of contract law in international claims is helping to construct transnational contact law. Tribunal awards have extensively discussed subjects such as damages, frustration, *force majeure,* hardship, and *pacta sunt servanda*gesin. It is clear that tribunal's jurisprudence can be very helpful in investment arbitration. Some commentators point out that, as investor--state arbitration continues to grow, the spate of rulings from the burgeoning number of other arbitrators may swamp the tribunal's output.[218] But recently the Permanent Court of Arbitration, in *Yukos* (2014),[219] several times referred to IUSCT jurisprudence. Specifically,

---

215.M. SORNARAJAH, *The International Law on Foreign Investment*, New York, Cambridge University Press, 2010.p.333

216.M. BRUNETTI, préc., note 212.p.207

217.J. A. WESTBERG, préc., note 135.p.66

218.Andrea J. MENAKER, « the enduring relevance of the expropriation jurisprudence of the Iran_U.S. Claims Tribunal for investor-state arbitrations », dans Christopher S. Gibson and Christopher R. DRAHOZAL (dir.), *The Iran-U.S.Claims Tribunal at 25: The Cases Everyone Needs to Know for Investor_State & International Arbitration*, United Stated of America, Oxford University Press, 2007.335-365, p.345

219.*YUKOS Universal LTD. (ISLE OF MAN) v The Russian Federation*, 2014 Permanent Court of Arbitration, Case No 2005/04-AA227, en ligne : <https://pcacases.com/web/sendAttach/420>.The award encompasses the reference to Iran-U.S. awards in subjects including: the rate of interest that is referred to Sylvania Technical Systems v. Iran, 1985, 8 Iran–U.S. CTR. 298, the tribunal has cited awards regarding interest, existence of causal link, date of valuation, and attribution of damage.

Drahozal (2007) examined the citing of IUSCT jurisprudence in ICSID and NAFTA arbitration (see Tables 1 and 2).[220]

Table 1. The number of citations of Iran-U.S. awards in ICSID arbitration until 2007

ICSID arbitration	Citing tribunal precedent	Not citing tribunal precedent	Total
Award(on the merit)	17	21	38
Award denying jurisdiction	0	8	8
Decision -- jurisdiction	9	26	35
Total	26	55	81

320, the existence of causal link that is refereed to Otis Elevator Company v. Iran,1987, the date of valuation that is referred to Amoco International Finance Corporation v. Iran, 1987, 15 Iran–USCTR, 189, and the attribution of damage that is referred to Flexi-Van Leasing, Inc. v. Iran, Iran-U.S. 12 Iran-U.S.C.T.R. 335.

220.Christopher R. DRAHOZAL et Christopher S. GIBSON, « Iran_U.S. Claims Tribunal precedent in investor-state arbitration », dans Christopher S. Gibson and Christopher R. DRAHOZAL (dir.), *The Iran-U.S.Claims Tribunal at 25:The Cases Everyone Needs to Know for Investor_State & International Arbitration*, Oxford University Press.2007.1-29., p.25

Table 2. Frequency of citation of IUSCT precedent in party memorials in NAFTA arbitrations until 2006[221]

Party submission	Number (%) citing tribunal precedent	Average number of citations
Investor memorials (jurisdiction only)	5 out of 10 (50%)	1.8 per memorial
State memorials (jurisdiction only)	4 out of 10 (40%)	0.9 per memorial
Investor memorials (merits and jurisdiction)	14 out of 18 (77.8%)	4.6 per memorial
State memorials (merits and jurisdiction)	11 out of 16 (68.8%)	4.2 per memorial
Memorials of the Government of Canada	5 out of 6 (83.3%)	4 per memorial
Memorials of the United States	2 out of 4 (50%)	6.8 per memorial
Memorials of the United Mexican States	4 out of 6 (66.7%)	3 per memorial

Although, the massive use of precedents by investment tribunals in their reasoning is not the equivalent of the development of a rule of binding precedents[222] and, tribunals have no *obligation* to follow precedents. However, this conclusion should not undermine their practical importance. Thus, this de facto practice of precedents has had an impact on the development and harmonization of investment arbitration. There are some significant precedent which created in the practice of the Iran-U.S. Claim Tribunal. Definitely, the findings of this tribunal in expropriation issues are of significant importance. For instance, these are the cases where investment tribunals have relied on the 'sole effects' doctrine to determine whether a challenged measure

221.CHRISTOPHER S. GIBSON AND CHRISTOPHER R. DRAHOZAL, « Iran-United States Claims Tribunal Precedent in Investor-State Arbitration », (2006) 23-6 *J. Int. Arbitr.* 521-546.

222.P. DUMBERRY, préc., note 202.p.273

amounts to indirect expropriation. Since the sole effects doctrine is an exclusive creation of the Iran–U.S. Claims Tribunal it can be safely concluded that those investment tribunal relying on the sole effects doctrine are subconsciously relying on the decisions of the Iran–U.S. Claims Tribunal[223]. In some cases, investment tribunals have reproduced the pleadings of claimants, which in most cases inevitably rely on the decisions of the Iran–U.S. Claims Tribunal. Thus, whether or not investment tribunals expressly rely on the decisions of the Iran–US Claims Tribunal, as long as they rely on the sole effects doctrine the influence of the Iran–US Claims Tribunal is all-pervasive in investment treaty arbitration.[224].

1.9 Summary

After large-scale nationalization in Iran following the Islamic Revolution, the Iran-U.S. Claims Tribunal emerged in 1981 to settle nearly four thousand claims that American companies laid against Iran, relating mostly to expropriation and contracts. This tribunal has now rendered 881 awards, partial awards, decisions, and awards on agreed terms –the largest case load ever for international arbitration in investor-- state disputes.

Article V of the Claims Settlement Declaration requires that the tribunal base its decisions on "respect to law" and says so more clearly than do founding treaties for other international claims tribunals. Drafters supposed it essential to distinguish between the tribunal's work in public international law and that in private law so that it could develop an analytically consistent approach to such issues as nationality of claims and interest on awards. The tribunal has resolved these

223.Aniruddha RAJPUT, « Problems with the Jurisprudence of the Iran–US Claims Tribunal on Indirect Expropriation », (2015) 30-3 *ICSID Rev.* 589–615.p 591

224.*Id.*p.592

questions in practice without distinguishing between the public- and private-law nature of the law it has applied. In effect, the tribunal practises a transnational legal process. The tribunal routinely applies general principles of transnational law and in fact has spurred development of that law, the judges holding very similar views regarding content. The tribunal's application of the general principles of law and extracting them from comparative analysis, doctrine, customary international law, and interpretation of them in awarding cases of the Tribunal fits with the goal of codifying the UNIDROIT, but for a long time the tribunal was reluctant to refer directly to the UPICC as a legal source in its awards. The study of tribunal practice shows that it interprets the principles carefully through a comprehensive legal analysis. Tribunal jurisprudence that applies the principle of compensation is often termed investment arbitration, and some authors have even claimed that the tribunal practice *jurisprudence constante* in investor--state arbitration.

Chapter Two

The Principle of Compensation in Transnational Arbitration

2.1 General

Damages have traditionally been a legal remedy available in cases involving an illegal act, including acts contrary to international law. Damages invoke the duty to pay for the harm that the victim has suffered. Typical breaches of contract include rescission, unjustifiable termination, non-performance, and imperfect performance. The obligation to pay may take various, interchangeable forms, such as compensation, damages, indemnification, or reparation.[225]the common law sees the primary remedy for a breach of contract as damages. In contrast, in most civil law countries, the primary remedy is to have the contract performed in the agreed manner. It is the difficulties of specific performance that usually results in a damage award[226]. While the type of damages will differ depending on the exact circumstances of each case, most are intended to restore the position of the party that has suffered harm. Accordingly, the quantification generally involves a comparison of two positions: the position the injured party is currently in as a result of the harm and the one he would have been in were it not the harm[227]. This is often referred as the "but for" rule.

The question of the amount of compensation payable by the

225.Irmgard MARBOE, « Compensation and Damages in International Law The Limits of "Fair Market Value" », (2006) 7 *J. World Invest. Trade* 723-759.p.723. see also T. DAI, préc., note 108.

226.Peter ASHFORD, *Hand Book on International Commercial Arbitration*, Second Edition, United States, JurisNet, 2014, p. 319.

227.*Id.*, p. 329.

breaching party has long vexed international arbitration. Claims for damages usually form the core of disputes before international commercial arbitration and create extensive debate in commercial and investment law, especially in international investment disputes. This uncertainty has prevented codification of rules on the subject.[228]

It is a universal axiom that the successful party on a claim of debt may recover the amount of the debt, and on a claim of a breach or repudiation of a contract may recover compensatory damages. The method to determine the precise amount, however, may vary among legal systems. In addition, while the normal remedy in compensation for the expropriated property is compensation, the standard for settlement may be variously 'appropriate,' 'equitable,' 'fair,' 'full,' or 'just.' Thus, the calculation of compensation is characterized by its inconsistency, variety and flexibility, which make difficult the global analysis of jurisprudence in such cases[229].

Generally, international law ensures entitlement to compensation for losses foreign investors suffer from the host state's wrongful acts, or because of a lawful expropriation.[230] International law dealing with reparation constantly uses the terms 'compensation' and 'damages'. Damage has a closer connection to unlawful conduct in general, and particularly breach of contracts. It is the legal duty to pay for the harm that the victim of an unlawful act has suffered. Compensation is the duty to make financial reparation for expropriation, usually of the lawful kind.[231]

---

228 . Borzu SABAHI, « The Calculation of Damages in International Investment Law », dans Philippe KAHN (dir.), *New Aspects of International Investment Law*, Leiden/Boston, Martinus Nijhoff Publishers, 2007. 553-595, p.553

229.T. DAI, préc., note 108.

230.S. RIPINSKY, préc., note 56.p.64

231.Borzu SABAHI et Thomas WALDE, « Compensation, Damages and Valuation », dans Peter Muchlinski and Federico ORTINO (dir.), *The Oxford*

Compensation is the usual term for the amount a state has to pay in case of an expropriation; damages are the amount due after a violation of a legal obligation.[232] The statement that the aggrieved party is entitled to full compensation for harm sustained as a result of the non-performance requires further elaboration. There are three elements which are in need of addition explanation. The first is meaning of the words "full compensation".

The second concerns the meaning of the words "harm sustained". The third concerns the nature of the causal link which must exist between the harm sustained and the non-performance. In this chapter the application of the full compensation, is studied and the other two elements will be studied respectively in next chapters.

This study treats the two terms as largely synonymous. We have already looked at the practice of the Iran-U.S. Claims Tribunal with regard to these concepts. The international instruments define damages for breach of contract as monetary compensation for the injured party's loss. The examples above show that the distinctions between compensation and damages are often blurry. The CISG aims to restore an injured promisee to the position he or she would have enjoyed "but for" the breach, thus protecting that party's expectation interest.[233]

2.2 Cause of Action

To have the right to claim damages for breach of contract, the injured party usually must prove that the other party has breached a

---

Handbook of International Investment Law, New York, Oxford University Press, 2008.1049-1124, p.1052

232.Irmgard MARBOE, *Calculation of Compensation and damages in international investment law*, United States, Oxford University Press inc., 2009.p.9

233.Joseph M. LOOKOFSKY, « Consequential Damages in CISG Context », (2007) 19 *Pace Int. Law Rev.* 63-88.p.74

contract; that it has suffered loss that the instruments recognize as recoverable; and that the alleged loss flowed from the breach of obligation.

The international instruments rely on a comprehensive and uniform concept of breach (or non-performance) of contract –that it gives an aggrieved party the right to claim damages. In the view of the transnational contract law, the nature of the non-performance is irrelevant: the aggrieved party must only prove non-performance, whether it is an obligation to achieve a certain result *(obligation de resultat)* or an obligation of best effort *(obligation demoyens).* It is not necessary to prove fault in addition to the non-performance of the contractual obligation. Damages are due for all kinds of non-performance: total lack of performance, late performance or defective performance[234].Article 7.4.1 of UPICC states: "Any non-performance gives the aggrieved party a right to damages either exclusively or in conjunction with any other remedies except where the non-performance is excused under these Principles." This article establishes a general right to damages in the event of non-performance. It reminds us that the right to damages, like other remedies, arises from the sole fact of non-performance. The aggrieved party need only prove the non-performance, i.e., that it has not received what it was promised. In particular, it need not prove that the non-performing party caused the non-performance.[235] The respondent's termination of the contract obliges it to compensate the claimant for the resulting damages. This compensation includes reimbursement for costs incurred, represented by invoice amounts rendered and not paid, including profits up to the time of termination, as well as for other direct costs. The wording of the pertinent articles makes it clear that any claim for damage needs to prove

234.Denis TALLON, « Damages, Exemption Clauses, and Penalties », (1992) 40-7 *Am. J. Comp. Law* 676-686, 677.

235.*UNIDROIT principles of international commercial contracts 2010*, préc.,note 25 art.7.4.1.

two primary subjects: existence of the loss and the causal link between the loss and the wrongful act. The first tenet of the principle of compensation is that actual damage is a necessary condition of monetary compensation.[236]

In the Iranian government's claim against the U.S. government relating to U.S action to stop the export of certain properties to Iran,[237] "the Tribunal finds that Iran has not proven that, as a result of the United States' refusal, on 26 March 1981, to allow the export of Iran's export-controlled properties, it suffered a deterioration of its financial position. Iran has failed to prove that it in fact suffered any losses caused by the action taken by the United States in prohibiting export that would be compensable."

In the *Petrolane* case,the judges awarded compensation for drilling equipment that Iran expropriated. However, they did not allow the claimant to recover funds for equipment it withheld on behalf of third parties, instead mandating compensation for the property's owner rather than a bailee. The claimant, they held, had failed to prove that the taking of the third parties' equipment had harmed it.[238] As for method, international law classifies investors' claims for compensation in terms of three types of cause of action:[239]expropriation; breach of international law, and breach of contract.

We now look in turn at these causes of action as they surfaced in the tribunal's cases.

236.S. RIPINSKY, préc., note 56.p.113

237.*Iran v. United States, A/15, partial award*, [2009] 38 _IUSCTR_ 197 (Iran_U.S. Claims Tribunal).260

238.*Petrolane Inc. v the Islamic Republic of Iran*, [1991] case no.22, 27 _IUSCTR_ 22 (Iran_U.S. Claims Tribunal).para.104

239.S. RIPINSKY, préc., note 56., P.13, also I. MARBOE, préc., note 232. P.9

2.2.1 Expropriation

The terms expropriation, nationalization, taking, and confiscation seem almost interchangeable in the literature of the tribunal.[240] Also, nationalization or socialization is expropriation of one or more major national resources as part of a general new program of social and economic reform.[241] The state may restrict foreign investors' rights via interference principally with administrative or fiscal, contract, management, or property rights..[242] A deprivation or taking of property may occur under international law when a state interferes in its use or the enjoyment of its benefits, even where it does not challenge legal title to the property. It is accepted that in involuntary or efficient takings of investments, the goal of compensation ought to be to leave the investor in the same position it would have been in had the property not been taken[243].

In almost all its awards, the tribunal has enforced respect for property rights and compensation for their deprivation.[244] In the *Tippett* award,[245] it finds the claimant subject to "measures affecting property rights" by losing its property interests in TAMS-AFFA since at least

240.*Starrett Housing Corporations, Srarrett System, Inc. and Starrett Housing International, Inc. v. the Islamic Republic of Iran*, [1987] case no.24, 16 _IUSCTR_ 113 (Iran_U.S. Claims Tribunal)., concurring opinion of judge Holtzmann

241.J. CRAWFORD, préc., note 201. P.534

242.S. RIPINSKY, préc., note 56.p.47

243.LOUIS T. WELLS, « Double Dipping in Arbitration Awards? An Economist Questions Damages Awarded to Karaha Bodas Company in Indonesia », (2003) 19-4 *Arbitr. Int.* 471-482.p.474

244 . George H. ALDRICH, « What Constitutes A Compensable Taking of Property? The Decisions of the Iran-United States ClaimsTribunal », (1994) 88 *Am. J. Int. Law*.p.585

245.*Tippett, Abbett, McCarthy, Stratton v TAMSA_AFFA Consulting of Iran*, [1984] case no.7, 6 _IUSCTR_ 219 (Iran_U.S. Claims Tribunal).p.225

March 1980, and exculpates the Iranian government by virtue of its acts and omissions. International law and general principles of law enjoin compensation for the full value of the property. The tribunal prefers the term 'deprivation' to the largely synonymous 'taking,' which may imply that the government has acquired something of value, which is not required.

2.2.2 Breach of International Law

The title of breach of international law concerns a state's wrongful conduct in breach of investment treaty or customary rules of international law, but stands as a separate cause of action apart from expropriation claims, particularly vis-à-vis violations of treaty provisions such as fair and equitable treatment.[179] Generally, claims for damages arising out of state conduct that did not constitute expropriation, but breached treaty provisions, fall within this category. The U.S.-Iranian Treaty of Amity of 1955 described in detail state responsibility to support and compensate American investors. Neither party expressly repudiated the treaty after the Islamic Revolution, so it remained in force. The cases before the tribunal involved no such violation, so expropriation or breach of commercial contract underlay each claim. Thus, this category of claims is irrelevant in the practice of the Iran-U.S. Claims Tribunal.

2.2.3 Breach of Contract

International disputes often involve contracts between foreign investors and host states or state enterprises. Controversies typically arise when an investor commits capital or resources but fails to realize expected profits because of a breach or other interference attributable to the state. This situation often occurs when a new government no longer views a contract as beneficial. Where an act attributable to a state causes a breach, rules of damages derive from the contract itself and from the law governing the contract.

The tribunal holds non-performance, such as failure to deliver goods or to pay for delivered goods, or generally any non-compliance to contractual obligations, as breach of contract and arising from the state's responsibility as the contract party. In the *Pomeroy* case,[246] it held that the navy's purported termination of the contract constituted a breach of contract, entitling the party in breach to compensation: "The Navy having terminated the Contract for no fault of Pomeroy Corporation, the Tribunal finds that the Claimants are entitled to compensation for their losses caused by the termination."

Judge Mosk, concurring, justified the principle giving rise to a right to damages: "It is a widely recognized and elementary principle of law that when there has been a breach of a contract, the claimant is entitled to a remedy which would put it in the economic position it would have occupied had the respondent-obligor performed its obligations."

2.3 Principle of Full Compensation

Some commentators argue that the right to damages flows directly from the principle *pacta sunt servanda*, which substitutes a pecuniary obligation for the obligation that was promised but not performed. It is therefore natural that the creditor should thereby receive full compensation, including the loss suffered (*damnum emergens*), the expense of performing the contract, and *lucrum cessans*,the profit lost[247]. Abby Cohen Smutny states the aspects of the compensation:

"In a typical breach of contract case, the injured party, in reliance upon the contract, may have incurred expenses placing himself in a position to perform the contract with an expectation of receiving

---

246.*Pomeroy Corporation v. the Islamic Republic of Iran*, [1983] case no.41, 2 _IUSCTR- 391 (Iran_U.S. Claims Tribunal).p.398

247.L. CHENGWEI et M. S. NEWMAN, préc., note 17.p.179

some revenue in return that would both reimburse expenses incurred, plus provide some degree of profit. When the other party fails to perform in a situation where the injured party already incurred expense, in order to wipe out the consequences of the breach, the injured party must be compensated for the expenses already incurred and must be awarded the profits lost--as those two elements would be the equivalent of substituting for contract performance, that is, together, they are economically equivalent to obtaining the revenue not earned (or, in common law terms, giving the party the 'benefit of his bargain."[248]

Full compensation seems broad enough to provide a remedy for cases of both extra-contractual and contractual liability.[249] Therefore the application of the principle (with its roots in private law) requires payment of money for both the actual material damage (*damnum emergens*) and lost profits (*lucrum cessans*).[250]

Typically, damages protect one or both of two interests: reliance and performane/ expectation. Reliance interest attempts to put the claimant in the same position as if there had been no contract.[251] This usually includes the costs of preparation and performance under the agreement and the costs of preparation for collateral transactions that became necessary during the performance of the contract.

Protection of performance or expectation interest ideally places the claimant in the position that would have followed the contract's completion (including the loss of profit) –or 'market value of benefits,' which comprises incidental and consequential losses. Incidental costs arise because of breach, such as the buyer's costs of preserving the

---

248.Abby Cohen SMUTNY, « Some Observations on the Principles Relating to Compensation in the Investment Treaty Context », (2007) 22-1 *ICSID Rev.*p.16

249.Borzu SABAHI, *Compensation and Restitution in Investor_State Arbitration*, New York, Oxford University Press, 2011.p.31

250.*Id.*

251.S. RIPINSKY, préc., note 56.p.108

defective goods. While the term Consequential damages comprises the loss, which is not immediate and usually suffered in the remote third parties relations such as loss of profit[252].

Today most legal systems, including common and civil law, protect the performance interest and include legal measures to ensure full compensation. This concept has entered into the instruments of transnational contract law. Both CISG and the UNIDROIT Principles, provide that a contracting party aggrieved by the other party's non-performance of its obligations has a right to compensation for the full amount of the loss it suffered as a result of the breach. In other words, the damages provision protect a claimant's performance interest. Damages for breach of contract compensate the injured party for the loss it suffered. The principle of full compensation also informs both transnational instruments. Article 74 of CISG sets the standard for compensation at an amount equal to the injured party's loss --"a sum equal to the loss, including loss of profit, suffered as a consequence of the breach."

Problems arise with remedies under the convention because its rules concerning payment of damages and interest are very general.[253]In fact, what the CISG provisions try to do is "state basic principles to govern compensation" when a breach occurs[254]. Technically, Article 74 of the CISG does not explain how to calculate damages but allows courts and tribunals to do as circumstances dictate.[255] According to Zeller,

---

252.J. M. LOOKOFSKY, préc., note 233.p.64

253.J. Y. GOTANDA, préc., note 104.,p.96

254.John Y. GOTANDA, « Using the Unidroit Principles to Fill Gaps in the CISG », dans Djakhongir SAIDOV et Ralph CUNNINGTON (dir.), *Contract Damages; Domestic and InternationalPerspectives*, Portland, Hart Publication, 2008, p. 107-124.p.108

255.John Yukio GOTANDA, « Damages, Article 74 », dans Stefan KROLL et loukas MISTELIS (dir.), *UN Convention on Contracts for International Sale of Goods*, munchen, Germany, C.H.Beck, 2011.990-1054, p 995

"What article 74 suggests is a mechanical way rule to calculate losses, but without defining loss or full compensation.[256] Article 74 sets forth the general rules for the recovery of damages for breach of contract. In fact, it aims to place the aggrieved party in the same economic position as if the breach had not occurred –giving it the benefit of the bargain or its expectation/performance interest. This approach is the principle of full compensation.[257]

Also, UPICC article 7.4.2(1) states: "1) The aggrieved party is entitled to full compensation for harm sustained as a result of the non-performance. Such harm includes both any loss which it suffered and any gain of which it was deprived, taking into account any gain to the aggrieved party resulting from its avoidance of cost or harm. (2) Such harm may be non-pecuniary and includes, for instance, physical suffering or emotional distress."

Thus, the action for damages restores the injured party to a completed- contract economic position.[258]International arbitrations consider all claims for direct, incidental, and consequential loss. These tribunal findings reveal the autonomy of each tribunals in determining damages standard of non-expropriation violations is left to the discretionary decision of each arbitral tribunal.[259]

Under customary international law, a fundamental principle of reparation is to wipe out all the consequences of the illegal act[260]. In modern public international law, this principle traces back to the *ChorzowFactory* case (1927) before the Permanent Court of International Justice:[261] "The essential principle contained in the actual notion of an illegal act --a principle which seems to be established by

---

256.B. ZELLER, préc., note 103., p.39

257.J. Y. GOTANDA, préc., note 255.p.991

258.*Id.*

259.T. DAI, préc., note 108.p.318

260.Z. DOUGLAS, préc., note 194, 179.

261.*Chorzow Factory case,(Germany v. Poland) Merits*, préc., note 59. Para.125

international practice and in particular by the decisions of arbitral tribunals -- is that reparation must, as far as possible, wipe out all the consequences of the illegal act and re-establish the situation which would, in all probability, have existed if that act had not been committed."

The court adds that commission of an illegal act in international law--here an unlawful expropriation--requires reparation. It sets out the general principle of reparation by explaining that reparation must as far as possible eliminate the consequences of an illegal act and re-establish the situation likely in the absence of its commission. The *Chorzow Factory* principle then enjoins compensation equivalent in present-value terms to the value that the claimant lost.[262]

A key element in the *Chorzow*award is the remedy's practicality. It supports this idea that, while restitution (restoring the *status quo ante*) may be preferable in theory, it is not practical. First, the respondent state may be unwilling or unable to undo what it did. Second, compelling a state to annul its own measures may appear undue interference with its sovereignty. Third, the situation may have evolved so as to make restoration impractical or impossible. Fourth and final, the rule *non ultra petita* limits the discretion of an arbitral tribunal, so that if the parties have not asked for a particular remedy, then the tribunal should not award it.[263] Tribunals often decide that actual restitution cannot take place and proceed to determine a sum corresponding to the value that restitution in kind would bear in accordance with the Chorzow

262.William H KNULL, Scott T JONES, Timothy J TYLER et Richard D DEUTSCH, « Accounting for Uncertainty in Discounted Cash Flow Valuation of Upstream Oil and Gas Investments », (2007) 25-3 *J. ENERGY Nat. Resour. LA W* 268-302.p.268

263.B. SABAHI et T. WALDE, préc., note 227. P.1058

dictum[264]Therefore, compensation is the typical remedy in arbitration on states' wrongful acts; where restoration is not possible, compensation becomes the goal.[265]

The issue of the compensation standard in customary international law has lost a lot of its urgency with rapid expansion of investment treaties that specify the amounts to indemnify expropriation. Few, if any treaties contain the standard "full compensation," even among BITs between two industrialized states. Instead, the standard "adequate, prompt and effective" appears in a vast number of BITs.[266] A *lex specialis*is taking form in investment treaties that contain provisions on expropriation, and the provisions of arbitral tribunals will prevail over rules of customary international law. Thus, the specific binding treaty language decides the level of compensation for lawful expropriations in investment arbitration. This 'compensation rule,' which permits expropriation conditional on the payment of "prompt, adequate, and effective" compensation, has been widely, if not always unanimously, embraced by jurists and scholars throughout the twentieth century.[267]

The term 'compensation' had appeared previously in international law to refer to the consequences of states' lawful exercise of their sovereign rights, especially the right to expropriate foreign-owned property.[268] This study uses the terms 'compensation' and 'damages'

264.Jose' ALBERRO, « Estimating Damages Using DCF: From Free Cash Flow to the Firm to Free Cash Flow to Equity (and Back) », (2015) 30-3 *ICSID Rev.* 689–698.p.690

265.S. RIPINSKY, préc., note 56.p.55

266.I. MARBOE, préc., note 225.p.730

267.W. Michael REISMAN et Robert D. SLOANE, « Indirect Expropriation and its Valuation in the BIT Generation », *Yale Univ. Fac. Scholarsh. Ser.* 2004.115-150.

268 .In the ILC Articles on responsibility of states for internationally wrongfully acts, the term compensation is used to refer to a form of reparation

interchangeably to cover consequences of both lawful and unlawful breaching-party conduct encompassing state actions. It is sensible that, the standard for determining the amount of compensation has been contested between advocates of capital-exporting states and supporters of capital importers.

However, more than one standard is recognized, and differing opinions as to the appropriate one have been reflected in arbitral awards and scholarly writing. Traditionally, developed and developing countries have championed different standards. The former have defended the Hull formula for compensation–"prompt, adequate and effective"-- while the latter have argued for appropriate compensation, which is something less.[269] Most investors favour the former. U.S. Secretary of State Cordell Hull wrote to government of Mexico in 1938 that "under every rule of law and equity, no government is entitled to expropriate private property, for whatever purpose, without provision for prompt, adequate, and effective payment therefore."[270]

Two international instruments – from the International Law Commission (ILC) and the World Bank--present a formula for reparations in state--investor disputes. The International Law Commission Draft Articles on State Responsibility for Intentionally Wrongful Acts (2001) states the standard reparation in article 35, which

---

wrongful acts of sates. The commission thus clearly opted for a broader meaning of compensation. International Law Commission, *Draft Articles on Responsibility of States for Internationally Wrongful Acts*, préc., note 118.

269.Borzu SABAHI, « The Calculation of Damages in International Investment Law », dans Philippe KAHN (dir.), *New Aspects of International Investment Law*, Leiden/Boston, Martinus Nijhoff Publishers, 2007. p.559

270.Campbell MCLACHLAN QC, Laurence SHORE et Matthew WEINIGER QC, *International Investment Arbitration, Substantive Principles*, Great Britain, Oxford University Press, 2008.p.316, Ignaz SEIDL-HOHENVELDERN, « L'évaluation des dommages dans les arbitrages transnationaux », (1987) 33 *Annu. Fr. Droit Int.* 7-31.p.8

starts with the restitution obligation but factors in consideration of impossibility and proportionality and in article 36 declares the compensation principle. The formulation of reparation in the form of compensation is widely viewed as being consistent with the principles of restitution laid out in Article 36 of the International Law Commission's (ILC) Articles on State Responsibility[271]. Article 36 states:

: "1. The State responsible for an internationally wrongful act is under an obligation to compensate for the damage caused thereby, insofar as such damage is not made good by restitution. 2. The compensation shall cover any financially assessable damage including loss of profits insofar as it is established."[272]

The World Bank Guidelines on the Treatment of Foreign Direct Investment (1992) advances the standard of 'appropriate compensation' in article IV, which paragraph 3 defines: "Compensation will be deemed 'adequate' if it is based on the fair market value of the taken asset as such value is determined immediately before the time at which the taking occurred or the decision to take the asset became publicly known."[273]

The different standards indicate the lack of consensus on the matter in international law.[274] The Iran-U.S. Claims Tribunal has encountered several interpretations in investor--State disputes, in which area it has rendered almost 60 awards. The next paragraphs examine its practice respecting the standard of compensation.

271.J. ALBERRO, préc., note 264.p.691

272.International Law Commission, *Draft Articles on Responsibility of States for Internationally Wrongful Acts*, préc., note 118.

273.*world Bank Guideline on the Treatment of Foreign Direct Investment*, préc., note 121.

274.C. MCLACHLAN QC, L. SHORE et M. WEINIGER QC, préc., note 270.P.317

2.3.1 The Standard of Compensation in the Iran-U.S. Claims Tribunal

As a practical matter, however, virtually all of the tribunal's decisions focus on returning to the claimant the value of the property interest lost. None of its awards have discussed or seriously contemplated restitution or specific performance. The reasons are evident: the tribunal cannot enforce such restitution, but can use the Security Account from the Algiers Accords for monetary awards.[275] In tribunal practice, U.S. lawyers sought the most recovery, and Iranian respondents wanted to give less. Arbitrators on the tribunal fought over the principle of compensation to apply. Some authors point out that even when the tribunal awarded full compensation, its measures did not fulfil that promise.

The arbitrators' responses to each other's views, sometime acrimonious, served only to highlight their differences. The Americans usually s asserted the Hull formula, which the Iranians rejected. The Iranian party responded in the *American International Group, Inc.* case;[276]

"Even assuming, that Iran violated principles of customary international law in the course of nationalizing the insurance industry, there is no international legal entitlement to compensation equal to the 'full value' of the property nationalized. The suggestion of full compensation derives from the traditionally asserted standard of 'prompt, adequate and effective' compensation [i.e., Hull] which has been repudiated by modern developments in international law; instead, a standard of 'partial compensation' should be applied, based on

275.CHARLES N. BROWER, « Current Developments in the Law of Expropriation and Compensation: A Preliminary Survey of Awards of the Iran-United States Claims Tribunal », (1987) 21 *Int. Lawyer.*639-669, P.639

276.*American International Group Inc. v the Islamic Republic of Iran*, [1984] case no.2, 4 _IUSCTR_ 96 (Iran_U.S. Claims Tribunal).p.103

references contained in resolutions of United Nations organs and from post-war settlement practice."

As we saw in chapter 1, the 1955 Treaty of Amity is still in force, despite decades of conflict between the states, and no one is pushing for its revocation. Several times the tribunal has referred to this document as lex specialis. There is general authority for considering a bilateral treaty a lex specialis, whose provisions will prevail over rules of customary international law. The tribunal said as much in the *Phillip Petroleum* award:[277]

"116. With regard to the standard of compensation, the Tribunal has pointed out, supra, that it applies the lex specialis of the Treaty of Amity and that it need not therefore make any finding with respect to customary international law."

As for compensation standard, the Iranian party argued that article 4 of the Treaty of Amity lays out just compensation.[278] Article 4 states:

"2) property of nationals and companies of either High Contracting Party, including interests in property, shall receive the most constant protection and security within the territories of the other High Contracting Party, in no case less than that required by international law. Such property shall not be taken except for a public purpose, nor shall it be taken without the prompt payment of *just compensation*. Such compensation shall be in an effectively realizable form and shall represent the full equivalent of the property taken, and adequate provision shall have been made at or prior to the time of taking for the determination and payment thereof."

Despite controversy over the treaty's validity, the tribunal has expressly affirmed the document as applicable law to resolve disputes.

277.*Phillips Petroleum Company v. the Islamic Republic of Iran and NIOC*, préc., note 157.p.125

278.*Treaty of Amity, Economic Relations, and Consular Rights. Signed at Tehran, on 15 August 1955, between Iran and United States*, préc., note 122

The question regarding standard of compensation related to the choice of the treaty's 'just compensation' or instead 'full compensation.' The tribunal's chambers have taken different positions, ranging from just compensation, through denying the treaty, to applying Hull foemula[279]. However, the leading awards involving compensation for expropriation indicate the range of possible views as well as the tribunal's evolving views on this crucial matter.

In the *INA Corp.* case,[280] the judges pored over the issue of standard of compensation. Judge Holtzman chose full compensation: "The Permanent Court of International Justice in the *Chorzow Factory*Case, held that, in an unlawful nationalization, there must be restitution to establish the situation that would otherwise have existed, or, if this is not possible, payment of a sum corresponding to the value which restitution in kind would bear." Judge Lagergren stated: "It is well settled that the measure of compensation ought to be such as to approximate as closely as possible in monetary terms to the principle of restitutio in integrem." According to Judge Ameli of Iran, "Where the conduct of a party is held to be unlawful, in terms of its contractual obligations, then the concept of restitution in integrem may perhaps properly be invoked." Finally, the majority, reflecting PCIJ jurisprudence and the Treaty of Amity, awarded full compensation for unlawful taking, including *damnum emergen* and *lucrum cessans.* It held that the words "the full equivalent of the property taken," from article IV of the Treaty of Amity, mean compensation equal to the fair market value of the claimant's shares in the expropriated company.

However, a number of judgments endorsed 'appropriate' compensation. For instance, in the *Shahin Shaine Ebrahimi* case, the

279.Homayoun MAFI, « Controversial Issues of Compensation in Cases of Expropriation and Nationalization: Awards of the Iran-United States Claims Tribunal », (2011) 18-1 *Intl J Humanit.* 83-102.p.98

280.*INA Corporation v. the Islamic Republic of Iran*, préc., note 160. at p.395, Separate Opinion of judge Holtzmann tribunal stated:

"The Tribunal believes that, while international law undoubtedly sets forth an obligation to provide compensation for property taken, international law theory and practice do not support the conclusion that the prompt adequate and effective standard represents the prevailing standard of compensation Rather, customary international law favors an '*appropriate*' compensation standard."[281]

There has been considerable controversy about what constitutes 'appropriate' compensation. While Western countries interpret this generally as full compensation, developing states insist that it must mean less than full. The chamber stated further that "once the full value of the property has been properly evaluated, the compensation to be awarded must be appropriate to reflect the pertinent facts and circumstances of each case."[282] Paragraph 88 states: "The gradual emergence of this rule aims at ensuring that the amount of compensation is determined in a flexible manner, that is, taking into account the specific circumstances of each case. The prevalence of the 'appropriate' compensation standard does not imply, however, that the compensation quantum should be always less than full."

In the *Sedco* case,[283] the tribunal maintained that customary international law and the Treaty of Amity set the same standard. The chamber's position in fact acknowledges the Hull formula.[284] This approach appears in its other expropriation cases. The tribunal found,

---

281.*Ebrahimi Shahin Shaine v. the Islamic Republic of Iran*, [1994] case no. 44&46, 30 _IUSCTR_ 170 (Iran_U.S.Claims Tribunal). p.198, para 88

282.*Id.*para.94

283.*SEDCO, Inc. v. the Islamic Republic of Iran and National Iranian Oil Company*, préc., note 159., p.189

284. The standard of prompt, adequate and effective compensation is usually referred as the Hull rule, which originated in a Note from the US Secretary of State, Cordell Hull, to the Mexican Government on 22 August 1938, J. CRAWFORD, préc., note 201.p.547

the Standard of compensation to be applied to a taking of property is the same whether viewed as a requirement of the Treaty of Amity or as an application of principles of customary international law. Stating that: "Therefore, the fact that SISA is a Panamanian corporation would not alter NIOC's obligation to pay full compensation for property appropriated, even if the Treaty of Amity were not applicable."

In the *Sola Tiles* case, the tribunal saw only minimal differences between the standards: "The amount of appropriate compensation is determined in flexible manner, that is, taking into account the specific circumstances of each case. The prevalence of the appropriate compensation standard does not imply, however, that the compensation quantum should be always 'less than full.'"

In the *ITT Industries, Inc.*[285] case, Judge Aldrich wrote, "I would be reluctant to decide it, particularly as the applicable rules of international law are not significantly different whether the Treaty applies or not. In either case, a taking of property must be accompanied by the prompt payment of just compensation which is effective and adequate to compensate fully for the value of the property taken. In the absence of a market to determine market value, the Tribunal must endeavor to find the value of the company as a going concern."

The full tribunal, in an inter-state Case B-1,[286] ruled for full compensation vis-à-vis the retention of the purchased goods in the United States because of a U.S. embargo on exports to Iran:

"Under international law the State responsible for such deprivation is liable to compensate for the full value of the deprived property at the date the deprivation became effective. Moreover, this is consonant with general principles of contract law pursuant to which the United States, as a Bailee of the Iranian-owned items at issue in this part

---

285.*ITT Industries, Inc v. the Islamic Republic of Iran*, [1983] case no.156, 2 _IUSCTR_ 348 (Iran _U.S. Claims Tribunal). p.354

286.*Iran v United States, Case B-1*, [1988] 19 _IUSCTR_ 273 (Iran_U.S. Claims Tribunal).p.295, para.70

of Claim, had the obligation to substitute compensation for the value of the items in place of their return."

Almost all the tribunal's awards have consistently applied the Treaty of Amity and its 'just compensation' standard of full compensation; most have also found the same standard of full compensation under both the treaty and customary international law.[287] Several of the tribunal's more recent awards have explored the interrelationship between the two standards of compensation. All have concluded "that the two sources impose essentially identical obligations on the expropriating state." In the *Phelps Dodge Corp.*[288] award, it suggested that the Treaty of Amity stipulated compensation standards "similar, if not identical" to those of customary international law."

The standard of compensation in non-expropriation contractual claims is also full compensation. In claims arising out of contracts, the tribunal ruled for full payment for damage. It factored in any actual, incidental, or consequential losses. In the *CMI International* case,[289]about illegal termination of the contract, the tribunal called for compensation for all the heads of damages the client suffered:

"3. Other Damages. The Claimant, like any seller whose buyer has breached the contract of sale, is entitled to compensation for the actual damages that can be proved. Obviously, that includes any losses on resale and, in the present case, it includes the cost of resales, such as commissions, and other costs caused by the breach, such as carrying and administrative costs (including insurance premiums, property taxes, and custodial costs), and most significantly the financial costs of the delays in payment from the dates due until the dates of resale."

Tribunal case law contains various forms of compensation:

287.J. R. CROOK, préc., note 154.p.301

288.*phelps Dodge Corp. v. the Islamic Republic of Iran*, [1986] 10 _IUSCTR_ 121 (Iran_U.S. Claims Tribunal).*para.28*

289.*CMI International, Inc, the Islamic Republic of Iran*, préc., note 151.p.270

various terms, such as full, adequate, equitable, fair, and full.[290] Although the tribunal approves of the principle of full compensation, it has never awarded the full value of the expropriated property. Sornaraja writes: "Though, the arbitrators supported the norm of full compensation, they regarded it only as a principle with which to start the inquiry and took several factors into consideration in reducing the compensation which was finally awarded so that on inspection it would appear that full compensation was never awarded by any of the individual tribunals/"[291] This outcome flowed from the distinction it made between lawful and unlawful expropriation–the subject of the following paragraphs.

2.3.2 Different Compensation Standards in Lawful and Unlawful Expropriation

The idea that lawful and unlawful expropriation might have different consequences for the expropriating state originated in the judgment of the now-superseded Permanent Court of International Justice. If and how the lawfulness of the expropriation affected compensation is rather unclear.[292] Under current customary international law, states have the right to expropriate the property of foreign nationals for a public purpose, as long as they do so in a non-discriminatory manner and pay compensation.[293] According to Sergey Ripinski, a lawful expropriation must be for a public purpose, non-discriminatory, lawfully executed, and accompanied by payment of compensation. Academic writings support this view and also mention

---

290.Khalil KHALILIAN, *Iran_United States Claims Arbitration*, U.S, Trafford, 201.2.p.298

291.M. SORNARAJAH, préc., note 215.p.432

292.I. MARBOE, préc., note 232.p.68

293.B. SABAHI, préc., note 249. P.92

these four points,[294]and numerous past cases support this stance.[295]Under international law, expropriation is not unlawful *per se*, falling within the state's prerogative.[296] International practice and scholarly writing have, however, not clearly differentiated lawful and unlawful expropriation.[297] There are several legal opinions about this issue, and the International Law Commission Draft Articles on State Responsibility for Intentionally Wrongful Acts (2001)[298] makes no distinction between lawful and unlawful taking vis-à-vis compensation.

The right to expropriate is unquestionable, though not unlimited;[299] see the four basic conditions above, and article 13 (1) of the Energy Charter Treaty (ECT) of 1994 [300]and article 1110 of

---

294.I. MARBOE, préc., note 232. P.43and Christopher S. GIBSON, « Yukos Universal Limited (Isle of Man) v The Russian Federation, A Classic Case of Indirect Expropriation », (2015) 30-2 *ICSID Rev.* 303-314.p.306

295.Jan H. Dalhuisen and Andrew T. GUZMAN, « Expropriatory and Non-Expropriatory Takings Under International Investment Law », *UC Berkeley Public Law Leg. Theory Res. Pap. Ser.* 2012.21., 1-21, available at SSRN: https://ssrn.com/abstract=2137107

296.S. RIPINSKY, préc., note 56. P.66

297.I. MARBOE, préc., note 232.,P.69

298.International Law Commission, *Draft Articles on Responsibility of States for Internationally Wrongful Acts*, prec.note 118.,footnote 549: "Controversy has persisted in relation to expropriation cases, particularly over standards of compensation applicable in the light of the distinction between lawful expropriation of property by the State on the one hand, and unlawful takings on the other, a distinction clearly drawn by PCIJ in Factory at Chorzów,"

299.Tarcisio GAZZINI, « Drawing the Line between Non-compensable Regulatory Powers and Indirect Expropriation of Foreign Investment - An Economic Analysis of Law Perspective », (2010) 7-3 *Manch. J. Int. Econ. Law*.36-51, p.36

300.Article 13of Energy Charter Treaty 1994 states: "Investments of Investors of a Contracting Party in the Area of any other Contracting Party shall not be nationalised, expropriated or subjected to a measure or measures having e ect

NAFTA.[301] Most bilateral investment treaties have followed the same rules, but seem not to offer any guidance on compensation for unlawful acts or differentiate compensation between lawful and unlawful taking.

Commentators note that compensation for lawful and for unlawful expropriation should not be the same, for every legal system should make a distinction between damages arising from lawful and from unlawful acts.[302] Hence the principle for determining compensation in case of unlawful taking would not be appropriate for a lawful taking. Hence, it would seem reasonable, "an unlawful taking or breach of contract may give rise to general damages, including loss of anticipating profits; but a lawful taking by exercise of prerogative or statutory right will give rise only to just compensation, which does not include anticipatory profits, and which is different from the concept of damages."[303]

As for evaluation of the compensation attributable to the state's

---

equivalent to nationalisation or expropriation (hereinafter referred to as "Expropriation") except where such Expropriation is: (a) for a purpose which is in the public interest; (b) not discriminatory; (c) carried out under due process of law", *Energy Charter Treaty (opened for signature 17 December 1994, entered into force 16 April 1998).COR-REG-36116-Sr-4622, at https://treaties.un.org/Pages/showDetails.aspx?objid =080000028009ac15 accessed 2 February 2017.*

301.Article 1110 of NAFTA states: "1. No Party may directly or indirectly nationalize or expropriate an investment of an investor of another Party in its territory or take a measure tantamount to nationalization or expropriation of such an investment ("expropriation"), except:(a) for a public purpose;(b) on a non-discriminatory basis;(c) in accordance with due process of law and Article 1105(1); and(d) on payment of compensation in accordance with paragraphs 2 through 6. *North America Free Trade Agreement (NAFTA)*, préc., note 92.

302.S. RIPINSKY, préc., note 56. P.65

303.DEREK W. BOWETT, « claims between States and private entities: the twilight zone of international law », (1986) 35-4 *catholic university law review* 929-942. P.938

breach of the law, it is essential to distinguish between unlawful and lawful takings of property. The former invokes damages; the latter, compensation. Damages are, of course, usually heavier than compensation.[304] In the *Chorzow Factory* formula, the reparation was to put the victim of an unlawful act in a position as if the illegal act had not happened. Brownlie has explained: "expropriation for certain public purposes, as in wartime, is lawful, even if no compensation is payable. Otherwise, the expropriation of property is unlawful without provision for effective compensation; nationalization that expropriates a major industry or resource is unlawful without compensation."[305] Expropriation that is lawful necessitates compensation only for direct losses, that is the value of the property, while expropriation that is unlawful *per se* involves liability also for consequential loss (*lucrum cessans*).[306]

The tribunal's rulings have referred to the *Chorzow* award (see the next section). An unlawful expropriation contravenes international law, and the culpable state must fully repair any financial harm. To follow the *Chorzow* award and come as close as possible to *restitutio in integrum*, the tribunal should consider the highest value of the enterprise as of the judgment date or the expropriation date. This should ensure that a decrease in value would not harm the former owner, and an increase would be of benefit. [307]

Lawfulness and its effects on compensation have engaged the tribunal from its start. Generally, all of Iran's expropriations involved nationalization or a public purpose and were non-discriminatory, so the respondent sought to lessen liability to compensate. The tribunal has

304.C. F. AMERASINGHE, « Issues of Compensation for the Taking of Alien Property in the Light of Recent Cases and Practice », (1992) 41 *Int. Comp. Law Q.* 22-65.p.22

305.J. CRAWFORD, préc., note 201.p.624

306.*Id.* P.625

307.I. MARBOE, préc., note 232. P. 132

held that lawfulness or economic, financial, social concerns cannot negate an expropriation claim. In the *Phelps Dodge* award,[308] the tribunal held:

"The Tribunal fully understands the reasons why the Respondent felt compelled to protect its interests through this transfer of management, and the Tribunal understands the financial, economic and social concerns that inspired the law pursuant to which it acted, but those reasons and concerns cannot relieve the Respondent of the obligation to compensate Phelps Dodge for its loss."

The duty to compensate both expropriations and nationalizations was explicit in the *INA Corp.* case: "nationalizations are not per se unlawful, and a lawful one would also "impose on the government concerned the obligation to pay compensation." In this award the tribunal commented: "It has long been acknowledged that expropriations for a public purpose and subject to conditions provided for by law, notably that category which can be characterized as 'nationalizations', are not per se unlawful. A lawful nationalization will, however, impose on the government concerned the obligation to pay compensation." Judge Ameli noted: [309] "In the event of such large-scale nationalization of a lawful character, international law has undergone a gradual reappraisal, the effect of which may be to undermine the doctrinal value of any 'full' or 'adequate' (when used as identical to 'full') compensation standard as proposed in this case."

The judges in the *American International Group* case[310] reaffirmed the tribunal's opinion it is not true that the nationalization of a foreign investor's asset was by itself unlawful, under either customary international law or the Treaty of Amity, as there is not enough evidence that the nationalization was not for a public purpose as part of a larger

308.*phelps Dodge Corp. v. the Islamic Republic of Iran*, préc., note 288.. para 22

309.*INA Corporation v. the Islamic Republic of Iran*, préc., note 160.

310.*American International Group Inc. v the Islamic Republic of Iran*, préc., note 276.

reform program or was discriminatory. The tribunal recognized the lawfulness of Iran's taking and nationalization.

In the next steps the tribunal sought to delimit the measures of compensation in case of lawful taking and its difference with compensation in unlawful taking. Obviously, the distinction between compensation for lawful behaviour and damages for unlawful behaviour is important only if it has practical effects.[311]

In the *Amoco* case[312], the award propounded and reflected parties' contentions. The claimant asserts that compensation for unlawful expropriation would be more than the 'full equivalent' for lawful expropriation. The respondents argue that lawful expropriation would deserve substantially less compensation than a wrongful expropriation and should cover only the state's unjustifiable enrichment but not lost profit and in this case should be the equivalent of the net book value of the residual nationalized assets. According to that view, lost profits deserve compensation only in unlawful expropriations, while in lawful ones the state must cover only what the owner has suffered (*damnum emergens*).

This, respondents claim, resembles what the PICJ held in the Chorzow Factory case, but this is not the amount the former owner has invested or the value of its tangible assets. The "value of the undertaking," according to the PICJ, comprises not only the value of its lands, buildings, equipment, and stocks, but also its supply and delivery contracts, its goodwill, and its future prospects.[313]

The distinction in the *Phillips Petroleum* case[314] between lawful and unlawful acts remains. The tribunal found the lawfulness of the

---

311.I. MARBOE, préc., note 225. P.726

312.*Amoco International Finance Corp. v the Islamic Republic of Iran*, préc., note 157.p.253

313.I. MARBOE, préc., note 225. P.727

314.*Phillips Petroleum Company v. the Islamic Republic of Iran and NIOC*, préc., note 157., para.110

taking under customary international law relevant to only two issues--"whether restitution of the property can be awarded and whether compensation can be awarded for any increase in the value of the property between the date of taking and the date of the judicial or arbitral decision awarding compensation." This ruling means that an unlawful expropriation immediately obliges the state to restore the property, not compensate. Further, an increase in the property's value between taking and decision is relevant only in an unlawful expropriation.

"110. The Tribunal believes that the lawful/unlawful taking distinction, which in customary international law flows largely from the Case Concerning the Factory at Chorzow (Claim for Indemnity) (Merits), P.C.I.J. Judgment No. 13, Ser. A., No. 17 (28 September 1928), is relevant only to two possible issues: whether restitution of the property can be awarded and whether compensation can be awarded for any increase in the value of the property between the date of taking and the date of the judicial or arbitral decision awarding compensation. The Chorzow decision provides no basis for any assertion that a lawful taking requires less compensation than that which is equal to the value of the property on the date of taking."

The tribunal's conclusion is legal recognition that damages may vary with the nature of the wrong, giving rise to the right to recovery and the remedy for that wrong. This rationale points to an awarding of damages either to punish the wrongdoer or to deter other wrongs, potentially useful in illegal, as distinct from lawful, expropriation.

Judge Brower, concurring in the *Amoco* award, states: "It is in fact obvious that the expropriator's responsibility must be increased by the fact that his action is unlawful. It is also obvious that the unlawful character of his action can never place the expropriator in a more favourable position by reducing the indemnity due. This point of view, with which the Court in its judgment has not thought fit expressly to deal, appears to me to be in accordance with the general principles of law."[315]

These aforementioned decisions suggest that both the PCIJ and the tribunal believed that in a lawful taking lost profits (*lucrum cessans*) as such were not payable as compensation, while they were in an unlawful taking. Lost profits are clearly an aspect of consequential damages and as such rightly belong in the damages payable for an unlawful taking, but not for a lawful taking.[316]The tribunal's *Amoco* award emphasized that the"first principle established by the Court in Chorzow Factory is that a clear distinction must be made between lawful and unlawful expropriations, since the rules applicable to the compensation to be paid by the expropriating State differ according to the legal characterization of the taking."[317] The tribunal continued: "The difference is that if the taking is lawful the value of the undertaking at the time of the dispossession is the measure and the limit of the compensation, while if it is unlawful, this value is, or may be, only part of the reparation to be paid."

The distinction between lawful and unlawful expropriations did not much affect the final award. Since modern valuation techniques can estimate investments' income-generating potential, lost profit was recoverable under both standards. This increased the chance of compensation for consequential loss. In the awards of *Philip Petroleum* and *Amoco*, the tribunal made it clear that a claimant in unlawful expropriation can recover two items not available in lawful expropriation: first, the investment's potentially higher value at the date of award, and, second, consequential expenses, especially lost profit

315.*Amoco International Finance Corp. v the Islamic Republic of Iran*, préc., note 161

316.C. F. AMERASINGHE, « Some Aspects of the Quantum of Compensation Payable upon Expropriation », (1993) 87 *Am. Soc. Int. Law.*,477-482, P.477

317.W. M. REISMAN et R. D. SLOANE, préc., note 267. p.136

(*lucrum cessans*). Therefore, these two elements were not recoverable in a lawful expropriation, such as Iranian nationalization.

Judge Brower disagreed on this subject, arguing for full compensation in both lawful and unlawful expropriation, but, for the latter, adding punitive or exemplary damages against a state. In his separate opinion in the *Sedco* award[318] he states:

"There are strong reasons in logic why it would be appropriate for an international tribunal to award punitive or exemplary damages against a State in such circumstances. In the absence of such damages being awarded against an unlawfully expropriating State, where restitution is impracticable or otherwise inadvisable, that State is required to furnish only the same full compensation as it would need to provide had it acted entirely lawfully. Thus, the injured party would receive nothing additional for the enhanced wrong done it and the offending State would experience no disincentive to repetition of unlawful conduct".

Sergey Ripinski states that finding *lucrum cessans* not payable in lawful expropriation derived from the tribunal's reading of the *Chorzow Factory* case; a number of authors have criticized that reading as incorrect.[319] Also McLachlan observes; the Tribunal's approach to Chorzow factory cannot be justified as a correct reading of that judgment.[320]

2.3.3 Creeping Expropriation; Lawful or Unlawful?

Constructive or creeping expropriation occurs where there is no law or official document about an alleged expropriation. The absence of

318.*SEDCO, Inc. v. the Islamic Republic of Iran and National Iranian Oil Company*, préc., note 159.Separate opinion on judge Brower.

319.S. RIPINSKY, préc., note 56.p. 208

320.C. MCLACHLAN QC, L. SHORE et M. WEINIGER QC, préc., note 270.P.324

an expropriatory decree, but the presence of an expropriatory consequence, defines a generic indirect expropriation. Were disclaimers of expropriatory intention sufficient to validate otherwise expropriatory acts, states could avoid their obligation to make reparation simply by asserting the absence of that intention. Because of their gradual and cumulative nature, creeping expropriations also render it problematic, perhaps even arbitrary, to identify a single interference (or failure to act where a duty requires it) as the 'moment of expropriation.'[321]Recently, in Yukos investment arbitration[322], the tribunal determined that the Russian Federation had breached its obligations under Article 13 (Expropriation) of the Energy Charter Treaty (ECT). The Tribunal held that while the Russian Federation 'has not explicitly expropriated Yukos or the holdings of its shareholders', nonetheless, the measures it had taken 'have had an effect "equivalent to nationalization or expropriation". The Tribunal's ruling was founded on a finding of indirect expropriation. In this respect, the Tribunal concluded that the primary objective of the Russian Federation was to bankrupt Yukos and appropriate its valuable assets.

Cases of indirect expropriation would, almost by definition, constitute unlawful expropriation, because the expropriating state does not usually acknowledge the very fact of expropriation.[323] Because of the absence of a manifest intention in such cases, Judge Brower once observed that "it is difficult to envision a de facto or 'creeping' expropriation ever being lawful, for the absence of a declared intention to expropriate." In the *Sedco* award,[324] his separate opinion states: "By

321.W. M. REISMAN et R. D. SLOANE, préc., note 267.W. Michael Reisman and Robert D. SLOANE, « Indirect Expropriation and its Valuation in the BIT Generation », *Yale Univ. Fac. Scholarsh. Ser.* 2004.115-150.P.125

322.*YUKOS Universal LTD. (ISLE OF MAN) v The Russian Federation*, préc., note 219. Para.1580. 756

323.S. RIPINSKY, préc., note 56. P.69

324.*SEDCO, Inc. v. the Islamic Republic of Iran and National Iranian Oil* definition, it is difficult to envision a de facto or 'creeping' expropriation ever being lawful, for the absence of a declared intention to expropriate almost certainly implies that no contemporaneous provision for compensation has been made. Indeed, research reveals no international precedent finding such an expropriation to have been lawful."

However, indirect expropriation simply does not meet some of these conditions, such as due process of law and payment of compensation. Marboe asserts: "For indirect expropriations such procedures will rarely be available to the investor because the expropriatory measures are normally regulatory acts that are not directed towards the investor. The absence of even the possibility to challenge the expropriation means that indirect expropriations normally are unlawful."[325]

It is firmly recognized in international law that 'regulations' do not give rise to a right to compensation, even if they restrict a foreign investor's use of its investment. In this context, almost all arbitral tribunals adopt the so-called police-power doctrine in deciding whether a general measure entitles an investor to compensation.[326] Drawing the line between non-compensable exercise of regulatory powers and indirect expropriation, however, remains rather problematic, as there is neither a clear definition of indirect expropriation nor an a priori limit on the kind of state measure or action that may amount to deprivation or expropriation.[327] In principle, there is widespread consensus that regulatory measures pursued for legitimate objectives cannot constitute indirect expropriation.[328]

Company, préc., note 159.

325.I. MARBOE, préc., note 232. P.61

326.C. N. BROWER et S. W. SCHILL, préc., note 51.P.485

327.T. GAZZINI, préc., note 299.p.38

328.I. MARBOE, préc., note 232. P.164, and, August REINISCH, « Expropriation », dans Peter MUCHLINSKI, Federico ORTINO et Christoph

These rules could be relevant to creeping expropriation that resulted from any non-expropriatory state conduct, but breached other investment-treaty provisions. Lawful regulation, that is, is not expropriation. Some self-described 'regulation,' however, can and should properly be deemed expropriatory. Thus, while a host state may, of course, regulate foreign investment, some of its regulations and, equally important, failures to regulate may rise to the level of expropriatory action.[329] The practice of the tribunal has endorsed this position. In the *Sedco*award,[330]the tribunal held: "It is also an accepted principle of international law that a State is not liable for economic injury which is a consequence of bona fide 'regulation' within the accepted police power of states."

Summing up: the tribunal in its practice has treated all the Iranian-government actions in question as regulatory, thus rendering all of these claims, including direct and indirect expropriation, as lawful actions of the state.

2.4 Unjust Enrichment as a Basis for Compensation

The doctrine of unjust enrichment had its origins in Roman law, where it emerged as an equitable device to cover cases in which a general action for damages was not available. Most of the world's municipal legal systems recognize and codify it, and it seems generally an element in the catalogue of general principles of law available for international tribunals to apply.[331] The rule against unjust enrichment is inherently flexible, as its underlying rationale is to re-establish a balance

SCHREUER (dir.), *the Oxford handbook of International Investment Law*, New York, Oxford University Press, 2008, p. 407-459.P.433

329.W. M. REISMAN et R. D. SLOANE, préc., note 267.P.129

330.*SEDCO, Inc. v. the Islamic Republic of Iran and National Iranian Oil Company*, [1985] 9 _IUSCTR_ 248 (Iran_U.S. Claims Tribunal).p.275

331.*Sea-Land Service, Inc. v. the Islamic Republic of Iran*, préc., note 60.p.168

between two individuals, one of whom has enriched himself or herself, with no cause, at the other's expense. Its equitable foundation necessitates delimiting all the circumstances of each specific situation. It involves a duty to compensate, which is entirely reconcilable with the absence of any inherent unlawfulness of the acts in question. Thus, the principle finds an obvious field of application in cases where a foreign investor has sustained a loss whereby another party has been enriched, but that does not arise out of an internationally unlawful act, which would found a claim for damages.

Although the theory of unjust enrichment is a general principle in contract law, the CISG does not expressly mention it. However, article 7.4.2 of UPICC does so implicitly, where comment 3 explains "full compensation," pointing out the theory's application: "However, the aggrieved party must not be enriched by damages for non-performance. It is for this reason that paragraph (1) also provides that account must be taken of any gain resulting to the aggrieved party from the non-performance, whether that be in the form of expenses which it has not incurred (e.g. it does not have to pay the cost of a hotel room for an artist who fails to appear), or of a loss which it has avoided (e.g. in the event of non-performance of what would have been a losing bargain for it)."[332]

The principle of unjust enrichment has surfaced vis-à-vis the legal justification for the obligation to pay compensation upon expropriation, whereby nobody should benefit from somebody else's financial disadvantage without a legal justification.[333] Sornarajah believes that the doctrine should not be applied independently to determine the full compensation in the case of expropriation against a foreign investor: "unjust enrichment cannot uniformly support full compensation when

---

332.*UNIDROIT principles of international commercial contracts 2010*, préc note 25.

333.I. MARBOE, préc., note 232. P.15

applied to a situation of expropriation. It will support less than full compensation when the past benefits of the investment had weighed heavily in favour of the investor. It may support more than full compensation in situations in which the foreign investment is relatively new, had been enticed into the host country and had involved the transfer of assets and technology which would not otherwise have been obtained by the host state. An equitable principle like unjust enrichment lends only equivocal support to full compensation. While there could be full compensation in appropriate circumstances, in other circumstances it could produce results varying from no compensation to less than full compensation."[334]

The IUSCT upheld unjust enrichment as a cause of action in a number of other cases, which helped establish it as an independent cause of action in international law. One author remarks:

"The Iran-U.S. Claims Tribunal definition, with disgorgement potential, creates a standard that can be applied universally. A universal standard does two things. First, it will limit abuses of unjust enrichment, both implicit (where it is silently imported into unrelated damage calculations and distorts the resulting quantum) and explicit. Second, a universal standard will create a well-defined and welcome space for unjust enrichment in international investment dispute resolution."[335]

The tribunal set out clear tenets for unjust enrichment as a cause of action. The most crucial is that it can be brought only where no other cause of action is available. Thus, claimants cannot bypass contracts to seek better results through an off-contract cause of action. This both protects the integrity of the contract and confines claims of unjust enrichment. Here, five elements appear to be the basis for holding unjust enrichment in the tribunal's jurisprudence:

334.M. SORNARAJAH, préc., note 215. p.419

335.Ana T. VOHRYZEK-GRIEST, « Unjust Enrichment Unjustly Ignored: Opportunities and Pitfalls in Bringing Unjust Enrichment Claims Under ICSID », (2009) 31-3 *Loyola Los Angel. Int. Comp. Law Rev.* 501-580.

•There must be an enrichment,

•with a corresponding loss.

•Close causal connection between the loss and the enrichment

•No justification for the enrichment

•No other cause of action available (thus, if you have a contract claim, you cannot rely on unjust enrichment, and unjust enrichment can be brought only in isolation).

This summary stems from what the tribunal held more specifically in the *Benjamin Isaiah* case:

"There must have been an enrichment of one party to the detriment of the other, and both must arise as a consequence of the same act or event. There must be no justification for the enrichment, and no contractual or other remedy available to the injured party whereby he might seek compensation from the party enriched."

This was the first case in which the tribunal decided a claim for unjust enrichment.[336] It found that the claimant was the beneficial owner of funds represented by a bank cheque drawn in January 1979 by the respondent bank's predecessor on an American bank, which cheque was subsequently dishonoured for insufficient funds. Because the payee of the cheque -- a business associate of the claimant's -- was an Israeli national, the tribunal had no jurisdiction over a claim based on the cheque, as such claim would not satisfy the jurisdictional requirement of continuous ownership of the claim by a U.S. national from the date it arose until January 19, 1981, the date of the Algiers Accords.

So, the claimant asserted a claim for unjust enrichment against the Iranian bank, arguing that the bank had been given funds of which he was the beneficial owner and that it retained those funds for its own benefit and to his detriment. Citing authorities, the tribunal observed: "Restitutionary theories such as unjust enrichment and *enrichissement sans cause* are found in the laws of many nations," and "in international

336.*Isaiah Benjamin v. Bank Mellat*, préc., note 173.

law unjust enrichment is an important element of state responsibility." The tribunal concluded that unjust enrichment was a general principle of law. In awarding the claimant of the cheque, the tribunal observed: "It would be inequitable for such a bank to be able to escape liability to the beneficial owner of the funds represented by such a dishonored check and retain the funds to which the bank has no claim."

In *Sea-Land* case,[337] the predominant view seems to favour assessing damages to reflect the extent by which the state has been enriched. Judge Jiménez de Aréchaga considers that where the 'enriched' state has obtained no benefit, no compensation should be payable at all. Sea-Land maintained that PSO (the Iranian Ports and Shipping Organization) or the Iranian government was unjustly enriched at the expense of Sea-Land, which accordingly deserves compensation. The tribunal has formulated the theory of unjust enrichment in its award:

"The concept of unjust enrichment had its origins in Roman Law, where it emerged as an equitable device 'to cover those cases in which a general action for damages was not available'. It is codified or judicially recognized in the great majority of the municipal legal systems of the world, and is widely accepted as having been assimilated into the catalogue of general principles of law available to be applied by international tribunals. The rule against unjust enrichment is inherently flexible as its underlying rationale is 'to re-establish a balance between two individuals, one of whom has enriched himself, with no cause, at the other's expense."

Wayne Mapp, who served as a judge on the tribunal, states: "The Sea-Land claim also included expropriation as a cause of action, and apart from the duty to compensate, expropriation is not necessarily a breach of international law. Although there is a close relationship between causes of action founded on expropriation and unjust

---

337.*Sea-Land Service, Inc. v. the Islamic Republic of Iran*, préc., note 60.P.168.169

enrichment they have been perceived by the Tribunal as quite separate. Thus, the Tribunal has awarded compensation to claimants if the respondent state has been enriched at the expense of the claimant, whether or not the respondent state has committed any act of expropriation."[338]

The tribunal in *Sea-Land* pointed out that, opinions differ as to the basis of computation of damages. The predominant view seems to be that damages should be assessed to reflect the extent by which the state has been enriched. Equity clearly requires that cognizance be taken of the de facto situation, and this explains why there is no discernible uniformity in the practice of international tribunals in this respect. Important factual circumstances to be taken into account are the level of investment; the period during which the foreign investor has been able to make a profit; and the benefit actually derived by the host country from its acquisition. Applying these considerations to the Sea-Land facts, the Tribunal held:

"Compensation for unjust enrichment cannot encompass damages for loss of future profits. The Tribunal must aim instead to place a monetary value on the extent to which PSO was enriched by its premature acquisition of the facility. The Tribunal must establish whether PSO did in fact avail itself of the facility after Sea-Land's departure."

The majority in this award had rejected breach of contract and expropriation claims amounting to $40 million and awarded a small sum as damages for unjust enrichment. The tribunal here estimated that premature use of the Sea-Land facility enriched the PSO by approximately $750,000.[158]This figure comes from the tribunal's projected gain for PSA, which it based on PSO documents discussing what PSO could have gained during the 611-day period that Sea-Land

338.W. MAPP, préc., note 127. P.215

remained unexploited (which figure the tribunal used to estimate the profits that occurred when PSO later began exploitation), coupled with documents showing in fact subsequent exploitation.[339]

Thus, in the tribunal's jurisprudence, unjust enrichment is a theory of 'last resort,' which may not be maintained when a valid and enforceable contract exists. Where a valid contract exists, unjust enrichment is a derivative, or at best a secondary alternative, legal theory to an action on the contract." In the *Sea-Land* case, chamber I set out certain conditions for the admissibility of a claim of unjust enrichment: "There are several instances of recourse to the principle of unjust enrichment before international tribunals. There must have been an enrichment of one party to the detriment of the another, and both must arise as a consequence of the same act or event. There must be no justification for the enrichment, and no contractual or other remedy available to the injured party whereby he might seek compensation from the party enriched."[340]

Based on this finding, the chamber denied the remedy the claimant sought. A breakdown of these conditions yields five elements in deciding a valid case of unjust enrichment: enrichment by one party, with loss and detriment affecting the other party; both enrichment and detriment arising from the same act or event; lack of justification; and lack of remedy for compensation. Generally speaking, restitutionary theories such as unjust enrichment figure in the law of many nations. In cases where a contract relationship did not emerge, unjust enrichment may constitute a cause of action. In investment disputes to date, it has not been accepted as a basis for determining compensation.[341]Regardin the UPICC the commentators mostly believe that the aim of the award of damages is to compensate the aggrieved party for the harm which it

339.J. A. WESTBERG, préc., note 135. P.208

340.*Sea-Land Service, Inc. v. the Islamic Republic of Iran*, préc., note 60.P.169

341.S. RIPINSKY, préc., note 56. P.134

has suffered; it is not to deprive the non-performing party of any benefit which it has obtained as a result of its non-performance. Thus, it appears not to be possible to recover restitutionary or gain-based damage under the UPICC[342]. There is some indication that the amount of unjust enrichment may serve as an equitable factor to the extent that the law permits application of equitable consideration. In sum, unjust enrichment claims are admissible only where there is no claim for expropriation and no contract, and where the five prerequisites in the *Isaiah* award are met.

In the *T.C.S.B., Inc.* case,[343] the tribunal stated: "Where a contract binding on both parties exists, the issue of whether a performance of the contract results in any 'enrichment' of a party and whether such enrichment is 'unjust' in relation to the other party, cannot be decided without specifically determining the contractual rights and obligations of the parties." Wayne Mapp writes in this regard, "The doctrine of unjust enrichment as an independent cause of action has been progressively developed by the Tribunal."[344]

2.4.1 Prohibition of Double Recovery

The principle of unjust enrichment prohibits the awarding to the party of damages greater than the amount of its loss and thereby placing it in a better position than where performance of the contract would have placed it. Preventing over-compensation necessitates taking into account all the extra gains and cost savings flowing from the breach

---

342.Ewan MCKENDRICK, « Damages », dans Stefan VOGENAUER et Jan KLEINHEISTERKAMP (dir.), *Commentary on the UNIDROIT Principles of International Commercial Contracts (PICC)*, United States, Oxford University Press, 2009 à la page 874.

343.*T.C. S. B., Inc. v. the Islamic Republic of Iran*, [1984] 5 _IUSCTR_ 161 (Iran_U.S. Claims Tribunal).p.172

344.W. MAPP, préc., note 127.p.215

of contract when calculating damages.Certain aspects of damages calculations are still undeveloped by investment arbitration tribunals, specifically whether benefits received by the claimant may be applied to offset the total damages to be paid by the breaching party[345]. Damages should not enrich the claimant or give it a windfall at the expense of the other party. Article 7.4.2 of UPICC expressly states: "(1) The aggrieved party is entitled to full compensation for harm sustained as a result of the non-performance. Such harm includes both any loss which it suffered and any gain of which it was deprived, taking into account any gain to the aggrieved party resulting from its avoidance of cost or harm."

This article further requires the tribunal to take into account any gain to the aggrieved party resulting from its avoidance of cost or harm. The aim here is to avoid the unjust enrichment of the aggrieved party. Equally any gain which accrue to the aggrieved party (such as income received from a substitute contract entered into by the aggrieved party) must be brought into account[346].

Because the purpose of damages for breach of contract is to compensate the injured party for the loss, benefits or gains the breach gave to the respondent are generally irrelevant for measuring damages.[347] Gains can be of two kinds: the value of what has been received under the contract (goods or purchase price) and the value derived from putting the subject-matter of the performance to a profitable use. The transnational instruments contain provisions relating to the return of what has been received under the contract in cases where the contract has been avoided (articles 81 and 82 of CISG and article 7.3.6 of

345.Christian TIETJE et Emily SIPIORSKI, « Offset of Benefits in Damages Calculation in International Investment Arbitration », (2012) 29-5 *J. Int. Arbitr.* 545-566.p.545

346.E. MCKENDRICK, préc., note 342 à la page 876.

347.Djakhongir SAIDOV, *The Law of Damages in International Sales*, Hart Publishing, Oxford, 2008.p.33

UPICC).[348]

As for the accounting for the gain in assessing compensation, UPICC article7.4.2 stipulates accounting for "any gain to the aggrieved party resulting from its avoidance of cost or harm." The comment to that article explains that the purpose of this language is to ensure that damages for non-performance do not enrich an aggrieved party. If a party is unjustifiably enriched at the expense of another, that party has to pay a sum equal to the enrichment's value, to be determined according to the contractually agreed price or market price, including full compensation for the use (usufruct) of the subject-matter of the enrichment.[349]

Article 75 of CISG states that the aggrieved party may recover the difference between the contract price and the price of the substitute transaction.[350] This article provides for the measurement of damages, eliminating the need for the claimant to prove the current or market price for the goods. when that party has entered into a substitute transaction after avoiding the contract. Article 75 permits calculating damages on the basis of the resale of goods or the cover purchase.

The tribunal has consistently required accounting for profits deriving from resale of goods that were the subject of breached sales

---

348 .Article 81 CISG states: "(2) A party who has performed the contract either wholly or in part may claim restitution from the other party of whatever the first party has supplied or paid under the contract. If both parties are bound to make restitution, they must do so concurrently."

349.*UNIDROIT principles of international commercial contracts 2010*, précnote 25.

350. Article 75 CISG states: "If the contract is avoided and if, in a reasonable manner and within a reasonable time after avoidance, the buyer has bought goods in replacement or the seller has resold the goods, the party claiming damages may recover the difference between the contract price and the price in the substitute transaction as well as any further damages recoverable under article 74."

contracts in calculating damages. Similarly, it insisted on accounting for the value of goods one party retained when a contract was terminated either by breach or in accordance with its terms. In the *CMI International, Inc.* case,[351] the tribunal -- in assessing whether to deduct profits on resales of equipment (claimant resold certain items of equipment at prices higher than those in the purchase order) from the damages for which it awarded compensation --applied the general principle of law that takes such profits into account and accordingly reduced the claimant's compensation.

The judges held that the claimant was entitled to claim the cost of resales, such as commissions, and other costs resulting from the breach, such as carrying and administrative costs (including insurance premiums, property taxes, and custodial costs), and, most significant, the financial costs of the delays in payment from the dates on which payment was due until the dates of resale of the equipment. In accounting for profits on resale, the tribunal applied the general principle of law that deducts profits on resales of equipment from the damages. It accordingly reduced the compensation by the value of the claimant's overall profit on the resale of certain items of equipment subject to the purchase orders.

In the *Harnischfeger Corp.* case,[352] the claimant, relying on Uniform Commercial Code (UCC) section 2-706(6), has not taken into account the resale profit on these two cranes in calculating the damages to which it is entitled. Under UCC section 2-706(1), however, the resale price and the contract price appear to be the price covering all the goods under the contract, not the price of each particular item. The tribunal therefore concluded that calculation of the resale price must take into

351.*CMI International, Inc, the Islamic Republic of Iran*, préc., note 151.p.269

352.*Harnischfeger Corporation v the Islamic Republic of Iran*, [1984] 7 _IUSCTR_ 90 (Iran_U.S. Claims Tribunal).p.111

account both the losses and the gains sustained on the resale of each individual item in the contract.

2.5 Equitable Considerations

The use of equitable considerations in computing compensation is not uncommon, even if it is not always admitted. It also lies just beneath the surface of many judicial and arbitral decisions.[353] The Iran-U.S. Claims Tribunal has introduced the notion of 'equity' into some of its awards, insofar as it has regarded equitable considerations as relevant in reducing compensation rather than increasing it.[354] One of the reasons that equitable principles surface in awarding of damages is that sometimes damages are impossible to quantify with certainty.[355]

In fact, where the amount of the damages cannot be established with a sufficient degree of certainty, the assessment of damages is stated to be at the discretion of the court. In this regard the official comments of UPICC refers to an equitable quantification of the harm sustained, but does not give any guidance as to the way in which this discretion should be exercised[356]. In this manner, the parties should endeavor to quantify the causal link between the harm and the onerous action as precisely as possible[357].

Equitable considerations can support less-than-full compensation, and some arbitral tribunals have sought to do just that.

353.Mark KANTOR, *Valuation for Arbitration: Compensation Standards, Valuation Methods and Expert Evidence*, The Netherlands, Kluwer Law International, 2008., p.117

354.C. F. AMERASINGHE, préc., note 316.,p.481

355.B. SABAHI, préc., note 269. p.581

356.*UNIDROIT principles of international commercial contracts 2010*, préc note 25. Comment on art.7.4.3

357.E. MCKENDRICK, préc., note 342 à la page 882.

Equity is a double-edged sword and can backfire on those who invoke it.[358] Aldrich, as one of the tribunal judges, submits: "I believe that when they are making a complex judgment such as one regarding the amount of compensation due for expropriation or rights to lift and sell petroleum products, equitable considerations will inevitably be taking into account, whether acknowledged or not."[359]

The notion of equity is inherently subjective: a conception of what is equitable or fair in particular circumstances will differ with viewpoint, so there can be little certainty about how to apply it. Much depends on the personal and collective views and beliefs of the members of the arbitral tribunal and their reading of the facts of the case.[360]This approach, gives to tribunals more flexibility in reaching result which seems to be just on the facts of the case and helped them to avoid the all-or-nothing consequences of the low degree of certainty. This seems to be what has happened in practice and number of cases can be found in which the Iran-U.S. Claims Tribunal awarded damages.

Equitable considerations have helped determine compensation by the Iran-U.S. Claims Tribunal. We can find such an approach in the following four cases, as examples.

In the *Phillips Petroleum* case,[361] the tribunal reduced the compensation the expert's report proposed, stating that "the need for some adjustments is understandable, as the determination of value by a tribunal must take into account all relevant circumstances, including equitable consideration."

358.M. SORNARAJAH, préc., note 215. p.420

359.G. H. ALDRICH, préc., note 125. p. 241

360.S. RIPINSKY, préc., note 56.p.126

361.*Phillips Petroleum Company v. the Islamic Republic of Iran and NIOC*, préc., note 157.para.112

In a partial award, the *Amoco International Finance* case[362], the judges' ruling noted the role of equitable consideration in its valuation of the compensation. It stated that there was no scientifically accurate method of valuation and that the phrase 'market value' was of no help in the absence of regular transactions in a free market:

"The choice between all the available methods must rather be made in view of the purpose to be attained, in order to avoid arbitrary results and to arrive at an equitable compensation in conformity with the applicable legal standards."

The judges also commented that the traditional view saw the expropriated person's loss, rather than the expropriating state's gain, as the reference point for assessing compensation. They argued that, vis-à-vis nationalization of a going concern, the difference between the expropriating party's enrichment and the claimant's loss would be minimal: "As the nationalization state normally intends to maintain such an undertaking as a going concern and to benefit from its profitability the value of the expropriated assets as a going concern will be the measure of the enrichment of the nationalizing state as well as of the deprivation of the expropriated owner."

The tribunal indicated that it would consider enrichment by either party in calculating compensation –its first duty is to avoid any unjust enrichment or deprivation of either party. This last statement may imply that a tribunal may include unjust enrichment as part of equitable consideration. In the *Starrett Housing* case,[363] the tribunal awarded less compensation than its expert had recommended, citing its discretionary power to 'determine equitably' the amount. It reduced the

---

362.*Amoco International Finance Corp. v the Islamic Republic of Iran*, préc., note 161..para.220

363.*Starrett Housing Corporations, Srarrett System, Inc. and Starrett Housing International, Inc. v. the Islamic Republic of Iran*, préc., note 240.p.221, para.339

expert's assessment of Rials 377 million for a particular property to Rials 27 million. The tribunal, ruling in the *Eastman Kodak* case, stated:[364]

"Compensation awarded was based on promissory notes the expropriated subsidiary had issued to the claimant. A 50 percent downward adjustment of the value of these promissory notes, owing to uncertainty as to whether the subsidiary would ever have been able to reply them in full, was considered equitable in all the circumstances."

As for equitableness of compensation, the tribunal concludes that this means that awards should take into account all the circumstances of the case. In the *Phillips Petroleum* award,[365] it referred to legitimate expectations and concluded that a willing buyer at the time of the expropriation must have counted on modifications of the concession: "153. The Tribunal concludes that the value of the Claimant's JSA (joint venture agreement) interests in September 1979 would have been reduced very significantly by virtue of the perceived risk that a buyer might encounter irresistible future pressures to modify the JSA in ways that would greatly reduce the anticipated future profitability of those JSA interests."

The tribunal frequently references to 'equity' in its lowering of compensation and arriving at the amounts to award, although, in all the cases it decided, what it was awarding was, by its own admission, 'full' compensation.[366]

2.6 Summary

The decisions of the tribunal affect above all the development of international law on compensation in international disputes, since it

364.*Eastman Kodak Company v the Islamic Republic of Iran*, [1991] 27 _IUSCTR_ 3 (Iran_U.S. Claims Tribunal).p.21

365.*Phillips Petroleum Company v. the Islamic Republic of Iran and NIOC*, préc., note 157.

358.C. F. AMERASINGHE, préc., note 304.p 65

has largely rejected the view of developing states, which tend to favour 'adequate' compensation for expropriated property, and has upheld the traditional approach of full compensation. Therefore, its awards have ruled decisively in favour of traditional, full compensation.

Every award that addressed the issue has clearly endorsed that standard of compensation. Whether it looked to customary international law or to the Treaty of Amity of 1955, it found various terms, such as 'adequate,' 'equitable,' 'fair,' and 'full,' to express different aspects of one concept. In contractual disputes it usually compensated any actual loss (*damnum*) and lost profit (*lucrum cessans*). However, its application of the compensation principle in claims arising from contracts fits exactly with the rules in UNIDROIT Principles of International Commercial Contracts. Its interpretation of the Permanent International Court of Justice's jurisprudence in the *Chorzow Factory* award has led it to find a fundamental distinction between lawful and unlawful taking in the standard of compensation. Accordingly, it decided that, in lawful expropriation, only *damnum emergens* (loss suffered) would be compensable, and, because in all its cases the expropriation was lawful, it did not award lost profits there. It submits that in unlawful expropriation the claimant can recover the following two items rather than a lawful expropriation claim: the higher value that the investment might have acquired at the date of award, and consequential expenses, particularly lost profit (*lucrum cessans*).

The doctrine of unjust enrichment has penetrated most of the world's municipal legal systems and the arsenal of general principles of law for international tribunals to apply. In the Iran-U.S. Claims Tribunal's practice, the doctrine can both lead to action and rebalance the two parties. First, it serves as a cause of action, as the tribunal has affirmed in a number of cases and has helped enshrine it an independent cause of action in international law. Unjust-enrichment claims are justiciable only where there is no contract and no claim for expropriation. Second, the doctrine re-establishes a balance between two parties, one of which has enriched itself, with no cause, at the other's expense. The tribunal seems to have applied the doctrine in awards to compensate for the respondent's unjust enrichment.

The tribunal's practice has also engaged with two other legal concepts, prohibition of double recovery and equitable consideration, which derive from the principle of unjust enrichment. First, double recovery defies the embargo on unjust enrichment and would follow on the awarding of more damages than the amount of loss, which would more than restore the claimant's original situation. To prevent over-compensation, the arbiter must consider all gains and costs flowing from the breach. Second, equitable consideration in fixing damages has usually, in the tribunal's practice, reduced, rather than increased compensation. Equitable principles become relevant when damages are uncertain and equity diminishes the damages on behalf of the respondent.

In sum, this chapter shows that the tribunal's standard of compensation comports with UPICC and such auxiliary legal principles as unjust enrichment and equity, and the role of the equity in approximation of the quantum of damage in the Tribunal's awards is the same as set out in the UNIDROIT Principles.

Chapter Three

Limitations on Damage

3.1 General

Because the recovery of damages must be finite in quantity, the methods of limiting them is to restrict liability, which thus becomes a part of the general measure of damages. Most legal systems recognize the legal concepts of causation, certainty, foreseeability, and mitigation as the criteria for measuring damage.[367] Generally, a party's claim is subject to several other requirements that also limit damages 'methods of limiting damages.'

However, it is necessary in the first instance to explore the reasons which have been advanced to explain why damages need to be limited first explore the three principles for limiting damages. Arbiters award damages to put the claimant, as nearly as possible, "in the same position as he would have been in if he had not sustained the wrong for which he is now getting his compensation or reparation." The first principle, causation, establishes the general compensatory approach. The second and third principles -- foreseeability and mitigation -- limit the compensatory approach. For an award of damages, there must be a causal connection between the respondent's breach of contract and the claimant's loss. Even if the claimant can show that the respondent's breach caused his or her loss, the claimant must still show that the recovery of damages for loss is not too remote.[368]. However, the practice

367.Djakhongir SAIDOV, « Methods of Limiting damages under the Vienna Convention on Contracts for the International Sale of Goods », (2002) 14 *Pace Int. Law Rev.* 308-353..p.309

368.John Y. GOTANDA, « Recovering Lost Profits in International Disputes », (2004) 36 *Georget. J. Int. Law Fall 2004 61-112* 61-112.p.74

of the Iran-U.S. Claims Tribunal limits recovery to damages provable with certainty. In general, the claimant must prove lost profits with reasonable certainty, although the certainty rule applies only to the breach's reducing the claimant's future revenues, not to the amount of profits it lost. In fact, the certainty of damage would be a limiting factor that, particularly in consequential damages, can lead to dismissal of the claim.

These three principles –causation, foreseeability, and mitigation--like all such principles, are easy to state but more difficult to apply. These principles may limit compensation. Even when the arbiter holds lost profits foreseeable, it might still deny or reduce compensation by reference to other elastic doctrines, such as mitigation and the doctrine of avoidable loss.[369] This chapter reviews the IUSCT's application of these three, principles in cases of expropriation and in contractual claims.

3.2 Causation

The law requires a sufficient link or nexus between the wrongful act and the injury before any obligation to make reparations for that injury arises.[370] In fact, determining the "consequences of the illegal act" requires an assessment of the principles of causation in the law. Legal standards such as proximate cause or 'too remote' or indirect are used to make the inquiry into relevant causality end at some point, usually within the range of foreseeability of the omnipresent fictitious ordinary and reasonable, but for a well-informed and prudent person. causation is a mental concept, generally based on inference or induction from uniformity of sequence, because of a causal connection between

---

369.J. M. LOOKOFSKY, préc., note 233.p.67

370.A. C. SMUTNY, préc., note 248. P.3

two events.[371] Recognizing the causal link can be difficult in some cases. The damage results perhaps from a series of events (multiple causes) or from several concurrent causes. Suppose that it is demonstrable there are one or more causes of delay and disruption that are the defendant's fault, but that the claimant is similarly responsible.

Causation in modern legal systems has two elements: factual and legal. Factual causation requires establishing that a wrongful act physically, or objectively, caused the damage. The breaching party cannot be liable for a loss that its breach has not caused, and a causal connection is necessary to establish liability in damages.[372]. In this sense it may require constructing a chain of events that begins with the wrongful act and ends with the harm caused.

Legal causation determines whether to sever the chain because, beyond a certain point, the wrongdoer could not have foreseen the result of the acts, or because the results were too remote and not proximate.[373] It means determining in legal terms how much the alleged cause was responsible for the damage. Under the legal test of causation, the key issue is whether the wrongful conduct was a sufficient, proximate, adequate, foreseeable, and/or direct cause of the harm.[374] Injury may in fact be too 'remote' or 'consequential' to be the subject of reparation. In some cases, the criterion of 'directness' may be used, in others 'foreseeability' or 'proximity.'

Some commentators believe that foreseeability is sufficient grounds for causation, so that these two concepts strongly overlap.[375] Foreseeability helps determine causation and damages, but normally not

---

371.Vivian RAMSEY, « establishing claims for damages, costs and interest in international arbitration », (2011) 26-5 *Am. Univ. Int. Law Rev.* 1211-1239. p.1223

372.D. SAIDOV, préc., note 347.p.82

373.B. SABAHI, préc., note 245.,p.19

374.S. RIPINSKY, préc., note 56. P.135

375.D. SAIDOV, préc., note 367.p.345

the quantum of the damage.[376] The damage that constitutes the substance of an action must be due to a direct, proximate cause. Consequential damages, or those damages found to be remote, are in principle not recoverable in an international arbitration.[377] Therefore the responsibility for compensation due to a breach of contract does not entitle the injured party to consequential damages, as they are too remote or unforeseeable.

Although these two principles – foreseeability and causation -- in practice overlap, the transnational instruments deal with them under separate rubrics. Thus, the principle of foreseeability appears in the next section. The Vienna Convention (CISG) deals with causation in article 74. It allows for recovery of only damages for such loss as has been "suffered as a consequence of the breach," requiring the presence of a causal link between the breach and the loss. UPICC also requires the existence of a causal link (article 7.4.2: "(1) The aggrieved party is entitled to full compensation for harm sustained as a result of the non-performance."

In investment arbitration, the concept of causation serves several purposes. First, it establishes the state's liability for harm resulting from its unlawful conduct flowing from its action, or from its inaction, if it had a duty to act. Second, it helps establish the amount of compensation due. There must be a causal link, including monetary damages, between the unlawful act and the injury.[378] As for state responsibility, According to article 31 (2) of the ILC Draft Articles: "Injury includes any damage, whether material or moral, caused by the internationally wrongful act of a State.[379]" The commentary on this article sums up causality as a necessary but not a sufficient condition for

376.S. RIPINSKY, préc., note 56. P.140

377.K. KHALILIAN, préc., note 290. p.181

378.Andrea K. BJORKLUND, « Causation, Morality, and Quantum », (2009) 32 *Suffolk Transnatl. Law Rev.* 435-450.p.436

379.S. RIPINSKY, préc., note 56.p 74

reparation. In addition, full reparation, formulated in the *Chorzow* formula, invokes proximate or effective causality, limiting the object of damages to damage that has a causal link with the illegal act in question.

The decisions of the Iran-United States Claims Tribunal constitute a significant body of precedent on this project.[380] The judges had to address the intention of the wrongdoer state in cases of harm to the investor and adopted an effects solution. They found generally that worthy economic or social objectives for expropriation did not negate compensation.[381]

Tribunal awards adhere to a jurisprudence that ignores governmental intention in expropriation. For example, in the *Sea-Land* award,[382]it said:

"A finding of expropriation would require, at the very least, that the Tribunal be satisfied that there was deliberate governmental interference with the conduct of Sea-Land's operation, the effect of which was to deprive Sea-Land of the use and benefit of its investment. Nothing has been demonstrated here which might have amounted to an intentional course of conduct directed against Sea-Land. A claim founded substantially on omissions and inaction in a situation where the evidence suggests a widespread and indiscriminate deterioration in management, disrupting the functioning of the port of Bandar Abbas, can hardly justify a finding of expropriation." Since, *Sea-Land*, however, the insistence on intention as a necessary component of expropriation has "obtained no support in subsequent Tribunal awards. In creeping expropriations, states do not form an express intent to expropriate; indeed, they may not have such an intent at all.

380.G. H. ALDRICH, préc., note 125.p.219

381.Sebastian Lopez ESCARCENA, « Expropriation and other Measures Affecting Property Rights in the Case Law of the Iran-United States Claims Tribunal », (2013) 31-2 *Wis. Int. Law J.* 177-207,p.189

382.*Sea-Land Service, Inc. v. the Islamic Republic of Iran*, préc., note 60., p.166

In its *Phillips Petroleum Co.* award,[383] the tribunal argued that it need not determine the intent of the Government of Iran" and added that "a government's liability to compensate for expropriation of alien property does not depend on proof that the expropriation was intentional. It held: "98. Although a government's liability to compensate for expropriation of alien property does not depend on proof that the expropriation was intentional."

This statement is supported by commentators, truly, state; the state's responsibility to pay compensation for expropriation does not, in any event, 'depend on proof that the expropriation was intentional is considerable.[384]

The tribunal looks for causal links between the harm and the wrongful action. In the *Agrostruct* case, the claimant argued that the respondent caused delays that lost it projects it anticipated carrying out elsewhere. However, the claimant failed to establish a sufficient causal link between the alleged delay and the loss of business.[385]

The tribunal attempts to apportion the several causes accurately. Such analysis requires consideration of legal causation. It can mean interference with a contractual relationship. In the *Schering Corp.* case,[386] the judges awarded damages for an unlawful instruction from Iran's Central Bank, which refused payment of drafts for delivery of goods to a domestic company.

As for proximate cause, chamber II shed light on it in the *Hoffland* case, where the claimant alleged that the National Iranian Oil Company had sold crude oil to U.S. companies, which used it to make

383.*Phillips Petroleum Company v. the Islamic Republic of Iran and NIOC*, préc., note 157. para79

384.W. M. REISMAN et R. D. SLOANE, préc., note 267.P.130

385.*Agrostruct International, Inc. v the Islamic Republic of Iran*, [1988] 18 _IUSCTR_ 180 (Iran-U.S Claims Tribunal)., p.194, para.46

386.*Schering Corp v the Islamic Republic of Iran*, [361apr. J.-C.] 5 _IUSCTR_ (Iran_U.S. Claims Tribunal).p.367

agrichemicals that destroyed some 36,000 colonies of the claimant's bees. The tribunal held that sales of Iranian oil caused the loss only in the sense that the loss would not have occurred had there been no oil and thus no chemicals– i.e., it acknowledged factual causation. However, it denied proximate cause: "What we do mean by the word 'proximate' is that, because of convenience, of public policy, of a rough sense of justice, the law arbitrarily declines to trace a series of events beyond a certain point."[387].

In some cases, the acts attributable to Iran were a concurrent cause, but not sufficient or finding a compensable deprivation. Notably, this analysis insists on a causal link for a finding of expropriation, rather than introducing it at the damages phase of the proceeding. In its *Otis Elevator* award,[388] the tribunal could not establish that governmental interference with the claimant's shareholding interest in Iran Elevator substantially deprived the claimant of the use and benefit of its investment:

"A multiplicity of factors affected the Claimant's enjoyment of its property rights in Iran Elevator, among them its position as a minority shareholder in an inactive company and the changed circumstances of the Iranian elevator market. However, the Tribunal is not convinced that the Claimant has established that the infringement of these rights was caused by conduct attributable to the Government of Iran."

In some cases, the act attributable to Iran as the cause of the damage is very complicated. In fact, the cause per se consists of a series of acts that are not simple to analyse. The tribunal, in its *Phillips* award,[389]

387.*Hoffland Honey v. National Iranian Oil Company*, [1983] 2 _IUSCTR_ 41 (Iran_U"S. Claims Tribunal).p.42

388.*Otis Elevator Company v. the Islamic Republic of Iran*, [1987] 14 _IUSCTR_ 283 (Iran_U.S. Claims Tribunal).p.294

389.*Phillips Petroleum Company v. the Islamic Republic of Iran and NIOC*, préc., note 157.

the claimant and Second Parties jointly operated the offshore petroleum fields and shared 50--50 the crude petroleum produced by the fields prior to the events of 1979, thereafter the Claimant and the other Second Party companies no longer participated in joint operation of the fields, no longer received their share of the petroleum being produced, and were told by Iran that their agreement had been terminated and nullified. The Tribunal has summarized the effects of Iran's actions on the claimant's property rights:

"These changes resulted from the actions of Iran, which totally excluded the Second Party from any of its functions under the JSA (joint venture agreement) The conclusion that the Claimant was deprived of its property by conduct attributable to the Government of Iran, including NIOC, rests on a series of concrete actions rather than any particular formal decree, as the formal acts merely ratified and legitimized the existing state of affairs."

For recognition of any direct expropriation, the tribunal has moved beyond constructive expropriation and declared that any action by the judiciary affecting the investor's rights would make the state responsible. In the *Oil Field of Texas* case,[390] it held: "It is well established in international law that the decision of the court in fact depriving an owner of the use and benefit of his property may amount to an expropriation of such property that is attributable to the state of that court." We now turn to the different sorts of actions that the judges regarded as the cause of expropriation.

3.2.1 Direct and Indirect Expropriation

The question of expropriation is at the heart of modern foreign investment law, yet remains an area of great uncertainty and ambiguity. "Neither treaty law nor existing jurisprudence provides clarity on the

---

390.*Oil Field of Texas, Inc. v the Islamic Republic of Iran and NIOC,* [1986] case no.43, 12 _IUSCTR_ 308 (Iran_U.S. Claims Tribunal)., para.42, p.318

questions of when government action amounts to an expropriation or what to do if does"[391]. In its practice, the tribunal applied the term 'expropriation' to all sorts of property-rights deprivations. During the revolutionary turmoil in Iran after 1979, the Islamic government issued sweeping nationalization decrees in June and July 1979, covering banks (June 7), insurance companies (June 25), and certain heavy industries (starting July 5). On January 8, 1980, the Revolutionary Council adopted a Single Article Act nullifying any oil contracts inconsistent with the government's policy of a totally nationalized oil industry.[392]

These various, explicitly expropriatory actions, directly affected foreign investors' properties and contracts, such as oil and gas contracts. Therefore, the tribunal, in its practice, treated the dates above as the moments of direct expropriation. Direct expropriation results in the transfer of title and physical possession of the property or other assets from a foreign investor to the state.[393]

Besides direct expropriation, in some cases the state perhaps took earlier actions that led to deprivation of the foreign investor of its properties. For example, the nationalization of an Iranian company in which a U.S. claimant owned stock constituted an expropriation of the claimant's investment. Confiscation of property constituted an expropriation, as did the state's refusal to allow a claimant to ship property out of the country. A nationalized bank's refusal to honour a depositor's demand to close out an account also constituted an expropriation. The government's failure to pay a claimant a tax refund to which he or she was entitled constituted an uncompensated expropriation. Indirect expropriation involves a measure or series of measures of a party that have an effect equivalent to direct expropriation without formal transfer of title or outright seizure.[394] They leave legal

391.J. H. D. and A. T. GUZMAN, préc., note 295.

392.C. N. BROWER et J. D. BRUESCHKE, préc., note 124.p.371

393.S. RIPINSKY, préc., note 56. P.64

394.W. M. REISMAN et R. D. SLOANE, préc., note 267.p.134

title to the property intact but interfere with the investor's ownership rights through regulatory acts and omissions, producing the same effect as an expropriation. Indirect expropriations often take place in the form of creeping expropriation.

Indirect expropriation is deemed to occur when a state's measure has an effect similar or equivalent to direct expropriation, even though it does not seize the property nor tamper with legal title.[395] Today, the predominant form of expropriation is indirect expropriation. Other terms for it are 'consequential,' 'constructive' 'creeping,' 'de facto,' or 'regulatory' expropriation.[396] In some cases, expropriation may result from a series of acts or omissions that in effect take away property rights --creeping expropriation.

It is obvious that abstract legal principles may not be enough to identify expropriation, which may require case-by-case analysis of the specific facts. However, the tribunal focused on the impact of the alleged taking rather than on semantics. In the practice of the tribunal the boundary between regulation and expropriation becomes the unreasonableness of an interference, and the unreasonableness of an interference would depend on the nature of the affected property and the means used."[397] In its rich jurisprudence, the tribunal has repeatedly addressed the concept of indirect expropriation, as in its *Tippett* award:

"The Claimant is entitled under international law and general principles of law to compensation for the full value of the property of which it was deprived. The Tribunal prefers the term 'deprivation' to the term 'taking', although they are largely synonymous, because the latter may be understood to imply that the Government has acquired something of value, which is not required. A deprivation or taking of property may occur under international law through interference by a

395.S. Ripinsky, préc., note 56.p.65

396.A. Reinisch, préc., note 328.,p.422

397.S. L. Escarcena, préc., note 381. P.190

state in the use of that property or with the enjoyment of its benefits, even where legal title to the property is not affected, thus requiring compensation under international law. Such a conclusion is warranted whenever events demonstrate that the owner was deprived of fundamental rights of ownership and it appears that this deprivation is not merely ephemeral.[398]"

The precedent that has been created in this decision is regarded by the following investment tribunals as the doctrine of sole effect. these are the cases where investment tribunals have relied on the 'sole effects' doctrine to determine whether a challenged measure amounts to indirect expropriation[399]. to define indirect expropriation focus on the unreasonable interference, prevention of enjoyment, or the deprivation of property rights. The tribunal has also construed and applied the notion of other measures affecting property rights within its jurisdiction. By applying this concept, the tribunal could award compensation even where deprivation was not tantamount to taking.[400]We next consider the variety of actions that the tribunal has regarded as causing expropriation.

3.2.1.1 Interference with Contract Rights

There is a general understanding that expropriation may affect not only tangible property but also a broad range of intangible assets of economic value to an investor. Expropriable property may thus include immaterial rights and interests, most notably contractual rights.[401] There are two viable approaches to determining the quantum of damages for loss of contractual rights: expropriation/international law and contractual disputes. The former deems a contract as establishing an

398.*Tippett, Abbett, McCarthy, Stratton v TAMSA_AFFA Consulting of Iran*, préc., note 245.p.225

399.A. RAJPUT, préc., note 223.p.591

400.S. L. ESCARCENA, préc., note 381, p.188

401.A. REINISCH, préc., note 328.p.410

expropriable property right that may decline in value. The latter involves claims for lost profits arising from breaches of long-term contracts, which are inordinately complex cases, especially where the respondent's breach has not just injured the claimant's business but destroyed it, and the tribunal must determine the value it lost.[402]

In awarding damages for breach of an international investment contract, arbiters apply both domestic and international law, depending on whether they understand the contract as a source of obligation or as property. The former position calls on domestic law, usually that of the host state; the latter, on international law protecting property, including rules on compensation for expropriation.[403]. International law and investment-treaty arbitration offer two approaches to compensation for interference with contractual rights or breach of contract. The first, deems a contract a kind of property, vulnerable to expropriation or other interference. This invokes the reparation obligation in the *Chorzow Factory* ruling, which places the aggrieved party in the hypothetical position of assuming no interference. In the *Chorzow Factory* case, about Poland's unlawful taking of Germán-owned industrial property, the Permanent Court of International Justice held in 1927: "It is a principle of international and even a general conception of law that any breach of an engagement involves an obligation to make reparation." [404]The second approach treats an injurious act as a breach of contract, worthy of damages. Such damages would put the claimant in the economic position that it would have possessed if the contract had been performed.[405] International law recognizes contractual rights as expropriable.[406]

The Iran-U.S. Claims Tribunal recognizes also tangible

402.J. Y. GOTANDA, préc., note 362.,p.90

403.B. SABAHI, préc., note 263. p.555

404.*Chorzow Factory case,(Germany v. Poland) Merits*, préc., note 59.

405.B. SABAHI, préc., note 263.p.556

406.S. RIPINSKY, préc., note 56. P.69

property, such as shareholder and contractual rights, as open to expropriation. Its approach is very clear and effective: it treats any breach of long-term contract by the Iranian state, particularly vis-à-vis oil and gas, as expropriation of contractual rights. This assimilation of the breach of contract into expropriation has provoked little challenge, but it raises a variety of issues about the proper standard of compensation and valuation techniques in expropriation cases. The literature and arbitral practice generally agree that a state's mere breach of a contract does not violate international law and thus does not entail state responsibility, but is subject to applicable (domestic) contract law.[407] Clagett writes: "For the purpose of measuring damages under customary international law, it is of slight relevance whether a taking of rights has been characterized as a breach of contract or as an expropriation. The goal of contract damages has been to restore the injured party to the financial position he would have enjoyed absent the breach. The goal of compensation for expropriation has been to restore the value of his lost property rights,"[408] Judge Ameli, in his separate opinion in the *INA* award,[409] asserts that international law recognizes not only tangible property but also contractual rights as expropriable.

In the *Amoco International Finance Corp.* case,[410] the tribunal observed that it could treat termination of the Khemco agreement -- a joint-venture agreement to extract oil --as nationalization of the investor's rights: "It is because Amoco's interests under the Khemco Agreement have such an economic value that the nullification of those interests by the single article act can be considered as a

---

407.I. MARBOE, préc., note 232.p.30

408.Brice M. CLAGETT, « The Expropriation Issue Before the Iran-United States Claims Tribunal: is "Just Compensation" Required by International Law or Not? », (1984) 16 *Law Policy Int. Bus.*813-891,p.840

409.*INA Corporation v. the Islamic Republic of Iran*, préc., note 160.

410.*Amoco International Finance Corp. v the Islamic Republic of Iran*, préc., note 161.at pp. 242-243 nationalization."[411]

The tribunal appears here to have recognized finally this distinction in its reasoning on valuation of terminated contract. In this case, it was the Special Commission's decision nullifying the Khemco (joint venture agreement) that constituted the expropriation for which the claimant was seeking compensation. Formally, therefore, it deprived the claimant of its contractual rights under the Khemco Agreement, and the compensation due relates to these rights. It is accepted by the tribunal that the value of such rights equals the value of Amoco's shares in the joint stock company that was incorporated pursuant to the Khemco Agreement. The compensation therefore is half the value of Khemco at the date of valuation.

In the *Phillips Petroleum* case,[412] the tribunal's award clarifies this proposition that contractual rights are expropriable. The Phillips Petroleum Company brought two claims in the alternative, an expropriation claim in respect of its rights under the 1965 contract with the National Iranian Oil Company (NIOC) for exploiting petroleum resources in an offshore area of the Persian Gulf, and a breach-of-contract claim vis-à-vis the same contractual rights. There is a difference between an ordinary breach of contract, which may entail legal consequences according to the applicable law, and the expropriation of contract rights, which brings consequences under international law. The tribunal relied on this distinction in its *Phillips Petroleum* award. It agreed with the claimant's argument that termination of contract rights under a concession agreement constitutes an expropriation of contract rights. It held:

"75. The Claimant's principal contention is that the Respondents are liable for the expropriation of contract rights stemming

---

411.*Id.*para.220-221

412.*Phillips Petroleum Company v. the Islamic Republic of Iran and NIOC*, préc., note 157.

from the JSA (joint venture agreement), and that, alternatively, they are liable for breach and repudiation of that contract. The Tribunal considers that the acts complained of appear more closely suited to assessment of liability for the taking of foreign-owned property under international law than to assessment of the contractual aspects of the relationship, and so decides to consider the claim in this light."

Then, the tribunal expressly termed the contractual rights expropriable:

"76. expropriation by or attributable to a State of the property of an alien gives rise under international law to liability for compensation, and this is so whether the expropriation is formal or de facto and whether the property is tangible, such as real estate or a factory, or intangible, such as the contract rights involved in the present case."[413]

In the *Sttarett* case,[414]the judges found expropriation of the claimant's right to receive payment under existing inter-company loans: "It is apparent that the claimants would not be repaid such loans and that rights to repayment had been taken by the government."

The tribunal stated in the *SeaCo* case,[415]"The claimant could have prevailed upon its contention for the compensation if the actions had adversely affected a claimant's property rights." In all mentioned cases, unilateral termination of a contract takes contract rights. This action regarded by the tribunal as measure affecting property rights and result in expropriation.

413.*Id*,para.75-76

414.*Starrett Housing Corporations, Srarrett System, Inc. and Starrett Housing International, Inc. v. the Islamic Republic of Iran*, préc., note 240., p.150

415.*SeaCo, Inc. v. the Islamic Republic of Iran*, [1992] 28 _IUSCTR_ 198 (Iran_U"S. Claims Tribunal).

3.2.1.2 Taking Control Over the Property

Unlawful interference with management rights can disturb business activity and lead to temporary losses or a taking of a company.[416] In some claims before the tribunal, the government-appointed manager of the investor's company replaced the original managers, installed by the owners. Such "temporary" or "provisional" appointments occurred pursuant to Iranian legislation to protect worker's rights.[417] Despite the euphemisms it used, in practice the government was assuming control.[418] The scope of management functions is also a determinative factor. When the new managers have complete authority to run the business, displacing the former management and denying the owner any representation, the tribunal has unhesitatingly found an expropriation.

In the *Starrett* case,[419] the government has sent in a temporary manager to run the company, in which the claimant was a shareholder, and the tribunal treated this as a kind of expropriation: "It is recognized in international law that measures taken by a state can interfere with property rights to such an extent that these rights are rendered so useless that they must be deemed to have been expropriated even though the state does not purport to have expropriated them and the legal title to the property remains with the original owner."

In another decision, the *Saghi* award,[420] the tribunal summarized its practice in this field:

"The assumption of control over property by a government, for

---

416.S. RIPINSKY, préc., note 56.,p.10

417.M. BRUNETTI, préc., note 212.p.211

418.G. H. ALDRICH, préc., note 125. P 587

419.*Starrett Housing Corporations, Srarrett System, Inc. and Starrett Housing International, Inc. v. the Islamic Republic of Iran*, préc., note 240.,para.122-154

420.*Saghi v. the Islamic Republic of Iran*, [1993] 29 _IUSCTR_ 20 (Iran_U.S. Claims Tribunal).p.44

example, through the appointment of 'temporary management', does not, ipso facto, mean that the property has been taken by the government, thus requiring compensation under international law. The appointment of such managers is, however, an important factor in finding a taking. If the appointments were part of a process by which the owner of the property was deprived of fundamental rights of ownership and if the deprivation is not ephemeral, then one must conclude that compensation is required."

In its *ITT Industries*[421]award, Judge George held: "While assumption of control over property by a government does not automatically and immediately justify a conclusion that the property has been taken by the government, thus requiring compensation under international law, such a conclusion is warranted whenever events demonstrate that the owner was deprived of fundamental rights of ownership and it appears that this deprivation is not merely ephemeral."

In dealing with Iran's de facto nationalization of the petroleum industry in 1979, the tribunal carefully examined the behavior of the parties during that year to see whether Iran had taken the claimants' contractual rights or whether the parties had agreed to contractual termination.[422]

In the *Starrett* award,[423]the tribunal said: "2. It has therefore been proved in the case that at least by the end of January 1980 the Government of Iran had interfered with the Claimants' property rights in the Project to an extent that rendered these rights so useless that they must be deemed to have been taken."

These awards are often cited by tribunals in investor-state proposition that temporary interference with property rights cannot

421.*ITT Industries, Inc v. the Islamic Republic of Iran*, préc., note 285.Separate opinion of Judge George Aldrich

422.G. H. ALDRICH, préc., note 125.p.193

423.*Starrett Housing Corporations, Srarrett System, Inc. and Starrett Housing International, Inc. v. the Islamic Republic of Iran*, préc., note 240.

support a finding an expropriation. In the *Tippett* award,[424] the tribunal stated: "While assumption of control over property by a government does not automatically and immediately justify a conclusion that the property has been taken by the government, thus requiring compensation under international law, such a conclusion is warranted whenever events demonstrate that the owner was deprived of fundamental rights of ownership and it appears that this deprivation is not merely ephemeral." This award concentrated on the fundamental effects of the taking as of the point of expropriation. Investment arbitration refers frequently to this ruling.[425],

3.2.1.3 Interference with Administrative Rights

Foreign investors operate within the regulatory regime of the host state. Governmental measures undermining investor's rights, such as those relating to licences and permits, may cause harm.[426] Refusal by the state or its agents to permit the export of an alien's property, or to assist in its export where a contractual duty to give such assistance exists, creates liability.[427] In the *Sedco*award,[428] the IUCST found thatthe

424.*Tippett, Abbett, McCarthy, Stratton v TAMSA_AFFA Consulting of Iran*, préc., note 245.p.225

425 .In the S.D. Myers v. Canada case, the Tribunal denied an expropriation claim arising from a temporary closure of the Canada-U.S. border to export PCB waste from Canada to the United States. Canada, relying on Tippetts case, argued that there was no expropriation because, among the other reasons, the border was closed for only eighteen months and claimant's business had continued to operate.*SD Myers, Inc. v Government of Canada*, [2002] 8 ICSID Reports 4 (ICSID, NAFTA arbitration).

426.S. RIPINSKY, préc., note 56.p.10

427.George H. ALDRICH, « What Constitutes A Compensable Taking of Property? The Decisions of the Iran-United States ClaimsTribunal », (1994) 88 *Am.J. Int. Law* 585-610.P.609

party's failure to render contractually required assistance towards exportation could ripen into a taking or conversion of the property. In the *petrolane* case,[429] the tribunal ruled that the National Iranian Oil Company's denial of a permit for re-export of the claimant's equipment from Iran constituted expropriation;

"97. Based on the foregoing, the Tribunal finds that by preventing the Claimant from exporting its Service Plant, NIOC deprived the Claimant of the effective use, benefit and control of the equipment listed on the April and June RTEs in breach of contract, as well as constituting an expropriation for which the Government of Iran bears responsibility."

3.2.1.4 Reforming Legislation Affecting the Property Rights

The tribunal considered whether certain Iranian land-reform legislation resulted in the expropriation, under customary international law, of real property held by dual Iranian-American claimants. In the *Mohtadi* case,[430] the claimant asserted that certain Iranian reform laws cancelled the title deeds of any undeveloped urban land. The tribunal decided:

"69. While the interference created by the cumulative effect of the land reform legislation and related governmental action did not rise to the level of an expropriation, at least prior to 19 January 1981, it has been established that the interference was of such a degree as to constitute 'other measures affecting property rights' within the meaning of Article II, paragraph 1, of the Claims Settlement Declaration."

428.*SEDCO, Inc. v. the Islamic Republic of Iran and National Iranian Oil Company*, préc., note 159.

429.*Id.*para.97

430.*Mohtadi v. the Islamic Republic of Iran*, [1996] 32 _IUSCTR_ 124 (Iran_U"S. Claims Tribunal).p.147

3.3 Foreseeability

The idea underlying the doctrine of foreseeability is that parties, while completing a contract, should be able to calculate the risks and potential liability they assume by their agreement. Then they should be able to predict their liability resulting from breach of obligation. Foreseeability should limit the risk of liability to what the party can determine at the conclusion of the contract, thus enabling it to take the risk, acquire insurance, or abstain from concluding the contract. The well-known English case of *Hadley v. Baxendale.*[431]laid out the doctrine of foreseeability. The Hadley rule states that promisors are not liable for losses that are not 'foreseeable'[432]. In this case judge Alderson B stated that : "where two parties have made a contract which one of them has broken, the damages which the other party ought to receive in respect of such breach of contract should be such as may fairly and reasonably be considered either arising naturally, that is, according to the usual course of things, from such breach of contract itself, or such as may reasonably be supposed to have been in the contemplations of both parties, at the time they made the contract, as the probable result of the breach of it."

Ferrari's study of the rule's origin rooted the concept in Roman law and thence into the French code long before the Hadley decision. In modern times it makes its first appearance in French law, from which it spreads to most legal systems, fashioned after French codification. The *Code civil* itself expressly states (Article 1231-3) the requirement of foreseeability in determining the amount of damages[433]. Art. 1231-3 of French civil code (2016) states: "A debtor is bound only to damages

---

431.*Hadley v. Baxandale,* [1854] 156 Eng. Rep.145. Court of Exchequer

432.Eric A. POSNER, « Contract Remedies: Forseeability, Precaution, Causation, and Mitigation », dans Bouckaert BOUCKAERT (dir.), *The Encyclopedia of Law and Economics*, U.K, Edward Elgar, 2000, p. 162-178.p.164

433.Lajos VEKAS, « The Foreseeability Doctrine in Contractual Damage Cases », (2002) 43-1-2 *Acta Juridica Hung.* 145-174.p.150

which were either foreseen or which could have been foreseen at the time of conclusion of the contract, except where non-performance was due to a gross or dishonest fault.[434]. Therefore, the history of the "foreseeability" limit confirms that the principle laid down in CISG article 74 cannot be a common law rule because the source of the *Hadley v. Baxendale* rule can be found in French law[435]. Questions of causal connection in breach-of-contract cases arise primarily as questions of fact. Therefore, a final conclusion would depend, to a great extent, on the amount of discretion the judge has. At the same time, in most situations this would harness techniques relating to foreseeability.[436]the foreseeability limitation evolved to a test that is comprising two rules: (1) the injured party can recover for losses that "may fairly and reasonably be considered as arising naturally, according to the usual course of things, from such breach of contract itself, and (2) that there should be no consequential damage recovery except such as may reasonably be supposed to have been in the contemplation of both parties, at the time they made the contract, as the probable result of the breach of it[437].

The CISG Convention's foreseeability standard uses only

434.Ingeborg SCHWENZER et Christiana FOUNTOULAKIS, *International Sales Law*, London, Routledge. Cavandish, 2007.p.535. The new provisions of the Code civil created by Ordonnance n° 2016-131 of 10 February 2016 translated into english, enligne: http://www.textes.justice.gouv.fr/art_pix/THE-LAW-OF-CONTRACT-2-5-16.pdf

435.Franco FERRARI, « Comparative Ruminations on the Foreseeability of Damages in Contract Law », (1993) 53-4 *La. Law Rev.* 1262-1269.p.1264

436.ALEXANDER KOMAROV, « the Limitation of domestic and International contract damagesin domestic legal systems and international instruments », dans DJAKHONGIR SAIDOV et RALPH CUNNINGTON (dir.), *Contract Damages; Domestic and InternationalPerspectives*, United States, Hart Publication, 2008.245-264. p.253

437.Eric C. SCHNEIDER, « Consequential Damages in the International Sale of Goods: Analysis of Two Decisions », (2014) 16-4 *J. Int. Law* 615-668., p.631

information available to the breaching party at the time of the conclusion (making) of the contract.Article 74 makes it clear that it is only the party in breach who is required to foresee. foreseeability "must refer to losses that can be a possible consequence of a breach of contract, consequently, "The foreseeability of a breach of contract or fault regarding breach does not matter."[438] Such damages may not exceed the loss which the party in breach foresaw or ought to have foreseen at the time of the conclusion of the contract, in the light of the facts and matters of which he then knew or ought to have known, as a possible consequence of the breach of contract.

The second sentence of article 74 counterbalances strict liability with the so-called foreseeability rule. The aggrieved party is compensable only for damages the other party subjectively had foreseen or –from an objective point of view– could have foreseen when concluding the contract. Article 74 states the limitations that exist in claiming damages:

"Damages may not exceed the loss which the party in breach foresaw or ought to have foreseen at the time of the conclusion of the contract, in the light of the facts and matters of which he then knew or ought to have known, as a possible consequence of the breach of contract."

That is 'the facts and matters must have existed at the time of the conclusion of the contract and/or must be foreseeable at the conclusion of the contract.' Events that occur subsequent to the making of the contract have no bearing on foreseeability of loss. Similarly, what was foreseeable at the time of the breach is irrelevant. However, foreseeability relates to the nature or type of the harm but not to its extent unless the extent is such as to transform the harm into one of a

---

438.Franco FERRARI, « Hadley v Baxendale v Foreseeability under Article 74 CISG », dans Djakhongir SAIDOV et Ralph CUNNINGTON (dir.), *contract damages. domestic and international perspectives*, United States, Hart Publication, 2008, p. 305-329.p.309

different kind.[439]Article74 employs both an objective and a subjective test of foreseeability. The objective test asks whether a reasonable party in the same situation could expect the loss from its non-performance. According to this view the foreseeability doctrine should be interpreted in a way that the party in breach is to be liable for even those damages that a logically reasoning person in his position ought to have calculated with[440].

Article 7.4.4 of UNIDROIT Principles outlines a virtually identical concept of foreseeability: "The non-performing party is liable only for harm which it foresaw or could reasonably have foreseen at the time of the conclusion of the contract as being likely to result from its non-performance." Like the CISG Convention, UPICC contains both subjective and objective tests for foreseeability. However, while the CISG requires that the foreseeable harm be a "possible" consequence of non-performance of the contract, UPICC states that such harm must be a "likely" result of the breach - more restrictive view. In addition, the concept of foreseeability which is enshrined in theses instruments is said to be narrow one. The test is based on the foresight of the non-performing party or the foresight of the reasonable person in the position of the non-performing party. The knowledge of the aggrieved party appears to be irrelevant[441].

In the civil law countries where foreseeability is one of the criteria, such as in article 1150of the French Civil Code, the rule is more refined: foreseeability is a limit to compensation for direct harm; it is an exception to the full compensation principle in favor of the performing party when the latter acted in good faith. The limit does not apply in case of deliberate or grossly negligent non-performance. This stems from the more acute "moralist approach" of the civil law. After many

---

439.*UNIDROIT principles of international commercial contracts 2010*, préc note 25.art.7.4.4

440.L. VEKAS, préc., note 433.p.162

441.E. MCKENDRICK, préc., note 342 à la page 886.

discussions -and numerous versions, it was decided to follow more or less the CISG rule-the idea to treat differently the non-performing party according to its good or bad faith was rejected. Although, Tallon submits that, "but there is no certainty that article 7-4-4will be construed identically bya French or an English court. A French judge may consider that it is contrary to public policy to allow a party having committed a deliberate breach to resort to foreseeability in order to limit his ability".[442].

The Iran-U.S. Claims Tribunal has applied the doctrine of foreseeability to recoverable damages resulting from breach of contract. It has frequently invoked foreseeability as a general principle of law for disputes arising from investor--state contracts. In a few cases, it acknowledged that the expenses investors incurred to terminate the contract and dissolve the business ('termination cost') could be foreseeable at the contract's conclusion and accordingly awarded consequential damage. In the *Sea-Land* case,[443] which challenged breach of the joint-venture contract, the claimant had to relocate its personnel and equipment, pay severance allowances to local personnel, dispose of equipment dedicated to its Iranian service for which it had no other uses, and incur numerous other expenses that are normal in closing down a substantial operation. The tribunal awarded costs: "These expenses were the foreseeable consequences of PSO's breach, and Sea-Land is entitled to recover them. Sea-Land has extensively documented a claim for such damages in the amount of $2,034,952. The Respondents have never seriously challenged Sea-Land's documentation or the calculations of damage based upon it."

In this award, Judge Holtzman, addressing two other claims by the claimant, referred to foreseeability. He later recognized one of them

442.D. TALLON, préc., note 234.p.679

443.*Sea-Land Service, Inc. v. the Islamic Republic of Iran*, préc., note 60.

as foreseeable. In that claim, Sea-Land asked for $174,000 for "emergency payments" it had to make to obtain permission to remove 401 of its chassis from Iran. Holtzmann states: "I believe, however, that the necessity of removing the containers was a foreseeable consequence of the breach, and that Sea-Land is entitled to compensation." In the other claim, Sea-Land further claimed $502,000 for ocean-freight charges on cargo it delivered to or shipped from Iran, which, it alleged, it was unable to collect because of termination of its Iranian service. Sea-Land likewise called for $320,158 for miscellaneous receivables it was unable to collect from its customers. Judge Holtzmann observed: "It is not clear from the evidence that PSO (joint venture contract) could have foreseen the loss of receivables due from third parties as a consequence of the breach of its contracts with Sea-Land. I therefore would deny these claims."

It is obvious that, in these expropriation claims, the tribunal did not apply the doctrine of foreseeability. Because of the nature of the nationalization, the state need not foresee the consequences of its action at the time it concluded its contract by the foreign investor. In its *INA Corp.* award,[444]the tribunal has regarded this argument and award for any unforeseen factors in valuation the expropriated company. However, the dissenting opinion of Judge Ameli states that the depreciation of the value of an expropriated entity was not foreseeable and he dismissed this claim: "If we accept the principle that the debtor is only liable for foreseeable damages in particular with regard to compensation for nationalization, which is lawful per se, then recovery for unintended depreciation in international law for a case such as the one at hand must be rejected."

Although the tribunal in its practice did not indicate to the foreseeability rule, it certainly did apply the remoteness criteria, usually to find whether the damage in question is compensable. As one author

444.*INA Corporation v. the Islamic Republic of Iran*, préc., note 160.

asserts, foreseeability is closely linked with remoteness: "The contractual remoteness test is more restrictive to remoteness test in the following three ways: (i) the contractual test takes account of what was foreseen at the time of contracting, (ii) under the contractual test losses are recoverable if foreseeable as not unlikely to occur; and (iii) implied assumption of risk (inferred from the relationship, price, etc.) has an effect on contractual test."[445] Therefore any expression of "remote loss" indicates that the tribunal was implicitly applying the foreseeability rule. It translates foreseeability to the remoteness of cause. In the *McCollough* Case, it found the absence of any evidence of causation between the non-payment of the debts and the loss to the claimant's financial health (a virtual ruin of its business, requesting an estimated $1 million in damages) and denied the claim as consequential damages.[446] This ruling shows the tribunal's reasoning on the connection between causation and consequential damage, translating foreseeability the remoteness of cause:

"50. The Claimant has asserted that the failure of the Respondent timely to remit the sums due to the Claimant made it impossible for the Claimant to assemble adequate working capital and thus it could not continue profitable activity in the field of its endeavor. 51. In particular, the Tribunal notes the absence of any evidence of causation between the non-payment of the debts and the damages allegedly caused to the Claimant. Under such circumstances the Tribunal considers that the mere non-payment of debts cannot give rise to consequential damages as claimed. This claim is therefore rejected."

445.ADAM KRAMER, « Remoteness: New Problems with the Old Test », dans DJAKHONGIR SAIDOV et RALPH CUNNINGTON (dir.), *Contract Damages Domestic and International Perspectives*, Hart Publication, 2008.277-304, p.279

446.*McCollough& Company, Inc. v. Ministry of Post, Telegram and Telephone*, [1986] 11 _IUSCTR_ 3 .page18, para50,52

3.4 Certainty

Both the occurrence and the extent of the harm must be established by injured party, with a reasonable degree of certainty the same principle is applicable to future harm, that is to say, harm which has not yet occurred. The tribunal's practice limits recovery of damages to damages that the claimant can prove clearly, although the certainty rule applies only to the breach's resulting in claimant's loss of future revenues, not to the amount of profits it lost. The UNIDROIT Principles requires establishment of lost profits with reasonable certainty. By contrast, the CISG Convention does not expressly mandate certainty about damages. The "reasonable certainty" limitation - that damages are recoverable only to the extent that they can be proved with reasonable certainty - is a creation of U.S. law and does not exist in the CISG[447].

Article 7.4.3 states: "(1) Compensation is due only for harm, including future harm, that is established with a reasonable degree of certainty."

This is an important point given that the requirement is applicable both to the existence and the extent of the harm. In English law, the requirement is that the claimant must prove its case on a balance of probabilities, then, an aggrieved party who can establish 50 percent or greater likelihood that it suffered harm of a particular type and extent as a result of the non-performance of the defendant is able to show that the loss and its extent have been established with a reasonable degree of certainty[448].

In fact, the calculation of the loss reflects the probability of the chance. This article reaffirms the well-known requirement of certainty of harm, since the non-performing party need not compensate non-existent harm, harm which may not have occurred or which may never

447.E. C. SCHNEIDER, préc., note 437.p.636

448.E. MCKENDRICK, préc., note 342 à la page 881.

occur.[449] Article 7.4.3 can sustain two guiding principles: the need to establish the likelihood of further harm, but not to quantify the claim. A measure of judicial discretion will allow for an equitable result where the harm is certain but not readily quantifiable.

The border line between direct and indirect damages, or between prospective and merely speculative profits, is seldom clear, and the arbitrator's subjective estimate is often decisive. In his separate opinion on the issues at the quantum phase of in *CME v. The Czech Republic*, Brownlie concurred: "The principle denying recovery for speculative damages has long been recognized in the practice of international tribunals."[450]

There is considerable support for this conclusion in the Iran-U.S. Claims Tribunal's practice. In the Amoco case,[451] the tribunal held: "One of the best settled rules of the law of international responsibility of States is that no reparation for speculative or uncertain damage can be awarded. This holds true for the existence of the damage and of its effect as well. Such a rule does not permit the use of a method which yields uncertain figures for the valuation of damages, even if the existence of damages is certain."

In other cases, arbitral tribunals have insisted on proof of future losses with "sufficient (degree of) certainty," "sufficient degree of probability," "some level of certainty," or "comparative likelihood" and that they must be "probable and not merely possible." Tribunals have disallowed claims for lost profits when they were "wholly uncertain" or

449.*UNIDROIT principles of international commercial contracts 2010*, préc note 25.

450.*CME Czech Republic B.V. v. The Czech Republic*, [2006] 9 ICSID Reports 113 (ICSID).

451.*Amoco International Finance Corp. v the Islamic Republic of Iran*, préc., note 161.p.238

"too uncertain and speculative," or if they contained "a great deal of uncertainty" or were "not probably realizable"[452]

The calculation of lost profits must be reasonably certain and not speculative. This means awarding of lost profits on the basis of past performance and application of higher evidentiary standards.[453] The Commentaries to the ILC Articles on State Responsibility refers to "sufficient certainty" as a requirement for legal protection of the anticipated income stream. Commentary on article 36 states: "In cases where lost future profits have been awarded, it has been where an anticipated income stream has attained sufficient attributes to be considered a legally protected interest of sufficient certainty to be compensable. This has normally been achieved by virtue of contractual arrangements or, in some cases, a well-established history of dealings.[454]"

Professor Gabrielle Kaufmann-Kohler chaired the ICSID's *Aucoven v. Venezuela* case, which dealt with a claim for lost profit. The tribunal noted "Decisions issued by ICSID tribunals and by the Iran-US Claims Tribunal have often dismissed claims for lost profits in cases of breach of contract on the ground that they were speculative and that the claimant had not proven with a sufficient degree of certainty that the project would have resulted in a profit."[455]

The opinion of the arbitrator in the *Sapphire* case [456]has been influential in this regard: "It is not necessary to prove the exact damage in order to award damages. On the contrary, when such proof is impossible, particularly as a result of the behaviour of the author of the damage, it is enough for the judge to be able to admit with sufficient

452.S. RIPINSKY, préc., note 56.p.16

453.B. SABAHI, préc., note 263.. P.572

454.J. CRAWFORD, préc., note 72.p.7

455.*Autopista Concesionada de Venezuela, C.A. (Aucoven) v Bolivarian Republic of Venezuela, ARB/00/5,* [2003] 10 ICSID Reports 309 (ICSID).

456.*Sapphire International Petroleums Ltd. v National Iranian Oil Company,* [1963] 35 I.L.R 136 (ad hoc Tribunal).

probability the existence and extend of the damage." Any difficulty in determining compensation does not prevent assessment of such damage where its existence is certain. In such circumstances, tribunals may exercise discretion and resort to approximation, because requiring certainty before awarding lost profits has invoked higher evidentiary standards at that first stage. Observers note oftenthat arbitrators seem to arrive at award figures in an imprecise manner, even in the presence of detailedsubmissions, expert analyses, exacting calculations, and alternative formulae and valuations.[457] Even though many final awards do seem to flow from an inexact approach, where precise calculation is difficult or impossible --for example, due to inconclusive evidence -- tribunals may exercise discretion and resort to approximation.[458]

UNIDROIT Principles envisions court discretion in cases of uncertainty. Article 7.4.3 states: "(3) Where the amount of damages cannot be established with a sufficient degree of certainty, the assessment is at the discretion of the court." Althoght, the tribunals build on their own collective sense of what is reasonable and equitable in the circumstances of the case. But they should be prudent that the harm to be compensated must not be hypothetical or speculative. It must be established with a reasonable degree of certainty, as to its existence and its amount[459].

This approach to approximation characterized many of the IUSCT's awards. In the *AIG* case, the judges noted: "It might be possible to draw some conclusions regarding the higher and the lower limits of the range within which the value of the company could reasonably be assumed to lie. But the limits are widely apart. In order to determine the value within those limits, to which value the compensation should be related, the Tribunal will therefore have to

---

457.A. C. SMUTNY, préc., note 248. P.22

458.S. RIPINSKY, préc., note 56.

459.D. TALLON, préc., note 234., p.678.

make an approximation of that value, taking into account all relevant circumstances in this case."[460] The tribunal made no attempt to explain how it determined amount of compensation but linked it to the various factors it had used to justify the amount of the award. Recently, in 2014, the Judges Abedi, Nikbakht, and Seifi, in an opinion in the case 602 Al5(IV)/A24-FT[461] submitted that:

"It is widely accepted that the approximation principle covers a variety of damage assessment situations and thus it is not limited to a situation where 'valuation' of a certain property is at stake. It must be noted that in no doctrinal authority has the power to approximate been limited to such a situation, for the simple reason that once breach and occurrence of loss have been proven, the adjudicating body should not refuse compensation for the mere reason of imperfection of evidence on quantum, international instruments suggest such a limited approach."

Notably, in this opinion directly referred to the Article 7.4.3 (3) of UNIDROIT 2010 sating that: '(3) Where the amount of damages cannot be established with a sufficient degree of certainty, the assessment is at the discretion of the court.' In the *Faithlita Khosrowshahi* case,[462] the IUSCT made an approximation of the impact of the Islamic Revolution on the value of the claimant's shares in expropriated companies between the date on which the shares were last publicly traded and the date of the taking.

460.*American International Group Inc. v the Islamic Republic of Iran*, préc., note 276.p.96, para.109

461.*Iran v United States, A15,* [2014] Award NO. 602-A15(IV)/A24-FT published on the tribunal official website (Iran_U.S. Claims Tribunal), en ligne :
<http://www.iusct.net/General%20Documents/AWARD/4-A-Joint%20Separate%20Opinion%20IR%20Members%2001%2007%202014%20(Final).pdf>.

462.*Khosrowshahi, Faith Lita v. the Islamic Republic of Iran,* [1994] 30 _IUSCTR_ 76 (Iran_U.S. claims Tribunal)., para.52.

In some cases, however, the tribunal has made a fairly sophisticated approximation of certain aspects of damages. In the *Shahin Shaine Ebrahimi* case, it used probabilities extensively[463] but did not explain how it linked the arbitrary amount of compensation to the factors it had used to justify the amount of the award. In a number of the claims the tribunal has so decided, it has said little about how it drew the compensation sum from its reasoning on the loss suffered.

In other cases, particularly the *Levitt* case,[464] the tribunal had required a "sufficient degree of certainty" in proving future losses. In this case the claimant, as a construction company undertaking a project in Iran, could not prove that the project being finished timely scheduled. The judges held: "58. For these reasons the Tribunal finds that the Claimant has not established with a sufficient degree of certainty that the project would have resulted in a profit. The claim in this respect is therefore dismissed."

In order to explain inexact calculations or estimations, the tribunal has frequently referred to reasonableness or the relevant circumstances. In its *Thomas Earl Payne* award,[465] it factored in all the circumstances of the case to ground its approximation:

"37. The Tribunal therefore finds that it must make an approximation of the value of the Claimant's interest in the two companies, taking into account all the circumstances of the Case. Accordingly, the Tribunal determines that the sum of U.S.$900,000 represents the fair value of the Claimant's interests in the two companies at the time of the taking."

463.*Ebrahimi Shahin Shaine v. the Islamic Republic of Iran*, préc., note 281.para.35,119

464.*William J. Levitt v the Islamic Republic of Iran*, [1987] 14 _IUSCTR_ 191 (Iran_U.S. Claims Tribunal).p.209, para. 55-56-

465.*Payne, Thomas Earl v. the Islamic Republic of Iran*, [1986] 12 _IUSCTR_ 3 (Iran_U.S. Claims Tribunal).p.15

In the *Phelps Dodge* case, construction of a factory for SICAB (which Phelps Dodge owned in part and controlled) began in 1976 and concluded in 1978. By late 1978 almost all the equipment was on site and installed, and limited production of certain product lines began. In mid-1979, Iran nationalized SICAB stock belonging to Iranian nationals, along with two domestic banks that were investors in the company. In November 1980, it transferred management of SICAB to its own agencies. The judges could not agree that the factory was a going concern at the time of the taking "so that elements of value as future profits and goodwill could confidently be valued." They determined that any conclusions on these matters would be highly speculative. "While no diminution in value should be made because of the anticipation of a taking, the Tribunal could not properly ignore the obvious and significant negative effects of the Iranian Revolution on SICAB's business prospects, at least in the short and medium term.[466]"

These risks can involve politics, market, or climate:

•political: changes to legal and regulatory regimes; partial or complete expropriation; involuntary changes to investment terms; political violence; war; and export and currency controls market: availability of transportation, internally and cross-border; regional economic conditions; and solvency of regional suppliers and customers

•natural: extreme weather and earthquake

The valuation process may exclude some risks for legal or equitable reasons[467]. In the *Sea-Land* case,[468]the claimant was a company doing shipping between Iran and United States. It had a service contract with the Iranian government, which nullified it in 1978. The claimant requested profit it lost from the unilateral termination of the service

466.*phelps Dodge Corp. v. the Islamic Republic of Iran*, préc., note 288.*para.30*

467.W. H. KNULL, S. T. JONES, T. J. TYLER et R. D. DEUTSCH, préc., note 262.P.278

468.*Sea-Land Service, Inc. v. the Islamic Republic of Iran*, préc., note 60.

contract. The tribunal saw this loss as a foreseeable result of PSO's breach, entitling Sea-Land to claim for its forgone profits, and to recover them if it could prove them with reasonable certainty. The tribunal did not recognize the proof of future revenue from the contract and dismissed the claim as speculative.

One of another limiting factor of damage which broadly is accepted by the transnational instruments is the duty to mitigate the damage. This kind of obligation has been frequently invoked by the tribunal. In next paragraph, the application of duty to minimize is examined.

3.5 Duty to Mitigation

Mitigation of damage is a contractual duty based on the principle of good faith. Some commentators have suggested that it is not fair to hold the breaching party liable for all loss resulting from the breach if the injured party can reasonably avoid or mitigate its loss, and some argue further that both fair dealing and good faith require the injured party to take into account the other party's interest.[469] Some observers would interpret the duty to mitigate as the sort of cooperation that these legal instruments enjoin. One frequent criticism of the duty to mitigate is the absence of sanctions for its breach, except perhaps a smaller recovery.[470] Essentially, the sanctity of contracts (or the principle of the necessity) does not permit the parties to resort to the substitute transaction, but in the case of duty to mitigate, rules allows the seller to not respect its contract. The wide acceptance of mitigation in international conventions and extensive application of it by international tribunals demonstrates that certain restrictions regarding

469.D. SAIDOV, préc., note 347.p.178

470.Alexander KOMAROV, « Mitigation of Damages », dans Yves DERAINS et Richard H. KREINDLER (dir.), *Evaluation of Damages in International Arbitration*, ICC Publication Department, 2006. 37-56, P.38

full compensation of an injured party do exist. Mitigation is a duty placed on the claimant as a means of controlling the total damages award. This duty to mitigate lowers the total damages award where the party has failed to take adequate measures[471].The mitigation doctrine requires the promisee to take steps to reduce the loss from breach after it learns of the breach or acquires reason to know of it. If the promisee fails to take such steps, it will not recover full expectation damages[472].This concept finds its ultimate source in the principle of good faith. Duty to mitigate loss has two aspects. First, it binds the claimant to taking positive steps to minimize the loss from the defendant's default. Second, it may bind the claimant to refrain from taking steps that, but for the default, it would properly have taken under the contract, but that, in view of the default, may justifiably augment the loss.[473] A claimant's failure to mitigate losses is one of the factors that arbiters may take into account to limit the amount of damages. The principle of mitigation refers to situations where the injured party reasonably can, but fails to, take measures to reduce the damage[474]. Existing evidence indicates that international investment law recognizes the duty of mitigation and that failure to comply, if a tribunal upholds it, will limit recoverable damages.[475] Both contributory fault and failure to mitigate the damage reduce compensation, and both of them relate to the more general matter of causation: in cases of both mitigation and contributory fault, the injured party's act or omission may be seen as concurrent cause for the ultimate injury suffered.[476] Both CISG and UNIDROIT Principles enunciate, the duty of mitigation. Article 77 of CISG states: "A party

471.C. TIETJE et E. SIPIORSKI, préc., note 345.p.560

472.E. A. POSNER, préc., note 432.p.169

473.A. KOMAROV, préc., note 470. P.40

474.Felix PRAENDL, « Measure of Damages in International Commercial Arbitration », (1987) 23-6 *Stanf. J. Int. Law* 263-302.p.297

475.S. RIPINSKY, préc., note 56.P.21

476.*Id.*P.19

who relies on a breach of contract must take such measures as are reasonable in the circumstances to mitigate the loss, including loss of profit, resulting from the breach. If he fails to take such measures, the party in breach may claim a reduction in the damages in the amount by which the loss should have been mitigated." Article 77 deals withthe duty to mitigate damages bythe innocent party which covers only one aspect of the issue at stake here, namely a failure to avoid further damages after the breach bynot taking reasonable steps. This dichotomy between contributory conduct and failure to mitigate, reflects the English position. In many European systems, failure to mitigate and contributory conduct are seen as species of the same phenomenon[477].

Article 7.4.8 of UPICC states: "(1) The non-performing party is not liable for harm suffered by the aggrieved party to the extent that the harm could have been reduced by the latter party's taking reasonable steps. (2) The aggrieved party is entitled to recover any expenses reasonably incurred in attempting to reduce the harm." UPICC also contains the civil-law rule that implies the duty to mitigate damages.[478] UPICC announces: "When the harm is due in part to an act or omission of the aggrieved party or to another event for which that party bears the risk, the amount of damages shall be reduced to the extent that these factors have contributed to the harm, having regard to the conduct of each of the parties."[479] The duty to mitigate also figures in the jurisprudence and instruments of international investment. As Sergey Ripinsky notes: "In public international law, the doctrine of mitigation has not been well developed. Nonetheless, there are indications that it is accepted as a matter of general principles."[480] Article 39 of the ILC Draft Articles states: "In the determination of reparation, account shall be

---

477.S. EISELEN, préc., note 31.p.39

478.A. KOMAROV, préc., note 470.p. 52, S. RIPINSKY, préc., note 56., p.19

479.*UNIDROIT principles of international commercial contracts 2010*, précnote 25.

480.S. RIPINSKY, préc., note 56.p.320

taken of the contribution to the injury by willful or negligent action or omission of the injured State or any person or entity in relation to whom reparation is sought." Also, commentary on article 31, about the elements of state responsibility, proposes: "(11) A further element affecting the scope of reparation is the question of mitigation of damage. Even the wholly innocent victim of wrongful conduct is expected to act reasonably when confronted by the injury. Although often expressed in terms of a 'duty to mitigate', this is not a legal obligation which itself gives rise to responsibility. It is rather that a failure to mitigate by the injured party may preclude recovery to that extent.[481]"

In its practice, the Iran-U.S. Claims Tribunal has invoked the principle of mitigation in a number of cases, but it seems to have no standard for reasonable mitigation, so everything depends on the facts of a case. It has applied the mitigation rule to sales transactions, proposing a substitute transaction as a typical measure to mitigate loss.

3.5.1 Reasonable Measures

The aggrieved party cannot sit idly while the losses resulting from the breach of contract accumulate and then expect to be entitled to recover the losses that could have been avoided. Instead, one is generally required to undertake all measures that are reasonable in the circumstances to mitigate the loss resulting from the breach[482]. It is clear that the duty does not require the injured party to engage in risky

481.International Law Commission, *Draft Articles on Responsibility of States for Internationally Wrongful Acts*, préc., note 118.

482.Peter RIZNIK, « Some Aspects of Loss mitigation in International Sale of Goods », (2010) 14-2 *Vindobona J. Int. Commer. Law Arbitr.* 267-282.p.268

activities. Whilst he may be expected to advance money he need not do so where there is a risk that the money will be lost[483].

The "obligation to mitigate loss' requires the victim of a loss to take all "reasonable measures" to limit or, indeed, reduce this loss. If the victim does not do this, it will not receive compensation for the part of the loss that it could have avoided.[484] To determine whether the duty to mitigate is applicable, courts use the standard of a reasonably prudent and diligent person who would have taken the same decisions in the same circumstances. They apply this standard *in concerto*, taking into account the circumstances of each particular situation. However, reasonableness is a question of fact. In other word, it depends on particular circumstances of factual situations, but usually the party claiming damages must take action to minimize its losses. The corollary of the duty to mitigate is that the party claiming damages cannot increase its damage by unreasonable conduct and, in this regard, must act with the defendant's interest in mind as well as its own. Furthermore, different types of factors are to be considered, such as perishability of the goods, fluctuation in market price, availability of a specific market, third party obligations etc.,"[485]. In fact, whether or not the substitute contract has been concluded within the reasonable manner depends upon the facts and circumstances of the case[486].

483.Solene ROWAN, *Remedies for Breach of Contract, A Comparative Analysis of the Protection of Performance*, United States, Oxford University Press, 2012, p. 144.

484.Stephan REIFEGERSTE et Guillaume WEISZBERG, « obligation to mitigate loss and the concept of "reasonableness" in international commercial law », *Int. Bus. Law J.* 2004.181-197., p.187

485.P. RIZNIK, préc., note 482.p.472

486.E. MCKENDRICK, préc., note 342 à la page 891.

In the *Questech Inc.* case,[487] the claimant asked for damages resulting from the respondent's failure to pay amounts it owes. The tribunal realized that the claimant did not take reasonable action by replacing the amount, which would have prevented the damages: "If it replaced the amounts and invested them, as appears to be the case, it has in fact already earned what it seeks, and so would recover twice. If it had not in fact replaced the amounts but instead had absorbed the larger loss, it might well have failed to take reasonable measures to mitigate damages as required by general contract law." In the *Houston Contracting Company (HCC)* case,[488] the claimant alleged that its equipment remained in Iran while it could not obtain the export permit from that country. The tribunal ruled: "467. HCC is still required to show that it took all reasonable steps to export the equipment, so as to satisfy the burden of proof to show that the losses suffered by it were incurred as a result of the acts or omissions of Iran and not by HCC's own failure to act."

In the *Behring* case,[489] the respondent declined to receive the goods under contract, and the claimant stored the sold goods in inadequate storage, so, claimant asked the tribunal to issue an interim measure to ensure removal of the respondent's goods to a modern, air-conditioned facility, which was essential to conserve the goods. The tribunal ordered the respondent to deposit money for rent for a new warehouse. In fact, changing the storage and moving the goods into a well-maintained place would seem a reasonable measure to mitigate the damage, to prevent the goods from perishing.

487.*Questech, Inc. v the Islamic Republic of Iran*, [1985] 9 _IUSCTR_ 107 (Iran_U.S. Claims Tribunal).p.128

488.*Houston Contracting Company v. the Islamic Republic of Iran*, [1988] 20 _IUSCTR_ 3 (Iran_U.S. Claims Tribunal).p.124, para.467

489.*Behring International, Inc. v the Islamic Republic Iran Air Force*, [1991] 27 _IUSCTR_ 218 (Iran_U.S. Claims Tribunal).p.241

3.5.2 Substitute Transaction

Arbitral case law has established that making a substitute transaction is a typical measure of mitigating loss. Where a buyer fails to pay and take delivery of the goods, a seller can mitigate its loss by reselling the goods, and a buyer that does not buy substitute goods after the seller failed to deliver will be found to have failed to mitigate. Apparently, this duty obliges the innocent party (seller) to not engage in its contract by breaching the buyer and to sell its goods to other buyers so as to mitigate its loss. If the seller does not do this, it cannot claim the loss of perishable goods because of late or non-delivery. In the *Endo Laboratories* case,[490] the tribunal decided that the claimant's failure to resell, especially manufactured and packaged pharmaceuticals, did not result in breach of the duty to mitigate:

"The packaging of the goods was printed with registration numbers and label information that had been specifically required by the Iranian Government. In addition, the size of the packages and dosage forms were unique to Iran. To resell outside Iran would have required repackaging. The Claimant alleged that to repackage the goods would have required manual opening of the bottles, a procedure both contrary to accepted cleanliness and control standards of the pharmaceutical industry and prohibitively expensive ... The Tribunal finds the Claimant's explanations reasonable. The goods appear not to have been re-saleable."

In addition, the Tribunal took into consideration the fact that continued storing of the goods would have caused the Claimant to incur additional warehousing costs and that shipment of same likewise would have caused it to incur costs with no prospect of reimbursement. On balance the Tribunal held that the Claimant, under the circumstances,

---

490.*Endo Laboratories, Inc. v the Islamic Republic of Iran,* [1987] 17 _IUSCTR_ 114 (Iran_U.S. Claims Tribunal).p.127

acted reasonably and consequently is not in breach of the obligation to mitigate damages.

In the *Harnischfeger* case,[491] the claimant mitigated damages by reselling the goods for which the respondent had failed to open a letter of credit. Chamber III approved the operation and further allowed the claimant even to recover the difference between the contract price and the resale price. It ruled also that the claimant was not accountable to the respondent for any net profit it made on the resale of all the goods under the contract. But in determining the loss, the tribunal would give credit for those items it sold at a profit.

3.5.3 Anticipatory Breach

The existence of the right to withhold the performance, or breach the contract, against the fundamental breach by the other party constitutes both a right for the aggrieved party and a duty on it According to Saidov the notion of anticipatory breach as a right stems from the principle of *favor contractus*: "One aim of the remedy of withholding performance is to maintain the balance between the interests of the parties ... The Principles' purpose of maintaining fairness in international commerce, an element of uncertainty inherent in the nature of the doctrine of anticipatory non-performance, and the Principles' policy of *favorcontractus* that the need for the balance between the two parties cannot be ignored."[492] A general rule is that when one party repudiates the contract prior to the performance date, the other party has an option. It can refuse to accept the repudiation and treat the contract as subsisting. As for a fundamental breach, some commentators have postulated that if it is clear that such a breach will

491.*Harnischfeger Corporation v the Islamic Republic of Iran*, préc., note 352.

492.Djakhongir SAIDOV, « Anticipatory Non-Performance and Underlying Values of the UNIDROIT Principles », (2006) 11 *Rev. Droit Unif.* 795-823, P.795

take place, the party concerned "cannot await the contract date of performance before he declares the contract avoided and takes measures to reduce the loss arising out of the breach by making a cover purchase, reselling the goods or otherwise."[493]

The theory of anticipatory breach of contract surfaced in a very few of the tribunal's awards. In the *Watkins-Johnson* case,[494] the claimant sold equipment it manufactured under contract in order to offset the proceeds against its outstanding claim for performance costs. Iran disputed Watkins-Johnson's right to dispose of the equipment. The tribunal ruled "that the Claimant, having notified the Respondent several times of the planned sale without receiving any objection, was entitled to sell the equipment to mitigate damages." Also, the tribunal acknowledged the right to sell the undelivered goods according to the rules set out in CISG. The Tribunal recognized that Watkins-Johnson's right to sell undelivered equipment in mitigation of its damages is consistent with recognized international law of commercial contracts, stating:

"95. The conditions of Article 88 of the United Nations Convention on Contracts for the International Sale of Goods (1980) all are satisfied in this case; there was unreasonable delay by the buyer in paying the price and the seller gave reasonable notice of its intention to sell."

In the *Ford Aerospace* case,[495] the claimant terminated various subcontracts when the respondent failed to provide necessary instructions and to pay outstanding invoices. The respondent argue that this termination amounted to breach of contract. The tribunal held that the claimant terminated the contract to mitigate the damages:

493.D. SAIDOV, préc., note 367.

494.*Watkins-Johnsons Company v. the Islamic Republic of Iran,* [1989] 22 _IUSCTR_ 218 (Iran_U.S. Claims Tribunal).p.244

495.*Ford Aerospace Communications v the Islamic Republic of Iran,* [1987] 14 _IUSCTR_ 255 (Iran_U.S. Claims Tribunal).

"44. Under these circumstances there was perhaps even an obligation on the Claimant to curtail work in order to mitigate damages.... 46. Indeed, the Claimant may have even been obliged to reduce work on the subcontractor level as much as possible to mitigate the Respondent's damages, in the event it decided not to continue the Contract."

The tribunal also rejected the respondent's argument that the claimant was in breach of contract when it sold certain equipment, which it had ordered for the respondent, to third parties in order to mitigate the damage.

"71. The Respondent alleges that the Claimant breached the Contracts when it sold the equipment. The Claimant contends that the equipment would have become obsolete otherwise. It notified the Respondent of its intention to dispose of the equipment in order to mitigate damages in a letter dated 18 September 1979, without receiving any objection ... 72. The Tribunal finds that the Claimant, having notified the Respondent several times of the planned sale without receiving any objection, was entitled to sell the equipment to mitigate damages."

In the *General Electric* case,[496] the claimant stated that it suspended shipments under purchase orders, allegedly in response to IACI's breaches of contract. On December 11, 1978, it extended the suspension to cover the remaining orders placed pursuant to the distribution agreement. General Electric (GE) claimed that this was a proportionate and reasonable measure it took to mitigate its losses. GE stated that it had intended to resume deliveries once IACI cleared its payment deficit, but that further shipments became impossible, and, in view of IACI's failure to designate a substitute freight-forwarding agent.

496.*General Electric Company v the Islamic Republic of Iran,* [1994] 26 IUSCTR 148 (Iran_U.S. Claims Tribunal).p.160

GE notified IACI of the suspension. As we saw above, however, the tribunal found that GE was correct under the circumstances to mitigate its damages in this manner.

The respondents also contested the sufficiency of the proof supporting this element of the damages. They questioned whether GE ever produced the items for IACI and, if so, whether the alleged sales took place at such discounted prices. GE presented summaries of all resales at a discount that make reference to the IACI purchase order, part number, quantity resold, IACI's net unit price, and the resale price. Moreover, the independent auditor examined the summaries and stated: "The Claimant present fairly the items, and the quantities thereof, ordered by IACI, sold to third parties at a discount, and the differences between the IACI contract price and the prices paid to GE by third parties for such items."

The tribunal ruled that IACI must pay GE for the items it manufactured for IACI and that GE was unable to resell, and it must also cover the differences between the discounted resale price and the contract price, as part of its mitigation efforts. The tribunal held that, as a general matter, the claimant's efforts to mitigate its damages were reasonable.

In the tribunal's decisions, it accepted claimants' timely disposition of goods or cancelling of subcontracts or orders relating to agreements in the wake of the events that took place in Iran as reasonable ways to mitigate damages.

3.6 Summary

Damage limitation based on the idea that there must be limits to the recovery of damages, which restricts the liability in damages. Most legal systems acknowledge causation, foreseeability, certainty, and mitigation as criteria for measuring damages. The law requires a sufficient link or nexus between the wrongful act and the injury before imposing any obligation to make reparations for that injury. In this analysis, a causal link was a necessary element of the finding of expropriation. Expropriation may take different forms and does not necessarily imply transfer of the title of property. It includes not only open, deliberate, and explicit taking of property, such as outright seizure or formal or obligatory transfer of title in favour of the host state, but also covers any incidental interference with the use of property that deprives the owner, in whole or in significant part, of the use or reasonably-to-be-expected economic benefit of property, even if not necessarily to the state's obvious benefit. This kind of interference, or indirect expropriation, occurs when a state's actions have an effect similar or equivalent to direct expropriation, even though it does not seize the property or alter legal title to it. The tribunal recognizes interference with contract or administrative rights, taking control over property, and unlawful interference with management rights as causes of action for compensation.

Foreseeability also limits the recoverability of damages. The underlying doctrine is that parties, while completing a contract, should be able to calculate the risks and potential liability they assume by their agreement. Foreseeability should limit the risk of liability to what the party can determine at the conclusion of the contract, thus enabling it to take the risk, acquire insurance, or abstain from concluding the contract. Both transnational instruments incorporate this idea. According to article 7.4.4 of UPICC, the non-performing party is liable only for harm that it foresaw or could reasonably have foreseen while concluding the contract as being likely to result from its non-performance, and article 74 of CISG makes it clear that it is only the party in breach that must foresee. The Iran-U.S. Claims Tribunal has invoked foreseeability regarding to recoverable damages following breach of contract. Judges applied the doctrine in several rulings, such as the *Sea-Co* award.

As for certainty, Usually the claimant must prove lost profits with reasonable certainty. Arbitral tribunals have insisted on a "sufficient (degree of) certainty" in proof of future losses. UPICC requires reasonable certainty, and article 7.4.3 of CISG states: "(1) Compensation is due only for harm, including future harm, that is established with a reasonable degree of certainty." The Iran-U.S. Claims Tribunal's practice limits recovery to certainly provable future damages. The border between direct and indirect damages, or between prospective and merely speculative profits, is seldom clear, and often depends on the arbitrator's subjective estimate. The claim's size neednot always be so certain, and the tribunal often deals with approximation. When precise calculation is difficult or impossible, as with inconclusive evidence, tribunals may exercise discretion and estimate. According to CISG article 7.4.3: "(3) Where the amount of damages cannot be established with a sufficient degree of certainty, the assessment is at the discretion of the court" In limiting damages, the general rule is that a victim must minimize the damage sustained and a debtor must reimburse solely the immediate and direct damages. This concept finds its ultimate source in the principle of good faith.

Both CISG and UPICC call for mitigation. Article 77 of CISG states: "A party who relies on a breach of contract must take such measures as are reasonable in the circumstances to mitigate the loss, including loss of profit, resulting from the breach." According to article 7.4.8 of UPICC: "The non-performing party is not liable for harm suffered by the aggrieved party to the extent that the harm could have been reduced by the latter party's taking reasonable steps." IUSCT awards for contract breach or repudiation seem to have recognized and invoked an almost absolute duty to mitigate damages, forcing the judges to estimate and deduct amounts where the injured party itself had failed to mitigate. The awards we examined indicate that the tribunal factored in profits from resale of goods or the value of retained goods in its efforts to be fair and equitable. In its practice, several awards pointed out the claimant's duty to take reasonable steps to minimize damages. For example, changing the storage and moving goods into a well-maintained place would seem a reasonable measure to mitigate damages. The tribunal's awards frequently announced the anticipatory breach. When a buyer fails to pay and take delivery of goods and the unpaid seller resells the items, the tribunal accepts the substitute transaction as necessary to mitigate damages.

Chapter Four

Category of Losses

4.1 General

This chapter explores how the Iran-U.S. Claims Tribunal interprets the notion of loss in its practice, that is, what losses does it treat as recoverable? What types of loss does it consider sufficiently 'real' and serious to qualify for legal protection? To answer these questions, we look at losses under several broad headings and attempt to assess the utility of the classifications of losses that appear in the legal literature.

The meaning and definition of loss lie at the very heart of the law of damages. The Roman-law concepts of *damnum emergens*(damages arising) and *lucrum cessans* (profits lost) arise constantly in many civil-law systems, often in determining the heads of damages potentially available for breach of contract and tort claims, sometimes in delimiting remedies for wrongful acts generally, and in international law.[497] In Roman law, damnum was a loss the plaintiff suffered because of the defendant's wrongful act. For the loss to be damnum, it must have resulted from a positive act or an act of omission. Damnum included consideration of both the diminution in value of property resulting from the act and the gains that the plaintiff could have made in the absence of the injury -i.e., lost profits.[498]

European lawyers later named these two types of loss *damnum emergens* (actual damage or loss) and *lucrum cessans* (gain prevented or lost profits, respectively).[499]'Loss suffered' is generally, a reduction in existing assets, property, or financial situation, and here, what the

497.A. C. SMUTNY, préc., note 248.p.15

498.D. SAIDOV, préc., note 347.

499.B. SABAHI, préc., note 245.p.20

innocent party has actually lost or will lose. 'Loss of profit,' in contrast, refers to what the party has never had but would have had if the contract had been performed. What is the purpose of this distinction? Generally, the transnational instruments restrain from delimiting the categories of loss. The drafters of the CISG Convention deliberately did not enunciate what constitutes a loss, nor did they outline any categories of losses, except for loss of profit, which is the only form of loss article 74 specifically provides for. Because not all legal systems allow damages for loss of profit (gains prevented), article 74 mentions it to indicate its recoverability.[500]

The UNIDROIT Principles of International Commercial Contracts mention recoverable losses in article 7.4.2. UPICC, like the CISG, regards both suffered loss and forgone gains as the major elements of recoverable damages[501], but, unlike its counterpart, expresses the compensability of non-pecuniary damages; according to article 7.4.2: "(1) The aggrieved party is entitled to full compensation for harm sustained as a result of the non-performance. Such harm includes both any loss which it suffered and any gain of which it was deprived, taking into account any gain to the aggrieved party resulting from its avoidance of cost or harm. (2) Such harm may be non-pecuniary and includes, for instance, physical suffering or emotional distress."

This chapter examines the practice of the Iran-U.S. Claims Tribunal to find out what kinds and heads of losses it deems compensable.

4.2 Damnum Emergens (suffered loss)

A party to a contract often incurs expenses that constitute part of its performance of (or preparation to perform) the contract, expecting to recoup them from the value it receives from the other party's

---

500.J. Y. GOTANDA, préc., note 250.p.998

501.D. TALLON, préc., note 234, 677.

performance. If, however, that other party fails to perform the contract, these expenses may, wholly or in part, turn out to be for naught. thereby causing loss. Generally, two kinds of losses constitute *damnum emergens*, or suffered loss: actual, or performance loss and incidental loss. performance costs that one party may suffer in performing its contractual obligations or that an investor may bear for implementation of the investment. Incidental damages are for losses beyond the loss in value from non-performance under the contract. Such losses may arise where the breach of contract causes an aggrieved party to incur additional costs in an attempt to avoid further loss.[502]

Subject to two requirements, such costs are, in principle, recoverable. First, the claimant must show a reasonable connection with further use of the subject- matter of the contract. Second, such costs must be reasonable or expedient in the circumstances.[503] In international arbitration, losses such as damage resulting from exchange rate fluctuation, and damage for inflation and also arbitration expenses have frequently been at the heart of the debate. The IUCST has propounded these matters in its awards, and we now turn to its jurisprudence vis-à-vis these sorts of losses.

4.2.1 Damage in Devaluation of the Currency

It is a general rule that full compensation for an aggrieved party require calculating damages in the currency of the loss, although it is possible to pay compensation in another currency. When claims for damages in currencies differ from those in which they were incurred, normally, tribunals face three issues: first, choosing the currency for issuing the award; second, picking the date for conversion, if necessary; or third, selecting the exchange rate. If the currency in which an award is made depreciates between occurrence of the damage and issuing of the

502.J. Y. GOTANDA, préc., note 250.p.996

503.D. SAIDOV, préc., note 347.p.219

award, the tribunal will need to decide which party is to bear the costs of such depreciation or devaluation.

In international transactions, delay in performance may give rise to losses flowing from a change in the value of the currency in question. Two types of situations can cause such losses --a change in a currency's 'internal' or 'real' value (usually from inflation or deflation) and a change in the 'external' or 'international' value of one currency vis-à-vis another.[504]Article 74 of the CISG does not explicitly state when an aggrieved party may recover as damages losses that arise when a breaching party wrongfully delays payment *and* the exchange rate between the currency of the agreement and the aggrieved party's local currency declines. Some authors see a need to protect the party's 'expectation/performance' interest and suggest that the fact that the currency-depreciation loss is a real financial loss makes it recoverable under the international instruments.[505] None of the CISG or UPICC principles provide an express remedy for declining exchange rates after maturity of the debt.

4.2.1.1 Currency of Damage

Generally speaking, a variety of currencies could be taken into account when determining the currency in which damages are actually to be paid[506]. Obligations to pay may be in different currencies to reflect the trading done around the world. The primary contractual obligation will be to pay in the original currency. To pay in any other currency risks shifting the exchange rate risk to the recipient[507]. To determine the proper currency of an award, tribunals often rely on the parties'

504.*Id.*p.257

505.*Id*. p.258

506.Ingeborg SCHWENZER, Pascal HACHEM et Christopher KEE, *Global Sales and Contract Law*, Great Britain, Oxford University Press, 2012, p. 602.

507.P. ASHFORD, préc., note 226, p. 349.

agreement, national laws, treaties, or general principles of law. Sometimes they simply issue awards in the currency most appropriate under the circumstances.[508] Thus tribunals often look for a contract provision to find place or currency of payment. There is a general rule that full compensation requires calculation of damages in the currency of the loss.[509]Article 7.4.12 of UPICC states: "Damages are to be assessed either in the currency in which the monetary obligation was expressed or in the currency in which the harm was suffered, whichever is more appropriate." The harm resulting from the non-performance of an international contract may occur in different places, so which currency to use for assessment? (This issue is distinct from that of the currency of payment of the damages, for which see UPICC, article 6.1.9). Article 7.4.12 offers a choice between the currency of the monetary obligation and that of the harm, whichever seems more appropriate. While the first choice seems unexceptionable, the second deals with expenses the aggrieved party may have incurred in a particular currency to repair damage that it has sustained. Such a case would warrant claiming damages in that currency. even if it is not the currency of the contract. Another possible currency to use might be that of the profit. The aggrieved party chooses, as long as it receives full compensation. Finally, in the absence of any indication to the contrary, a party is entitled to interest and to liquidated damages and penalties in the same currency as that denoting the main obligation.[510] The second option is the currency in which the harm was suffered. For example, sometimes the aggrieved party needs to repair damages in a particular currency and in this case it may be more appropriate to assess damages in that currency than in the

---

508.John Yukio GOTANDA, *Supplemental Damages in Private International Law*, The Hauge, Kluwer Law International, 1998.p.128

509.J. Y. GOTANDA, préc., note 250.p.999

510.*UNIDROIT principles of international commercial contracts 2010*, préc note 25.

currency of the contract[511]. If valuation of damages occurs in a foreign currency, what should be the currency of payment? Most essential, what is the date for determining rate? Some authors submit, if there is to be payment in any other currency rather than contract currency, to apply for full compensation, the determining date should be the date of payment, so that recipient can exchange it back to the original currency and be left with right amount[512].

Let us examine the practice of the Iran-U.S. Claims Tribunalin this regard. Issues about rates for currency conversion arise in many types of international business transactions. The tribunal, in order to determine the currency for awards for damages, has looked to a number of factors, including the 1955 treaty between Iran and the United States, the nationality of the party owed monies, and the terms of the parties' agreement.

In most cases, it has issued awards to American parties in U.S. dollars, as a result of the 1981 Algiers Accords, which set up a security account in U.S. dollars to pay awards. Aldrich has observed: "While many contracts between American claimant and Iran provided for payment in Iranian Rials, the 1981 Algiers Declarations established a security account in U.S. Dollars for the payment of all claims against Iran. Therefore, the Tribunal issued most of the awards to American parties in dollars, even though the contracts in claims called for payment in Rials."[513] For instance, in the *Howard Needles Tammen* case,[514] it mandated issuing of the award in U.S. dollars, even though most of the claims related to fees or invoices or both in rials.

511.E. MCKENDRICK, préc., note 342 à la page 918.

512.P. ASHFORD, préc., note 226, p. 350.

513.G. H. ALDRICH, préc., note 125.p 373

514.*Howard, Needles, Tammen & Bergendoff v the Islamic Republic of Iran*, [1986] 11 _IUSCTR_ 302 (Iran_U.S. Claims Tribunal).p.344

A few tribunal decisions have departed from this practice. For instance, in the *McCollough* case,[515]the judges ruled for an award in rials. The Algiers Accords did not insist on dollars, and the tribunal felt that it had to give effect to a "valid and enforceable" contract that required payment of part of the amount owing in rials.

Regarding awards against American respondents, the Accords set up no security account for payment to Iranians. As a result, the tribunal usually let the nature of the debt determine the currency of the award. In general, if the debt to Iranian parties was in dollars, the tribunal issued the award in that currency.

In *Parguin Private Joint Stock Co. v. The United States,*[516] the tribunal expressed its rationale for rendering the award in the currency of the contract: "First, there did not exist for these awards a security account mandating payment in a certain currency. Second, issuing the award in the currency of the contract gave effect to the intentions of the parties."

In such a process, the tribunal must determine the conversion date and the exchange rate. Once it has selected a date to convert the foreign money owed, it must determine the exchange rate for the conversion. This decision comes very significant when there are several rates such as official rate or market rate.

4.2.1.2 Date of Conversion

Once a tribunal decides to issue an award in a currency different from that in which it has calculated damages, it must select the date for the conversion. In general, tribunals convert foreign currency

---

515.*McCollough& Company, Inc. v. Ministry of Post, Telegram and Telephone,* préc., note 446.p.13, para, 31-33

516.*Parguin Private Joint Stock Co v United States,* [1986] 13 _IUSCTR_ 261 (Iran_U.S. Claims Tribunal).p.267, para29 obligations on one of three dates:1) the breach date, 2) the award date, or 3) the payment date.[517]

The Iran-U.S. Claims Tribunal has not settled on a particular one of the three dates and fixed it. Rather, it usually tries to choose the date that would most effectively compensate the claimant for its loss. Nationalization in Iran followed the Islamic Revolution of 1979, and in most expropriation claims the arbitral award came down at least seven years after the date of the property taking. During this period, Iran's economy had collapsed because of its war with Iraq, and the rial's value had fallen drastically against the U.S. dollar, which was the standard currency for the Iran-U.S. Claims Tribunal.

In expropriation cases, as we see in the next chapter, damages calculated in rials convert into dollars as of the date of the property taking. For instance, in the *Starrett Housing Corp.* case,[518] the tribunal awarded the claimant for the expropriation of its property and converted the damages from rials into U.S. dollars on the date of the taking. Aldrich states: "It is a fair assumption that an alien investor whose property rights were taken by a government would, if compensated in the local currency at the time of the taking, be likely to seek to exchange that currency for his own currency or a freely convertible currency."[519]

Similarly, a majority of the awards in favour of American parties involving breach of contract use the breach date for conversion. For instance, in the *Westinghouse Electric Corp.* case,[520] the judges applied the breach date as the conversion date, because there was nothing to suggest that the claimant would not have repatriated the contractual payments had they been made on time.

517.J. Y. GOTANDA, préc., note 502., p.134

518.*Starrett Housing Corporations, Srarrett System, Inc. and Starrett Housing International, Inc. v. the Islamic Republic of Iran*, préc., note 240 p.182

519.G. H. ALDRICH, préc., note 125. p.329

520.*Westinghause Electric. Corporation v. the Islamic Republic of Iran*, [1997] 33 _IUSCTR_ 60 (Iran_U.S. Claims Tribunal).

In a few claims against the government of Iran involving breach of contract, the tribunal selected the date of the award for conversion.

In the *T.C.S.B., Inc.* case,[521] the tribunal used this approach, reasoning first, that the claimant had assumed under the contract the risk of the exchange-rate variation and, second, that even though the claimant would have immediately sought to convert those rials into dollars, had it received them when due, Iran had imposed exchange controls to approve or refuse foreign exchange. Under the contract, the Housing Organization was obligated to make payments to TCSB in rials, not dollars. The Claimant has argued that any rial amount to which it is entitled should be converted into dollars for payment at the rate of exchange prevailing as of 20 July 1979, the date upon which the contract terminated, at which time the rate of exchange was 72.5 rials to 1 U.S. dollar. The Housing Organization maintains that the rate of exchange should be the rate in effect on the date the Award is issued, which is 85.9 rials to 1 dollar. Accordingly, the tribunal recognized the date of award as the criterion for finding the conversion rate:

"With a debt of this kind, where there has not been a devaluation and where it is not clear that the claimant would have promptly converted the rials into dollars if they had been paid when due, the Tribunal believes the better rule is that conversion should be made as of the date of the award. The Claimant assumed under the contract the risk of exchange rate variations. The fact that by virtue of the Algiers Declarations payment of the present award is to be made in U.S. dollars, should not, by itself, relieve him of that risk. In the instant case it is clear that, had TCSB received the rials owing to it in 1979, it would have immediately sought to convert those rials into dollars."

However, the Tribunal noted that by July 1979 Iran had imposed exchange controls that gave the Iranian Central Bank considerable discretion to approve or refuse foreign exchange, so it is

521.*T.C. S. B., Inc. v. the Islamic Republic of Iran*, préc., note 343. P.169

uncertain whether the Claimant would have been successful in obtaining conversion of rials to dollars. The Tribunal concluded that, on the record before it, conversion in this case should be made as of the date of the award. On the same date, chamber III, in the *Pereira* case,[522]recognized another way to find the date of conversion. In this case respondent's failure to pay the debt amount not only deprived claimant of the funds, but also deprived it of the opportunity to convert them into foreign exchange. Then the tribunal in selecting the date of conversion stated:

"In light of the fact that Claimant was a non-Iranian company and in the absence of any indication that the funds were to be used in Iran or were not to be exchanged for United States currency, the Tribunal determines that the amount due should be converted into United States dollars payable at the official rate of exchange in effect at or around the time when it became payable."

The contradiction between these two awards *T.C.S.B., Inc.* and *Pereira* -- arises from the principle that a contractor should bear the risk of variation in conversion. While chamber III in its *Pereira* award submits that such risk should be the respondent's, because its conduct has prevented the contractor from converting at the best rate. A substantial majority of tribunal awards have followed the *Pereira* approach. In the *Tippett* case,[523] the claimant alleged that some of its invoices for contractual services have not been paid, and also that it had performed certain services for which it had not yet sent invoices. It therefore demanded payment of the as-yet unpaid invoices and payment

---

522.*Pereira, William L Associates v. the Islamic Republic of Iran*, [1984] 5 _IUSCTR_ 198 (Iran_U.S. Claims Tribunal). also, This rule was followed by Chamber 3 in its award in *Rexnord, Inc. v. the Islamic Republic of Iran*, [1983] 2 _IUSCTR_ 6 (Iran_U.S. Claims Tribunal).

523.*Tippett, Abbett, McCarthy, Stratton v TAMSA_AFFA Consulting of Iran*, préc., note 245.p.254

of its fees for the services that it had performed and for which it had not yet sent invoices. It demanded in total U.S.$8,885,589. The fee was payable in rials. The claimant had calculated and converted its accounts payable at a rate of 70.6 rials to the dollar, but if it was to use the rate existing at the time of the award -- i.e., at least 86.32 rials to the dollar -- then its demands would amount to U.S.$7,267,507.

The tribunal in 1984, obligated the respondent to compensate the claimant in the amount of U.S.$5,594,405, which was the equivalent on March 1, 1980, of 400 million rials. This means that the tribunal applied the rate of 70.6 to 1 that was in effect at the time of the non-payment of the invoices in 1979 and declined to use the rate at the time of the award in 1984.

4.2.1.3 Rate of Conversion

Once the tribunal has selected the date of conversion, it must determine the exchange rate to use in the conversion – complex when there are several. In fact, International tribunals have tended to choose among the official rate, the market rate, and the published rate.[524] The majority of IUCST decisions invoke official rates – all of them, according to Aldrich.[525] In the *Starrett* case,[526]the tribunal applied the official exchange rate as of January 31, 1980. Although the majority of its awards apply the official rate, market and published rates have also been in play. In the *Aeronutronic Overseas Service* case,[527] the tribunal held: "The proper exchange rate to apply is the market rate applicable at the date each of the obligations become due." In some cases, the tribunal

524.J. Y. GOTANDA, préc., note 502. P.140

525.G. H. ALDRICH, préc., note 125., p.379

526.*Starrett Housing Corporations, Srarrett System, Inc. and Starrett Housing International, Inc. v. the Islamic Republic of Iran*, préc., note 240.para.182

527.*Aeronutronic Overseas Service, Inc. v. the Islamic Republic of Iran*, [1986] 11 _IUSCTR_ 223 (Iran_U.S. Claims Tribunal).p230 has accepted the latest published rate. In the *Reliance Group* case,[528] the judges named the latest published rate available prior to issuance of the award. The same method reappeared in the *Blount Brothers Corp.* case, with a clarification on the published rate. In this case,[529] the tribunal applied the official rate of exchange from *International Financial Statistics, Supplement on Exchange Rates*. It signed the award for the *George E. Davidson* case[530] on March 5, 1997. The claimant owned one-seventh of the Kamran Building, one-eighth of the Manouchehri Building, and five thirty-sixths of the Jalleh Building, all located in Tehran, Iran that were expropriated by the government. Its compensate on was as follows: "17 As a result, the Tribunal decides that the Respondent should pay the Claimant U.S. $277,556 with interest, calculated at a rate the Tribunal considers appropriate, from the date on which the Claimant's property is deemed to have been taken, on 1 July 1980. The exchange rate applied is the average exchange rate for June 1980 (69.920 rials to one U.S. dollar) as listed by the International Monetary Fund."

In the *William J. Levitt* case,[531] the tribunal on September 3, 1991, awarded the claimant U.S.$214,285 (as the equivalent of 15 million rials), together with simple interest thereon at the rate of 10 per cent per annum from January 1, 1980, the date of breach of contract. The tribunal converted the amounts at 70 rials to the dollar. This rate was valid in 1980 (date of breach); in 1991, because of Iran's unstable economy, the rate had dropped to 700 rials to the dollar

Respecting the agreed rate, the tribunal has enforced

528.*Reliance Group, Inc. v National Oil Company*, [1987] 16 _IUSCTR_ 257 (Iran_U.S. Claims Tribunal).p.274

529.*Blount Brothers Corporation v. Ministry of Housing and Urban Development*, [1983] 3 _IUSCTR_ 225 (Iran_U.S. Claims Tribunal).p.233

530.*George E. Davidson v. the Islamic Republic of Iran*, [1998] 34 _IUSCTR_ 3 (Iran_U.S. Claims Tribunal).

531. *William J. Levitt v the Islamic Republic of Iran*, préc., note 464.para.124

contractual provisions that address conversion. In fact, it has turned in those cases to the parties' agreement, applicable law, or the circumstances of the dispute.

In the *General Dynamics* case,[532] it respected the mutually agreed rate of conversion from the contract, noting: "Unlike most of the cases in which the Tribunal has faced a choice of conversion rates, in this case the parties used in the contract the rate of 70.75 rials to the dollar in calculating the rial payment for services priced in dollars in appendix 5. In view of a conversion rate in the contract, the Tribunal believes it is justifiable to use the same rate for purposes of the award."

With regard to currency conversion, the tribunal's awards have reflected the long-standing disagreement among international tribunals over converting with the rate of exchange on the date the obligation occurred, on the date payment was due, or on the date of the award.

4.2.2 Damage for Foreign Currency Exchange

International tribunals have generally not allowed depreciation of the respondent's currency between the loss and the arbitral decision to prejudice the claimant.[533] The IUCST has supported this principle by reference to equitable consideration. In its *McCollough* award,[534] held:

"110. The Tribunal notes that the average Iranian rial/US dollar conversion rate for the years 1977--1979, covering the years when approximately 90% of the obligations arose, was approximately 70.52 Iranian rials/US dollar, whereas the present conversion rate, according to the latest published rate available prior to the issuance of this Award, is 80.70 Iranian rials/US dollar. The Tribunal finds that it would be

---

532.*General Dynamics Tel., Inc. v. the Islamic Republic of Iran*, [1985] 9 IUSCTR_ 153 (Iran_U.S. Claims Tribunal).para.163

533.S. Ripinsky, préc., note 56. P.395

534.*McCollough& Company, Inc. v. Ministry of Post, Telegram and Telephone*, préc., note 446. Para.110

inequitable to oblige the Claimant now to suffer the full extent of such a depreciation when the payments it should have received were delayed as a consequence of breaches of contract by the Respondents."

In the *Atomic Energy Organization of Iran* award,[535] the claimant sought payment of "damages in the amount of U.S. $5,230,722.96 to compensate for the devaluation of U.S. Dollars, from July,1974 to the end of 1981." AEOI's subsequent pleadings, however, contained no further mention of this claim. The United States called claim frivolous and unfounded. The tribunal concurred: "2. Damages for Devaluation, no evidence or argument has been advanced by AEOI to substantiate either the legal or factual basis for its claim for damages for the alleged devaluation of the U.S. Dollar. The Tribunal accordingly dismisses this claim."

Summing up, it appears that, although the tribunal considered devaluation in its discussions, it did not award such kinds of losses.

4.2.3 Damage for Inflation

The tribunal has occasionally received claims for losses due to t inflation, particularly in the value of expropriated assets. It has declined to award for inflation because such payment had no legal justification. In the *CMI International, Inc.* case, the claimant asked to adjust purchase prices to account for inflation. It sought compensation for U.S. inflation by adjusting ministry of transportation's contract price to reflect changes in the U.S. producer's price index during the period from breach to resale. The tribunal found no legal basis for compensation for inflation, except that which flows from the award of interest.[536]

In effect, the tribunal treats the interest award as indemnity for any loss resulting from inflation in payment of debts. In its *McCollough*

535. *Atomic Energy Organization of Iran v the United States of America*, [1986] 12 _IUSCTR_ 25 (Iran_U.S. Claims Tribunal).p.27

536. *CMI International, Inc, the Islamic Republic of Iran*, préc., note 151.p.270

case,[537] in its view, interest indemnified any loss coming from inflation: "97. Most awards allocate only simple interest, but occasionally compound interest has been awarded and sometimes a percentage is added to the interest in consideration of the rate of inflation. It is difficult to draw any distinct conclusions from so diverse a practice."

Some authors suggest that arbiters award interest basically to compensate for the time value of money --interest payment covers any loss in money's worth over the time. Lu Song writes: "The payment of interest is seen as compensation of the time value of a sum in arrears that is lost. This argument is founded on economic considerations and the financial attributes of money, and is viewed as common knowledge in modern society. The duty to pay interest arises from the need to compensate the lost time value of money."[538]

4.2.4 Adjudication Expenses

Generally, when dealing with appointment of costs related to arbitration, two important consideration arise: i) the discretionary powers confined to the arbitral tribunals; ii) the lack of specifity in the arbitration rules and laws[539]. International tribunals generally have the power to award attorney/lawyer's fees and costs. In every arbitration, the tribunal must find a source of authority for such awards, whether the parties' agreement, arbitral rules, or laws governing the dispute, including national law or international instruments. Then it deals with arbitration expenses, in three stages. First, it must locate such expenses under either substantive or procedural law. Second, it determines which

537.*McCollough& Company, Inc. v. Ministry of Post, Telegram and Telephone*, préc., note 446.para.97

538.Lu SONG, « Award of Interest in Arbitration under Article 78 CISG », (2007) 12-4 *Unif. Law Rev.* 719-732.p.722

539.Jose ROSELL, « Arbitration Costs as Relief/ or Damages », (2011) 28-2 *Kluwer Law Int.* 115-126.p.115

kinds of cost are allowable and have coverage as arbitration expenses.[540] Admissible charges include fees for expert and attorneys, transcription expenses, and the tribunal's fees. Third, it allocates the cost between or among the parties.

Tribunals usually consider two issues in allocating costs and fees; whether a party has prevailed in its claim and to what extent it has recovered the remedy it sought, and whether a party has acted in a reasonable manner or in a frivolous and annoying manner.[541]To date, no uniform practice currently exists for awarding costs and setting fees in investment treaty arbitrations. Some tribunals have ordered each party to bear its own legal fees and share equally the costs of the tribunal, while others have required the losing party to bear the costs and fees of the prevailing party[542]. Obviously, the situation over arbitration expenses varies case by case. In the absence of any agreement on allocating of fees, the tribunal will consider the circumstances in assigning any charges. If the arbitration is voluntary, then, unlike in court litigation, parties must agree to any assignment of expenses. Normally the arbitral tribunal will award costs to the prevailing party.[543]The expenses associated with an investment treaty arbitration fall into two general categories: costs of the proceedings and costs of the parties[544].

540.David D. CARON et Lee M. CAPLAN, *The UNCITRAL Arbitration Rules, A Commentary*, Second Edition, United Kingdom, Oxford University Press, 2013.p.831

541.J. Y. GOTANDA, préc., note 502., P.173

542.John Y. GOTANDA, « Consistently Inconsistent: The Need for Predictability in Awarding Costs and Fees in Investment Treaty Arbitrations », (2013) 28-2 *ICSID Rev.* 420–437.p.421

543.D. D. CARON et L. M. CAPLAN, préc., note 540.p.840

544.J. Y. GOTANDA, préc., note 536.p.422

4.2.4.1 Legal Fees in the Practice of the Iran-U.S. Claims Tribunal

The tribunal's arbitration process involves national governments, citizens, and business interests in two states, and so the two governments bear its costs. Article VI of its Claims Settlement Declaration states: "The expenses of the Tribunal shall be borne equally by the two governments."[545] What about legal fees for parties to bring their action and present their documents? The tribunal decides charges for witness affidavits, travel, lawyers, and so on. It based Tribunal Rules of Procedure (see chapter 1) – see articles 38—40, costs --on United Nations Commission on International Trade Law (UNCITRAL) Arbitration Rules (1976), which it modified to suits its own needs.

The tribunal worded article 38 to allow it the greatest possible discretion in fixing arbitration costs: "The arbitral tribunal shall fix the costs of arbitration in its award."[546] The final award fixes the arbitration costs and decides which parties bear them, and in what proportion. The final award will also delimit parties' costs. The arbitrators or the arbitration clause (not unusual) may, however, let each party pay its own expenses.

Legal and other charges of the process include the fees and expenses of legal counsel during the arbitration, but not necessarily all those that occurred prior to it. How do arbitral tribunals deal with the

545 .Article 38 of the Tribunal Rules of Procedure reaffirms this way: "2) The Full Tribunal shall fix the fees and expenses of the Tribunal which, in accordance with Article VI, paragraph 3 of the Claims Settlement Declaration, shall be borne equally by the two Governments." *tribunal rules of procedure*, préc., note 97.

546. The same language is implied in UNCITRAL Rules, the 2010 edition in article 40 states: "The arbitral tribunal shall fix the costs of arbitration in the final award and, if it deems appropriate, in another decision.", also, D. D. CARON et L. M. CAPLAN, préc., note 540.p.832

requirement for "reasonable" legal and other costs? According to article 38, "The term 'costs' includes only: a) The costs of expert advice and of other special assistance required for a particular case by the arbitral tribunal; b) The travel and other expenses of witnesses to the extent such expenses are approved by the arbitral tribunal; c) The costs for legal representation and assistance of the successful party if such costs were claimed during the arbitral proceedings, and only to the extent that the arbitral tribunal determines that the amount of such costs is reasonable."

The tribunal's practice on parties' costs is not clear. It neither approved nor disapproved of witnesses' travel expenses, so did not treat those costs differently from expenses for of legal representation and assistance.As for costs of experts the tribunal selected and appointed, the unsuccessful party bore all of them only very rarely, as in the *Richard D. Harza* case.[547] However, in the other cases with such experts, the tribunal let each party bear the 50 per cent of the costs that it had advanced.

Allocation of Costs: Investment-arbitration tribunals take into account several criteria in deciding whether to award costs against the defeated party and on what basis to allocate the costs. They generally consider the party's successes or failures and their behaviour.[548] Article 40 of the Tribunal Rules of Procedure states: "The costs of arbitration shall in principle be borne by the unsuccessful party. However, the arbitral tribunal may apportion each of such costs between the parties if it determines that apportionment is reasonable, taking into account the circumstances of the case."[549]

Although the rules expressly provide that the unsuccessful party shall bear the cost of the arbitration, the tribunal is often reluctant to award the cost to the successful party -- mostly American. As legal

547.*Richard D. Harza. V. The Islamic Republic of Iran*, [1986] 11 - IUSCTR-76 (Iran_U.S. Claims Tribunal)., *p.136, para 175*

548.B. SABAHI, préc., note 245.p 165

549.*tribunal rules of procedure*, préc., note 97.

expenses, typically are the largest cost of the arbitration, they often figure prominently in a party's request for compensation for costs. Vis-à-vis the costs of legal representation and assistance, the three chambers have different approaches. Chamber II has consistently refused to award costs, thus leaving each party to bear its own. While it has never explained its reasoning, Judge Khalilian has commented:

"There were several relevant considerations, among which were the facts that the costs incurred by American parties were usually far higher than those incurred by Iranian parties, that successful American parties had the enormous benefit of the Security Account to guarantee prompt and full payment of all awards against Iran, and that if the parties had been left to litigate their disputes in American courts, they generally would have had to bear their own costs. This policy, once adopted by Chamber two under the chairmanship of judge Bellet, was followed by each successive chairman of the Chamber."[550].

One author pointed out: "The reluctance of the Claims Tribunal to award cost and fees appear to be based on the following reasons:1) such costs are inappropriate because the governments of Iran and the United States are bearing the costs of the Tribunal. 2) The existence of the settlement fund relieves the claimants of the risks and costs of award collection. 3) It would be unfair to subject Iran to costs and fees because the United States is not subject to those costs and fees in the majority of claims. 4) The practice in the United States is that each party bears its own attorneys' fees."[551]

In interstate claims, the tribunal has consistently let each of the two governments deal with its own costs in all cases where they opposed each other. In the interstates cases, known as official claims, the tribunal has usually declined to award costs to the successful state party, because

---

550.K. KHALILIAN, préc., note 290.p.93

551.J. A. WESTBERG, préc., note 135. P.268

it feels that both states should bear equally all the tribunal's expenses.[552] In the Ministry of National Defence v. United States case[553], the tribunal insists on its practice in this regard, stating:

"8. Based on the above, the Tribunal does not deem it reasonable to deviate in these Cases from its practice not to award costs in cases involving disputes as between the two Governments."

Yet it has occasionally awarded the legal fee for which the claimant asked, adjusting the claimed amount by applying criteria such as reasonableness, party conduct, and the degree of success. We now turn to the tribunal's criteria in such cases.

Article 40 (2) of Tribunal Rules of Procedure allows parties' reasonable behaviour as a criterion for recovering legal and other costs of an arbitration. The same rule applies to the costs of fact witnesses --for preparation of witness statements, travel to the hearing, and accommodation and ancillaries, including telephone, telefax, and photocopies. [554]Next we look at which costs the tribunal sees as reasonable.

4.2.4.1.1 Reasonableness of the Costs of Arbitration

Pursuant to article 41 of the UNCITRAL Arbitration Rules,[555] the arbitral tribunal determines the reasonableness of any claims for legal

---

552.K. KHALILIAN, préc., note 290.p.93

553.*Iran v United States,A3, A8,* [1991] 27 _IUSCTR_ 256 (Iran_U.S. Claims Tribunal).p.258

554 .Article 40 of the Tribunal Rules of Procedure states: "2)With respect to the costs of legal representation and assistance referred to in article 38, paragraph 1(c) the arbitral tribunal, taking into account the circumstances of the case, shall be free to determine which party shall bear such costs or may apportion such costs between the parties if it determines that apportionment is reasonable ."*tribunal rules of procedure*, préc., note 97.

555.Article 41 of UNCITRAL Arbitration Rules 2010 states: "1. The fees and expenses of the arbitrators shall be reasonable in amount, taking into account costs, pursuant to article 40(2) before deciding whether to apportion such costs. The Iran-U.S. Claims Tribunal also has dealt with the issue. In the *Sylvania* case,[556] it articulated a criterion for evaluating claims for costs and attorney's fees -- "test of reasonableness" --taking into account three considerations:

- the circumstances of the case
- any additional costs for taking funds from the security account
- practice in U.S. commercial cases that each party generally pays for legal counsel

In a case where the American claimant claimed $830.000 for legal costs, the tribunal applied these criteria to award only $50.000: "In view of general considerations outlined above, and taking into account that the present case involves factual and legal issues that are neither extreme nor of quite ordinary complexity in comparison to other cases before the Tribunal, $50,000 was a reasonable amount of costs to be paid by the respondent." In this case, Judge Holtzmann proposed a different set of criteria:

- Were such costs claimed in the arbitration?
- Were lawyers necessary?
- Are such costs reasonable?
- Do the case's circumstances make it reasonable to apportion such costs?

Judge Holtzmann also noted that, in cases in which a business entity is requesting legal costs, there is an indication that this is reasonableness:

"A test of reasonableness is not, however, an invitation to mere

---

the amount in dispute, the complexity of the subject matter, the time spent by the arbitrators and any other relevant circumstances of the case."*en ligne: http://www.uncitral.org/uncitral/en/uncitral_texts/arbitration/2010Arbitration _rules.htm,l accessed 3 May 2017*

556.*Sylvania Technical Systems, Inc. v. the Islamic Republic of Iran,* [1985] 8 _IUSCTR_ 298 (Iran_U.S. Claims Tribunal).p.324

subjectivity. Objective tests of reasonableness of lawyers' fees are well known. Such tests typically assign weight primarily to the time spent and complexity of the case. The Tribunal should not neglect to consider the reality that legal bills are usually first submitted to businessmen. The pragmatic fact that a businessman has agreed to pay a bill, not knowing whether or not the Tribunal would reimburse the expenses, is a strong indication that the amount billed was considered reasonable by a reasonable man spending his own money, or the money of the corporation he serves.[557]"

Leading commentators note that, in most international arbitrations, tribunals that award costs in favour of the prevailing party consciously or unconsciously adopt Judge Holtzmann's approach.[558] In the *SD Myers* case, the Iran-U.S. Claims Tribunal explained its approach to reasonableness of Judge Holtzmann:

"The test is not how much the 'successful' party actually spent; and the fact that the client has initiated or approved that expenditure is a matter only between the client and his attorney. The actual amount spent may have been 'reasonable' in that sense. The test of reasonableness in the context of recovery from an 'unsuccessful' party does not seek to second-guess these decisions, but looks to what amount it would be 'reasonable' to require the unsuccessful party to pay; taking into account the circumstances of the case."[559]

In the *General Electric* case[560], GE claimed costs and legal fees relating to this arbitration in the amount of $945,709.77, including legal fees of $840,787.50 and non-legal costs of $104,922.27. In this case, involving extensive legal and factual issues, the claimant has prevailed on three of its four claims, but failed on its largest claim. All the counterclaims have been dismissed. Applying these factors, the tribunal

557.*Id.*p.329-331,332

558.N. BLACKABY et C. PARTASIDIES, préc., note 8.p.535

559.*SD Myers, Inc. v Government of Canada*, préc., note 425.

560.*General Electric Company v the Islamic Republic of Iran*, préc., note 496.

determined that $40,000 was a reasonable amount of GE's costs for the respondents to pay.

4.2.4.2 Cost Apportion

When deciding whether it is reasonable to apportion cost pursuant to article 40 of Tribunal Rules of Procedure,[561] the tribunal must "take into account the circumstances of the case." Generally, arbitral tribunals consider some factors in interpreting and applying the case's circumstances: the parties' success on their claims, their conduct during the proceedings, and the nature of the dispute-resolution mechanism.[562]There are two principal approaches for determining how to allocate costs and fees among the parties. One approach calls for each party to bear its own costs—the pay-your-own-way principle. This practice is generally followed in the United States and is known there as the American rule. The other approach provides for the losing party to pay the winning party's costs and fees. This practice is followed by most civil law and common law countries, and is often referred to as the loser-pays rule or the principle that costs-follow-the-event[563]. Both the pay-your-own-way and costs-follow-the-event principles have their advantages and disadvantages.

Arbitral tribunals have typically focused on a party's conduct during the arbitration in assessing the circumstances of the case, but they may consider also a claimant's motivation for bringing a claim or a counterclaim. When a private party was involved in one of those cases and requested costs, however, the tribunal was inconsistent, as we see in

---

561 .Article 40 of Tribunal Rules of Procedure states: 'However, the arbitral tribunal may apportion each of such costs between the parties if it determines that apportionment is reasonable, taking into account the circumstances of the case.'*tribunal rules of procedure*, préc., note 97.

562.D. D. CARON et L. M. CAPLAN, préc., note 540.p.870

563.J. Y. GOTANDA, préc., note 536.p.424

two cases. In the *Woodward-Clyde Consultants* case,[564] in the circumstances of this case, and applying articles 38 and 40 of Tribunal Rules of Procedure, the tribunal awarded the claimant U.S.$25,000 as its costs of arbitration, while claimant seeks US $83,231 as its costs of arbitration. Yet the tribunal occasionally awarded the legal fee for which the claimant asked, adjusting the claimed amount by applying criteria such as reasonableness, party conduct, and the degree of success as the circumstances of the case.

4.2.4.2.1 Parties' Degree of Success

Arbitral tribunals frequently consider the degree to which a party prevails on its claim. We can see the rationale for this variation of 'loser pays' in the NAFTA Arbitration in the SD Myers case:[565] "The logical basis for this policy appears to be that a 'successful' claimant has in effect been forced to go through the process in order to achieve success, and should not be penalized by having to pay for the process itself. The same logic holds good for a successful respondent, faced with an unmeritorious claim."

In the *Sylvania* Award, Judge Holtzmann offered two examples of how the degree of the parties' relative success may determine a tribunal's apportionment:

"As noted above, when one party wins a claim and another wins a counterclaim, apportionment is warranted. Similarly, some cases involve quite separate and independent causes of action, such as where a contractor claims under two separate contracts involving different building projects. If such a claimant were to be successful as to one project but lose as to the other, an apportionment of its total legal fees

---

564. *Woodward-Clyde Consultants v the Islamic Republic of Iran*, [1983] 3 _IUSCTR_ 239 (Iran_U.S. Claims Tribunal).p.253

565. *SD Myers, Inc. v Government of Canada*, préc., note 425.

would be appropriate. Where no such circumstances exist, the concept of apportionment is not applicable."

While apportioning costs in the *Agrostruct* case,[566] the tribunal considered the claimant's level of success:

"55. Taking into account that; (1) Agrostruct was awarded approximately 25 percent of the amount claimed, (2) all Counterclaims were dismissed, and (3) the Respondents incurred translation costs for providing an English translation of the Contract in an estimated amount of $1,000, which Agrostruct must bear, the Tribunal determines that $9,000 is a reasonable amount of costs to be paid to Agrostruct."

In the *Rockwell International System* case,[567] the claimant asked for U.S.$928,036 for legal fees, based on presented documents, but the tribunal, looking at *Sylvania*-type criteria and factoring in the case's complex factual issues, set $70,000 as reasonable costs to the claimant. It did not explain its criteria for reasonableness, which appears frequently in the tribunal's practice. But Judge Holtzmann, in his separate opinion, challenged the application here: "The Tribunal Rules should be applied to allocate legal costs of arbitration based on the degree of success that the prevailing party achieves. In my view, the degree of Rockwell's success is most appropriately measured by reference to the fact that it was awarded approximately U.S.$12 million of the U.S.$19 million it sought for work performed under the Contracts -- i.e. about 63%. Taking all of these factors into consideration, I believe Rockwell is entitled to legal costs of. approximately 60% of the legal costs it claims."

566.*Agrostruct International, Inc. v the Islamic Republic of Iran*, préc., note 385.para.55

567.*Rockwell International Systems, Inc. v the Islamic Republic of Iran*, [1989] 23 _IUSCTR_ 150 (Iran_U.S. Claims Tribunal)., p.228

4.2.4.2.2 The Parties' Conduct

A party's conduct during the arbitral proceedings may affect apportioning and awarding of costs, especially frivolous or bad-faith conduct. So too, costly non-cooperative acts such as failure to file a required submission, late delivery of evidentiary materials, or refusal to provide information. The tribunal has awarded costs against a party whose conduct, while not necessarily inappropriate, directly cost its adversary. As, for instance, in the *William J. Levitt* case,[568] the tribunal has on several occasions taken into account a party's conduct. Applying the criteria from *Sylvania*, it commented that the respondents' failure to comply with the tribunal's production orders had substantially increased costs of arbitration.

In the *Behring International*,[569] it held: "In accordance with the precedent, a party's conduct during the arbitral proceeding may be taken into account in determining the appropriate amount of costs to award." The arbitration panel observed the claimant's failure to respond to several of its orders.

In some cases, the tribunal has awarded costs to penalize a party for its obviously pesky claim.[570] In the *Dadras*case,[571]the tribunal has held that a party is entitled to the reimbursement of extra costs that it was forced to bear because of the other party's inappropriate conduct. The tribunal wrote:

---

568. *William J. Levitt v the Islamic Republic of Iran*, préc., note 464., para.126

569.*Behring International, Inc. v the Islamic Republic Iran Air Force*, préc., note 489.para.71

570.K. KHALILIAN, préc., note 290.p.93

571.*Dadras International and Per-Am Construction Corporation v the Islamic Republic of Iran and Thran Development*, [1995] case no. 213,215, 31 _IUSCTR_ 127 (Iran_U.S. Claims Tribunal).p.205, para.280

"The procedural history of Tribunal's Cases shows that the Respondents have caused considerable disruption of the arbitral process and have unnecessarily occupied the resources of this Tribunal by pursuing their unfounded allegations of forgery and belatedly proffering the unconvincing testimony of Mr. Golzar. These actions have caused the Claimants to incur substantial additional costs associated with obtaining legal advice on and responding to the late-filed post-Hearing documents, as well as expenses associated with preparing for and attending a second hearing in these Cases."

The Tribunal considered that these circumstances call for an award of costs against the Respondents more substantial than the amount customarily awarded by this Chamber of the Tribunal to a successful party.

4.3 Lucrum Cessans (Lost profit)

In theory, the injured party should be able to recover money for actual loss that results from the breach and any net gains it prevented, including lost profits flowing from the respondent's actions. Although an award of lost profits places the aggrieved party in a pre- or non-breach position, such decisions in transnational contract disputes do not always achieve full compensation, and claimants often receive only a fraction of what they seek.[572] Calculation of lost profits may achieve reasonable accuracy, but not certainty. The drafters of the CISG Convention deliberately did not define loss, and article 74 does not name any categories of losses, except loss of profit, which some legal systems do not recognize.[573] The UNIDROIT Principles of International Commercial Contracts (UPICC) limits damages through the concepts of certainty, among others: "Compensation is due only for harm, including future harm that is established with a reasonable degree of certainty." If the

572 .J. Y. GOTANDA, préc., note *360*,p.101

573.B. ZELLER, préc., note 103.p.72

claimant cannot establish the amount of damages with sufficient certainty, UPICC permits the tribunal to set the amount. Additionally, it allows recovery of damages for the loss of profits in proportion to the probability of its occurrence. This principle of recovery has emerged as a general rule of private international law,[574] entitling an aggrieved party not only to recovery for lost profits incurred prior to the judgment or award, but also for future lost profits, to the extent that it can prove them with reasonable certainty. Rightly, the commentators advocate the principle of compensation by finding that lost profits are too unpredictable, too unforeseeable, too remote, too speculative, too uncertain or too extreme[575].

The Iran-U.S. Claims Tribunal has referred to the international-law practice of the International Court of Justice in the Hague in figuring out how to award lost profit. The PCIJ observed in the *Chorzow Factory* case[576] that a tribunal applying the compensation standards of international law must "determine the monetary value, both of the object which should have been restored in kind and of the additional damage, on the basis of the estimated value of the undertaking together with any probable profit that would have accrued to the undertaking between the date of taking possession and that of the expert opinion."

The initial problem with lost revenue in expropriation cases is that an assessment of lost profits may depend on projections deriving from past profits, estimated profits included within the price, or, particularly for new companies or projects, historical or post-dispute market projections of future profit. However, the tribunal has seemed reluctant to award lost profits on unperformed work, and, even when it does so, to refer to them as lost profits. It appears that the tribunal generally considered claims for lost profits speculative.[577] Judge Brower,

---

574.J. Y. GOTANDA, préc., note 362.p.86

575.F. PRAENDL, préc., note 474. P.289

576.*Chorzow Factory case,(Germany v. Poland) Merits*, préc., note 59.at 52

577.G. H. ALDRICH, préc., note 125.p.294

concurring in the *Amoco* case,[578] examined the legitimacy of awarding lost profit: "Our precedents confirm therefore that expected future profits must be included in the calculation of compensation. A fortiori, where the expropriated property consists of contract rights, the compensation must be defined by the anticipated net earnings that would have been realized, as well as one can judge, had the contract been left in place until completion."

The tribunal has determined that it can award a claimant for lost profits either if it was a going concern at expropriation or if it could have reasonably expected profits under a contract absent termination of the contract. In the Tribunal's precedent, the claimant was entitled to lost profits after showing that it had reasonably expected to complete a contract and thus earn the profits the Iranian entity's breach denied it. The tribunal's practice, following international adjudication, treats lost profit (*lucrum cessans*) generally as consequential, indirect, and even remote damage, which is not compensable in lawful expropriations. This is the principle on which the tribunal rejects claims for lost profit.

The tribunal has usually distinguished diligently between expropriation and breach of contract, even in the same proceeding. We next look at its practice regarding lost profit in contractual claims and in expropriation claims.

4.3.1 Loss of Profit in Case of Contract Breach

For the tribunal, the validity of such an award for lost profits in contractual claims, depends on establishing the likelihood of such profit if the contract had not been breached. The tribunal rejected the claim for lost profit in this case as too speculative. Damages for lost profits are available when loss of profits is a foreseeable consequence of the breach and when such profits can be calculated with reasonable certainty. Inthe

578.*Amoco International Finance Corp. v the Islamic Republic of Iran*, préc., note 161.Concurring opinion of judge Brower.

Economic Forms Corp. case,[579] several Iranian purchasers breached their contracts to buy concrete forms that the claimant custom made for them. The forms remained with the claimant, who sought the full contract price, plus interest. The tribunal recognized that the American Uniform Commercial Code (UCC), section 2-709(1) b, entitled the claimant to recover the contract price, together with any incidental damage, if it were unable after reasonable effort to resell the forms at a reasonable price, but it awarded a lesser sum, because it believed the manufactured materials had considerable residual value to the claimant. The tribunal said that, in the absence of more specific evidence, it must determine 'equitably' the damages, which it then set at U.S.$1.5 million, including interest.

Judge Holtzmann, concurring, disagreed with this resort to equity, as the law was clear, and he believed the claimant had established its inability to resell the forms. In his view, the claimant should have received U.S.$2.766.024. While neither the award nor Judge Holtzmann referred to lost profits, the tribunal's use of equity to reduce the damages due under the applicable law may well have had the effect of denying recovery for lost profits.

The claim in the *Blount Brothers* case[580] was arose from termination of a construction contract, where the claimant called for 10 per cent of the profit as a management fee, as the contract prescribed. The claimant estimated the profit to be 15 per cent of the base contract price and supported the reasonableness of this estimate with the testimony of one former and one current employee. Recognizing the claimant's lost revenue, and "exercising its discretion in determining the amount due to Claimant as its share of the profit under the Management

579.*Economy Forms Corporation v the Islamic Republic of Iran*, préc., note 164.p.55

580.*Blount Brothers Corporation v. Ministry of Housing and Urban Development*, préc., note 529.

Contract, the Tribunal awards a lump sum of US $175,000, based on a rate of profit of approximately 10 per cent of the total contract price.

In the *Pomeroy* case,[581] chamber III concluded that the respondent had terminated the contract, through no fault of the claimant, entitling the claimant to compensation for lost profits. Noting circumstances that suggested that claimant's profits would probably have been lower than expected and its cost higher, the chamber awarded less lost profit than the claimant had requested:

"The Navy having terminated the contract, the Tribunal finds that the Claimant is entitled to compensation for its losses caused by the termination. The Claimant claims the outstanding portion of the firm fee provided for under the Contract, arguing that this amount equals the profits it lost through the Contract being terminated."

The tribunal has recognized the effects of the Islamic Revolution on the future profits of the contract: "In determining the measure of compensation due to the Claimants in this respect, the Tribunal notes that there is an indication that due to events surrounding the Revolution and other factors, Pomeroy Corporation's net profits would have been less than Claimants assert."

In the *Levitt* case,[582] Iran (respondent) had breached a contract for construction of a housing project. The tribunal has expressly recognized loss of profit as a head of damages to award for breach of contract. It has conditioned the establishment of the validity of such an award on the existence of such profit under non-breach of contract. The award rejected the claim for lost profit in this case as too speculative:

"55. In principle, loss of profits constitutes a proper head of damages for breach of contract provided the Claimant can establish to the Tribunal's satisfaction that such profits would have accrued if the

581.*Pomeroy Corporation v. the Islamic Republic of Iran*, préc., note 246

582.*William J. Levitt v the Islamic Republic of Iran*, préc., note 464.para. 55-56-58 contract had proceeded to completion. 56. In the present instance, however, the basis of the claim for $19,456,100 under this head is highly speculative. By the time the Contract came to an end only the initial stages of clearing and grading had been completed, and no construction work had begun on the buildings. The project had therefore reached only a very early stage."

For the reasons such as the project was not advanced and terminated in early stage, then the Tribunal finds that the Claimant has not established with a sufficient degree of certainty that the project would have resulted in a profit. The claim in this respect is therefore dismissed. Damages for lost profits are available when the loss of profits is a foreseeable consequence of the breach and when such profits can be calculated with reasonable certainty.

The tribunal, in the *Gould Marketing, Inc.* case, awarded the claimant costs incurred plus profit on the performed work on a contract where the work stopped because the respondent failed to open a letter of credit, as the contract stipulated. The tribunal noted that the claimant did not request compensation for its lost profits on the unperformed portion of the work.[583]

In the *Morrison-Knudsen Pacific Ltd.* case,[584] the tribunal awarded the claimant compensation for the final, unpaid invoices it had submitted for its work on a motorway project. While it did not refer to lost profits, and the claimant had evidently completedall its work on the project, the award included the profit component of the contract price.

The tribunal granted lost profits in the *DIC of Delaware, Inc. v. Tehran Redevelopment Corp.* case,[585], awarding the claimants an amount it estimated to be equivalent to that which they would have

583.*Gould Mktg., Inc. v. the Islamic Republic of Iran*, préc., note 179.page.151

584.*Morrison-Knudsen Pacific Ltd. v Ministry of roads and Transportation*, [1984] case No. 127, 7 _IUSCTR_ 54 (Iran_U.S.Claims Tribunal).

585.*DIC of Delaware v. the Islamic Republic of Iran*, [1985] case no.225, 8 _IUSCTR_ 144 (Iran_U.S. Claims Tribunal).*p.171* earned but for the respondent's breach of contract. Where one party to a contract had the right to terminate the contract at any time for its own convenience, claims for lost profits face obvious difficulties. The tribunal states:

"Accordingly, the Claimants are entitled to use as part of their damages, monies they would have earned but for TRC (respondent)'s actions. The Claimants cannot seek to recover as lost profit any amounts which would have been earned if all of the contracts had proceeded to completion and been fully performed. Instead they seek only damages for the contractual defaults of TRC as of 17 June 1978, the date they ceased work."

The tribunal rejected lost profits on the basis of a unilateral termination, where the contract foresaw such a right. In the *Sylvania Technical Systems, Inc.* case,[586] which it treated as termination for convenience, rather than breach, it compensated the claimant explicitly for profit it earned prior to termination and said about lost future profits:

"In determining whether lost profits should be paid in the event of termination of a contract by one party it is necessary to consider whether the other party could have reasonably expected to earn profits if the contract had not been terminated."

In this case, the claimant could not have reasonably anticipated that the respondent would never exercise its right under article 4-A of the contract to terminate for its own convenience, and therefore the claimant could not reasonably expect to receive profits for any period after the date of such a termination. In the *FMC Corp.* case,[587] the tribunal awarded lost profits, even though the ministry of national

586.*Sylvania Technical Systems, Inc. v. the Islamic Republic of Iran*, préc., note 556.

587.*FMC Corp. v the Ministry on National Defence,* [1987] case No.353, .14 _IUSCTR_ 111 (Iran_U.S. Claims Tribunal). p.122

defence had lawfully terminated the contract, but based the award on a provision that specified that 'reasonable termination charges' 'were to take into account anticipated profits.

In this case, On 5 February 1978, FMC and the Ministry of national defence of Iran entered into a contract for the sale to the Ministry of 155 armored vehicles. While none of the purchased vehicles was delivered to Iran, the Iranian party terminated the contract on 1980 provoking on the conditions of the contract.

The contract was subject to termination at the convenience of the buyer only upon payment to FMC of reasonable termination charges which shall take into account expenses already incurred and commitments made by FMC as well as FMC's anticipated profits. This clause was not without ambiguity, as shown by the terms "reasonable" and "take into account". The tribunal held: "According to the most fundamental principle of interpretation, the Article in question must be presumed to be capable of being given meaning and effect as the expression of the common intention of the Parties. the Tribunal finds that reasonable termination charges as defined by this clause are those that generally compensate the Claimant for not being able to perform the entire Contract as planned.

This conclusion is supported by a comparison of Article 12.2 with Article 12.1 which provides for compensation in the event the Ministry terminated the Contract as a result of FMC's default. In that situation, FMC would receive only the costs incurred up to the date of termination. In contrast, when the Ministry terminates for its own convenience, Article 12.2 provides that specific additional compensation is to be accounted for. That these additional amounts are designed to compensate the non-defaulting seller for loss of the contract is further borne out by the use of the term "FMC's anticipated profits". The Tribunal finds it evident that, at the time the contract clause containing the phrase "FMC's anticipated profits" was drafted and concluded and at the time the Contract was terminated, the profits so anticipated by FMC were those anticipated from the entire Contract, i.e., those arising from the sale of 155 vehicles, repair parts, and special tools. The Tribunal, therefore, cannot agree with the Ministry's position that termination charges should be limited to expenses already incurred and profits on work completed by the date of termination. In examining all of the elements that constitute termination charges under Article 12.2, the Tribunal has followed the contractual directive that they be "reasonable". Anticipated profits, which is the difference between the agreed prices and the anticipated costs, are the largest single element of the claim (U.S. $9,274,200). Given the specific wording of Article 12.2, anticipated profits must be taken into account. The Tribunal has done so by closely examining both of the factors making up anticipated profits. the Tribunal finds at the outset that anticipated costs -- principally as a result of inflation -- would have been about U.S. $15,900,000, approximately 10% higher than asserted by Claimant. Finally, the tribunal stated:

"43. As a result of the above considerations the Tribunal awards FMC a total of U.S. $6,665,514 as termination charges. the Tribunal holds that these termination charges were owing to Claimant as of 9 April 1979 and interest is due on that amount from that date."

The tribunal's award in the*Dadras International* case[588] rejected a claim for lost profits as unduly speculative, because conditions were unstable in Iran just before and during the Islamic Revolution. The claim was for anticipated profits under a housing- construction contract that the respondent breached in late 1978. The claimant had not established adequately that construction of the North Shahyad Development Project would have profited Peer-Am. Nevertheless, the tribunal reaffirmed that "in principle lost profits may be awarded provided that Peer-Am is able to establish to the Tribunal's satisfaction

588.*Dadras International and Per-Am Construction Corporation v the Islamic Republic of Iran and Thran Development*, préc., note 571.

that such profits would have accrued had the project proceeded to completion."

Several cases before the tribunal dealt with damages that consisted mainly in the loss of income or profit. In the *Seismograph Service Corp.* case,[589] an export ban, which the judges considered not an expropriation but "other measures affecting property rights," caused damage to a foreign investor. They measured the firm's loss exclusively by the profits it went without, by substituting the profits that it could have earned by renting out the seismic equipment in other places: "The Tribunal finds that the actual damage suffered by the Claimant as result of the deprivation of its right to export and, therefore, of the use of the Property outside Iran is limited to the loss of the profit that it would have earned with this Property during the working life of the Property."

The claimant contended that it was entitled to a "reasonable profit" vis-à-vis the contract's terminated portion. It maintained further that its average monthly sales from the contract were $520,765.58, for a gross profit of $192,683.26 per month--a profit margin of 37 per cent. According to the claimant, this was the contract's "reasonable profit." The claimant finally claimed the loss of revenue for 15 months, from the alleged termination to the contract's expiry date, or $2,953,834.38. The tribunal accepted the claimant's contractual right to damage for the terminated period of the contract, but slashed the period and the amount:

"137. The Tribunal holds that, the Claimant is contractually entitled to recover a reasonable profit lost during the standby period which the Tribunal has determined amounts to $52,076.56 per month. 138. In conclusion, the Tribunal awards the Claimant $223,929.21

589.*Seismograph Service Corporation v. National Iranian Oil Company and The Islamic Republic of Iran,* [1989] case no.443, 22 _IUSCTR_ 3 (Iran_U.S. Claims Tribunal).

constituting contractual profit lost on Contract for the period 16 January 1979 through 24 May 1979."

4.3.1.1 Lost-Volume Damage to Seller

An injured party may lose profit as a result of falling volume of sales. The seller's ability to supply goods or services then exceeds the demand for its goods. In such conditions, the buyer's refusal to accept and pay for the goods costs the seller 'one sale' or one unit of profit. even if it manages to resell the goods.[590] In this situation, the seller's resale does not replace the original contract, because, even if the original contract had been performed, the second buyer would have bought these goods from the seller anyway, and the seller has lost volume by having sold only one item instead of two. However, the second sale cannot replace the original contract. The second buyer would have purchased these goods from the seller, even if the original contract had been performed.[591]

The lost-volume concept has been strongly criticized on conceptual and economic grounds. Although this section will not analyse the issue, it points out the main grounds for the criticism. First, some commentators allege that the concept is not in line with the seller's duty to mitigate. Second, others have argued that the seller's expectation interest in the profit from the second sale is unprotected. Proponents would evaluate the seller's expectation only at the time of its entry into a valid contract.[592]

The consensus today is that this loss of profit is claimable also in the lost-volume cases. Such a situation arises when the seller has more goods in stock than it needs to serve its contracts, thus losing the profit on an additional transaction it could have carried out had the contract

---

590.D. SAIDOV, préc., note 347., P.66

591.*Id.*p.56

592.*Id.*p.66 Saidov writes: "there has been some uncertainty regarding whether or not this type of loss should be recoverable."

been performed. If the seller does not deliver the goods and the buyer is thus unable to fulfil contracts with its customers, the loss of profit consists of the resale price minus certain costs.

The Iran-U.S. Claims Tribunal has recognized the claim for the lost-volume seller as a matter of damage law. In the following awards, it acknowledges the damage's compensability under the title of lost-volume seller, but, where the claimant failed to present the evidence to prove its damages, the judges dismissed the claims.

In the *CMI International, Inc.* case, the tribunal rejected a claim for lost profits because the claimant was a "lost volume seller." While it agreed in principle that such a vendor would be entitled to recover its lost profits as a result of the breach of its sales contract, it concluded that the claimant had failed to prove it was a lost-volume seller.[593]Chamber II defined the theory of "lost volume seller damage" and accepted that it could constitute a basis for damage.

In the *General Electric Co.* case,[594] the claimant argued for damages for lost profits ($6,057,272) and unrecovered overhead ($2,671,705) as a lost-volume seller. It alleged that it resold $14,053,995 in items it manufactured for IACI (respondent) to its other customers in the ordinary course of business. It contended that it had the production capacity to manufacture both the IACI products and those it resold to other customers and, therefore, that IACI's breach of contract reduced its total sales volume. The theory underlying this claim is that GE is entitled to recover damages as a 'lost volume seller' under Uniform Commercial Code (UCC)| 2-708, which is applicable here. According to GE, this theory of recovery is also consistent with general principles of contract damages in international law. A seller that can establish that it had sufficient production capacity to supply not only the defaulting purchaser but also the customers to whom it resold the goods is deemed

593.*CMI International, Inc, the Islamic Republic of Iran*, préc., note 151.p.268

594.*General Electric Company v the Islamic Republic of Iran*, préc., note 496.

to have suffered a reduction in its total volume of sales. It can accordingly recover the profit and overhead it would have expected to earn on the lost sales if the breach had not occurred. The tribunal did not need to decide whether lost-volume seller damages are awardable in principle because the evidence the claimant submitted was inadequate, and it therefore denied the claim.

4.3.2 Loss of Profit in Expropriation

The Iran-U.S. Claims Tribunal generally accepts the compensability of lost profits (*lucrum cessans*).[595] In cases of lawful expropriation, as we saw in chapter 2, the tribunal has treated the actual, or suffered loss as the only compensable damage and not awarded lost profits. It treated Iran's massive expropriations of 1980 as large-scale nationalizations, and hence legal, and would not award lost profits. For a lawful taking, only *damnum emergens* is payable as compensation -- that is, the value of the property, however established -- omitting *lucrum cessans* (lost future profits) and other consequential damage.[596] Judge Khalilian in his concurring opinion in the *Petrolane* case,[597] pointed out the dominant principle the tribunal applied in this issue: "23. As a concept in terms of international adjudication, lost profit (lucrum cessans) is generally viewed as consequential, indirect, and even remote damage, which is not compensable in lawful expropriations. This is the principle upon which to base the argument for rejecting the claim for lost profits."

---

595 .In Levitt award the Tribunal stated: "55. In principle, loss of profits constitutes a proper head of damages for breach of contract provided the Claimant can establish to the Tribunal's satisfaction that such profits would have accrued if the contract had proceeded to completion. " *William J. Levitt v the Islamic Republic of Iran*, préc., note 464.para.55

596.C. F. AMERASINGHE, préc., note 304.p.67

597.*Petrolane Inc. v the Islamic Republic of Iran*, préc., note 238.para.23

In the tribunal's *Sola* case, an expropriated company asked for lost future revenue resulting from expropriation. For the tribunal, this was a lawful expropriation, so, lost profit is irrelevant: "62. The Tribunal assigns no value to future lost profits and therefore does not decide the question whether and to what extent lost profit can be claimed in expropriation cases in addition to the going concern value."

In some cases, the tribunal awarded the lost revenue from an asset Iran withheld, but for only the period before the expropriation. In the *Sedco Inc.* case,[598] it held that the replacement value of the oil rigs alone would not be sufficient, because the claimant also lost income from renting them during at least nine months, the time it takes to buy and install comparable oil rigs.

In its statement of claim, Sedco alleged that NIOC's appropriation of its rigs had deprived it of revenue of $5,000 per day per rig. Sedco also claimed that at the relevant time it took at most 60 days to place a rig on lease and move it to its new drilling location, and requested damages of $5,000 per rig per day starting 60 days after appropriation of the rigs and continuing "until the rigs' return." The tribunal accepted the claimant's lost revenue for nine months:

"86. It appears that recovery for the nine months during which Sedco could not have mitigated its damages should be reduced by the initial 60 days which Sedco admits it ordinarily would have taken to move and restart operations for another company. Thus, lost revenue damages are properly awardable for a period of seven months, beginning two months after appropriation. Accordingly, the Tribunal awards as damages for loss of its use of SISA's rigs $4,817,064, an amount equal to $3,787 per day for each of the six rigs for 212 days starting 2 October 1980 and ending 1 May 1981."

Awarding lost profit in terms of the actual investment is a good

598.*SEDCO, Inc. v. National Iranian Oil Company*, [1987] 15 _IUSCTR_ 23 (Iran_U.S. Claims Tribunal).p.53

starting point in such cases. If there are other indicators that strongly support future profitability, then it may be relevant to calculate lost profit from future projections, but the mere fact that a project was near completion says nothing about its future profitability. Tribunals have been reluctant to award lost profits for a beginning industry and unperformed work. In such cases the recovery is limited to the amount of the investment actually made, because the business has not had the time to develop a history of profitability on which to project with a reasonable degree of certainty the future cash flows. In next chapter, the tribunal's approach to consider the future profitability in assessment of the compensation, is extensively discussed.

4.4 Summary

In theory, the Iran-U.S. Claims Tribunal has largely accepted suffered loss (*damnum emergens*) and lost profit (*lucrum cessans*) in its application of full compensation. Only, it believes, recovery of all damages can make the aggrieved party whole, the concept which both of transnational instruments enshrine – CISG, in article 74, and UPICC, in article 7.4.2.

In practice, however, the tribunal has often set up obstacles to awarding them. In addition, to factoring in investment costs that evidence may uncover, the tribunal may consider recoverability of currency devaluation and legal fees as suffered losses. In expropriation cases, where the tribunal has calculated the value of the expropriated property interests in Iranian rials, it has consistently converted that amount to U.S. dollars, using the exchange rate from the time of expropriation. In other types of cases, especially for debts in rials, its practice reveals no firm decision, although it seems to have preferred the rate at the debt's due date. The tribunal has sometimes examined whether, if the claimant had been paid at the due date, it exchanged the amount to its own country's currency. Regarding devaluation of currency, the tribunal believes that the award of interest should s cover such damages.

As for legal costs, it is free to determine which party shall bear them in whole or in part. Because of its broad discretion in this matter, its practice has been less than fully consistent. In deciding the proper amount of such costs to award, it has considered the nature and outcome of the proceedings, including the case's complexity, the degree of the prevailing party's success, and both parties' attitude and demeanor. However, the tribunal awarded no costs at all to the successful claimants in full. In most cases, without explanation, it considered whether the claim for legal fees seemed reasonable or appropriate. The tribunal has usually awarded lost profit vis-à-vis expropriated investments or terminated commercial contracts, as part of paying full compensation. But it has often dismissed as speculative or too uncertain claims for lost profits in cases of breach of contract.

The tribunal has recognized claims by lost-volume sellers as a matter of damage law and been willing to make awards under this head of damage. In these awards, damages for lost profits are available when loss of profits is a foreseeable consequence of the breach and is calculable with reasonable certainty. In expropriation claims with strong indicators of future profitability, it considers lost profit based on future projections, but the mere fact of a project's nearing completion does not demonstrate its future profitability. The tribunal has argued that in lawful expropriation the actual or suffered loss is the only compensable damage and abstained from awarding lost profits, and it has applied that standard in cases arising from the massive nationalizations in Iran following its Islamic Revolution.

Chapter Five

Valuation

5.1 General

The value of anything is what somebody else is willing to pay for it.[599] But the valuation of assets and properties and rights is not as easy a task as appears from such definition, because often there is no purchaser in the market or the property in question is not for sale. In contractual disputes that lead to termination of contract, there are some fairly straightforward ways to determine damages, through the resale value or by comparing market values. But, in expropriation, particularly that destroys the business, as occurred through large-scale nationalization in Iran's Islamic Revolution, the lack of a market and the destructiveness of the revolution make valuation very difficult. The liquidation of an enterprise is conceivable in expropriation, but it could happen to a distributor or an agency through the breach of an international commercial contract. Therefore, the jurisprudence of the Iran-U.S. Claims Tribunal in the evaluation of intangible assets and future enterprise revenue might provide useful insights for international commercial arbitrations.

For the tribunal to award a claimant full compensation is not a complete answer. The judges must decide which valuation method to use. Full compensation may not mean what the claimant hopes.[600].The calculation of compensation and damages is always a challenge, especially in the light of unclear and unpredictable international practice vis-à-vis valuation.[601] Even so, the outcomes of various international

599.A. MOURI, préc., note 156., p.408

600.R. B. L. and D. J. BEDERMAN, préc., note 137.p.458

601.I. MARBOE, préc., note 232.p.723

proceedings may help us grasp the nature and methods of this costly undertaking. Valuation of assets is not a legal matter per se and belongs rather to accounting, but the elements of assets, such as lost revenue, future prospects, and certainty and probabilities in long-term contract terminations, have substantial legal components and ramifications. We focus here on the two principal approaches for the valuation of investments at the centre of disputes --namely income-, and asset-based-- and the corresponding valuation methods through which the Iran-U.S. Claims Tribunal implements such approaches.

5.2 Method of Valuation; Fair Market Value

The main concept or method for valuation of an enterprise in international arbitration is fair market value. Although most of the legal instruments in international investment prescribe fair market value for assessing compensation, none of them defines the concept.[602] A number of other subsidiary methods or techniques could be applicable – for example, going-concern value, replacement value, investment value, discounted cash flaw value, liquidation value, and book value. Sometimes, the valuation process for a single claim should y apply more than one method, and many use a number of subsidiary methods in combination, depending on the circumstances of the case and the nature and size of the loss. A difficulty, however, arises when the above tools are not available, which is more common with the tribunal than in other types of cases. Very often the expropriation of property happens in a monopoly market where there is no comparable property.[603] An objective or abstract valuation frequently leads to lower compensation

---

602 .Article 13 of Energy Charter Treaty states: "(d) Such compensation shall amount to the fair market value of the Investment expropriated at the time immediately before the Expropriation or impending Expropriation became known in such a way as to affect the value of the Investment." préc., note 300

603.B. SABAHI, préc., note 263.p.565

than the claimant's actual loss.[604]. World Bank Guidelines on the treatment of foreign direct investment offers about fair market value: "IV.3. Compensation will be deemed adequate if it is based on the fair market value of the taken asset as such value is determined immediately before the time at which the taking occurred or the decision to take the asset became publicly known."[605]

The concept of market value sits atop a pyramid of assumptions, because it assumes a hypothetical sale in a hypothetical open market between a hypothetical willing vendor and a hypothetical willing purchaser. 'Fair market value' is a more technical valuation, often bearing the signature of expert or certified auditors, with its aim "to be equitable to both parties."[606] There need not be an 'active market' for the property in question, but compensation should reflect an objective, real, and full value -and, in that sense, a 'market' measure.[607]

For a value to be fair to all parties, it should take into account all the circumstances and the absence of an open market. A number of methods work for valuing individual tangible and intangible items of properties or property rights. Reference to the marketplace also has certain disadvantages. It does not generally represent the property's value for a particular owner. It does not reflect the specific competences, skills, know-how, mobility, plans, estimations, perceptions, or risk-acceptances of the affected individual. Further, it does not take into account whether the property in question forms a component part of a greater entity or if personal rights attach to it. Compensation that equals the fair market value of an expropriated asset therefore often does not provide full reparation to the former owner.

604.I. MARBOE, préc., note 232. P.35

605.*world Bank Guideline on the Treatment of Foreign Direct Investment*, préc., note 121.

606.A. MOURI, préc., note 156.P.410

607.A. C. SMUTNY, préc., note 248.P.9

However, international practice often neglects the reality that 'value' is not an objective quality of things. Appreciation by persons is what creates it. Without their needs and affections, things would not have any value. Value is therefore a relative concept.[608] The legal norms on expropriation implicitly accept this when they refer to fair market value as the standard of compensation.[609] Although most expropriation clauses require that the compensation must amount to the investment's value, they usually do not specify how to calculate its fair market value. Article 1110 of NAFTA declares fair market value to be the standard for compensation valuation but fails to define the criteria for valuation:

"2) Compensation shall be equivalent to the *fair market value* of the expropriated investment immediately before the expropriation took place ... Valuation criteria shall include going concern value, asset value including declared tax value of tangible property, and other criteria, as appropriate, to determine fair market value."[610]

The above expropriation clause specifies that the compensation must amount to the value of the investment, but it makes no mention of how to calculate the fair market value of the investment.

Therefore, as demonstrated, the BIT is often limited as a source of guidance in determining damages[611]. This classic formulation of market value, which is viewed as being consistent with the international standard embodied in the Chorzo'w dictum and the ILC Articles, provides the framework for the application of valuation methodologies in investment cases[612].

The commentary on article 36 of ILC Draft Articles, about compensation against a state's wrongful action, declares fair market value as the criterion for compensation: "Compensation reflecting the

608.I. MARBOE, préc., note 225.,p.724

609.Id.

610.*North America Free Trade Agreement (NAFTA)*, préc., note 92

611.A. LO, préc., note 107.p85

612.J. ALBERRO, préc., note 264.p.691

capital value of property taken or destroyed as the result of an internationally wrongful act is generally assessed on the basis of the 'fair market value' of the property lost."[613]

IUCST practice has seen much discussion of the methods of valuation. The tribunal stated in the *Amoco* award,[614]

"For the purpose of valuing the compensation due in case of the lawful expropriation of an asset, market value, apparently, is the most commendable standard, since it is also the most objective and the most easily ascertained when a market exists for identical or similar assets, i.e., when such assets are the object of a continuous flow of free transactions. The price at which these transactions take place is the reflection of the perceptions of value of a great number of willing buyers and sellers."

One determines an object's fair market value by looking at actually paid prices for comparable items on the market. However, due to the difference between price paid and fair market value, a valid assessment requires enough comparable transactions and available data.[615] Only, these conditions make it possible to balance the different subjective perceptions of the object's value.

Next comes calculation of the investment's fair market value to find the actual amount owing to the investor. To do so, the IUSCT must choose the best valuation method. It explained the hypothetical position of market value in the expropriation in *Amoco* award when an open market does not exist for the expropriated asset or for goods identical or comparable to it., like transactions relating to large corporations the shares of which are not traded on stock exchanges. The tribunal held:

613.International Law Commission, Draft articles on Responsibility of States for Internationally Wrongful Acts. préc.note 118..

614.*Amoco International Finance Corp. v the Islamic Republic of Iran*, préc., note 161.para.217

615.C. N. BROWER et J. D. BRUESCHKE, préc., note 124. P.596, I. SEIDL-HOHENVELDERN, préc., note 270.p. 17

"218. Actually, market value has frequently been used for the valuation of compensation in case of expropriation. 219. Market value, on the other hand, is an ambiguous concept,............ In such circumstances, referring to market value for the purpose of determining compensation in case of expropriation inevitably leads to a pyramid of hypotheses, since it is necessary to conjecture as to the price on which a hypothetical willing buyer and a hypothetical willing seller negotiating at arms length would eventually agree. Such a conjecture is more especially artificial as the owner of the expropriated asset usually is not a willing seller."

The fair market value of the investment must then be determined to find the actual amount owed to the investor. To do so, the Tribunal must choose the best valuation method out of numerous possible methods[616].

5.2.1 Valuation of Business Enterprise

The most challenging sort of problem the tribunal faced was the ending of activity by the businesses in question or their expropriation through nationalization. In these cases, there was no existing market with which to determine the value of the expropriated property. For a business that the respondent's breach of contract (which would include lost profits) has destroyed, parties and tribunals usually use the going-concern method to assess its value. Obviously, when the state exproprates a business, it will profit from the future revenue of the expropriated entity[617]. The Iran-U.S. Claims Tribunal ruled for "the full value of the asset taken" or "the full equivalent of the property" as the appropriate way to assess the going concern. The value encompassed "not only the physical and financial assets of the undertaking, but also the intangible values which contribute to its earning power, such as

616.A. LO, préc., note 107.p.77

617.I. SEIDL-HOHENVELDERN, préc., note 270.p.22

contractual rights ... as well as goodwill and commercial prospects." Intangible assets, explained the tribunal, link closely to profitability but are not the same as the financial capitalization of the revenues that might emerge after the transfer of property. Here it distinguished explicitly between the business's existing value and its future profitability power. The tribunal evaluated the business's lost future income by looking at its discounted cash flow (DCF)–the value of its money over time.

5.2.1.1 Income-Based Methods

Income-based valuation provides a more direct way to measure expected revenues and corresponding future cash flow. As modern valuation methods do not used fixed assets to assess an enterprise, but look rather at its capacity to generate future income for the owner, the expectations of future profits are already equivalent to the value of the enterprise itself. Awarding lost profits in addition to this value in case of unlawful expropriation would risk double counting.[618] Therefore income-based valuation not only factors in physical assets but also "takes into account the loss of future profits and, often, intangible assets such as goodwill as well. This method treats value as a forward-looking concept. At any given time, the value of an income-producing asset will depend primarily on the net cash flow it expects to generate in the future, 'discounted' (reduced) to a 'present value' (value as of the valuation date) at a percentage rate that accounts fully both for the time value of money and for all relevant risks.[619]

The tribunal considers an asset's income-producing ability using two separate methods or phases. The first is going concern, which relates closely to profitability and is not the same as the second, financial capitalization of the revenues after post-expropriation property transfer. In fact, the tribunal treats phase II as a DCF projection of future

618.I. MARBOE, préc., note 232. P.73

619.B. M. CLAGETT, préc., note 408.p.843

revenue. While the first method looks backward, examining the records of profit, the second peers forward, projecting future revenue to assess business value.[620] In its practice, the Iran-U.S. Claims Tribunal has applied both methods frequently.

5.2.1.1.1 Going-Concern Value

According to World Bank Guideline on the Treatment of Foreign Direct Investment, "a going concern means an enterprise consisting of income-producing assets which has been in operation for a sufficient period of time to generate the data required for the calculation of future income and which could have been expected with reasonable certainty, if the taking had not occurred, to continue producing legitimate income over the course of its economic life in the general circumstances following the taking by the State."[621] Going-concern value is the full value of the property, business or rights in question as an income producing asset.

The Iran-U.S. Claims Tribunal considered the going-concern value for the first time in its *American InternationalGroup* award.[622] It held that it must valuate Iran America, an operating entity, as a going concern and consider all the elements that contribute to its worth, including prospective income. The term 'going concern' connotes "the undertaking itself considered as an organic totality the value of which is greater than that of its component parts, and which must also take account of the legitimate expectations of the owners."

620.Manuel A. ABDALA, « Key Damage Compensation Issues in Oil and Gas International Arbitration Cases », (2009) 24-3 *Am. Univ. Int. Law Rev.* 540-570. p.541

621.*world Bank Guideline on the Treatment of Foreign Direct Investment*, préc., note 121.

622.*American International Group Inc. v the Islamic Republic of Iran*, préc., note 276.p.107

The first point at issue was the method to assess Iran America's shares. The tribunal opted for a going concern, including net book value of assets, goodwill, and likely future profitability, had the company continued its business under its former management. The judges avoided the book-value method, which is mainly for liquidations. In takings that involve ongoing businesses, the tribunal has ruled that full compensation requires going-concern analysis. Accordingly, in the *American International Group* award, held that, "the appropriate method is to value the company as a going concern, taking into account not only the net book value of its assets but also such elements as goodwill and likely profitability, had the company been allowed to continue its business under its former management."

In Amoco award, the tribunal, while advocates that, in case of expropriation of an enterprise the compensation to be paid is calculated according to the net value of the expropriated assets, defines the concept of the going-concern stating that:[623]

"228. As we have seen the net value of the expropriated assets can extend to physical properties, movable and immovable, as well as to intangibles, including profitability in the case of an ongoing enterprise: the 'going concern' value. To this element of damnum emergens, a complementary one is added where the expropriation is unlawful: the value of the revenues that the owner would have earned if the expropriation had not occurred, i.e., lucrum cessans."

The tribunal outlined the elements of going concern; as the physical and financial assets and the intangibles that contribute to earning power, such as contractual rights (supply and delivery contracts, patent licences, and so on), as well as goodwill and commercial prospects. Those assets are not same as financial capitalization of future

623.*Amoco International Finance Corp. v the Islamic Republic of Iran*, préc., note 161.para.228

revenues after the post-expropriation transfer of property.[624] According to the award, going concern was the model for assessing financial or intangible assets.

In general, the tribunal looks at intangible assets in terms of profitability, i.e., what means would help it become profitable? Such awards consider goodwill and future prospects as the main intangible assets, so, any damage to them requires compensation. But is goodwill a separate property right in the determination of market value, especially under revolutionary conditions? The tribunal's practice shows that it did not find elements such as good will, future prospects (or profitability) and loss of future profits to be property rights or to have value independent of the value of a particular property or entity.[625] In the *Sola Tiles* case,[626] the claimant requested compensation for an expropriated enterprise, and the tribunal held that recovery of damage to goodwill depends on recognition of the enterprises as being a going concern: "61. Sola also seeks compensation for Simat's goodwill and for its lost future profits. The Tribunal must therefore determine whether Simat qualifies as a 'going concern." In the next paragraph, the tribunal defines the notion of goodwill:

"62. Goodwill can best be defined, as that part of a company's value attributable to its business reputation and the relationship it has established with its suppliers and customers. 64. Given the picture that emerges, Simat's prospects of continuing active trading after the Revolution were not, in the view of the Tribunal, such as to justify treating Simat as a going concern so as to assign any value to goodwill. The decision to assign no value to Simat's goodwill suggests a similar result as to future lost profits, which also depend upon the business prospects of a going concern."

624.*Id.* , para, 264

625.A. MOURI, préc., note 156.p 58

626.*Sola Tiles, Inc. v the Islamic Republic of Iran*, [1985] 14 _IUSCTR_ 223 (Iran_U.S. Claims Tribunal).p.241

In this case, claimant had the briefest past record of profitability, having shown a loss in 1976, its first year of trading, and a small profit the next year. Accordingly, the Tribunal assigned no value to future lost profits and therefore did not decide the question whether and to what extent lost profit can be claimed in expropriation cases in addition to the going concern value.

In the *Payne* award,[627] the tribunal reaffirmed going concern as the way to assess assets: "29. The appropriate method is to value the company as a going concern, taking into account not only the net book value of its assets but also such elements as good will and likely future profitability, had the company been allowed to continue its business under its former management."

In the tribunal's *Ebrahimi* award,[628] Judge Richard Allison, in his concurring opinion, illustrated the circumstances that led the tribunal to establish GostareshMaskan as a going concern. Gostaresh was a construction company with current projects in Iran that the government expropriated in 1979. He stated that: "In 1979 GostareshMaskan was an established income-producing going concern. Based on (i) the Company's historical earnings (averaging 30 [%] profitability or 634 million rials per year), (ii) its staff of 1000 regular employees and the available pool of additional unskilled labor, (iii) its manufacturing assets and capabilities, (iv) accelerated write-off of heavy capital expenditures, (v) shrinking competition from foreign sources, (vi) the Iranian Government's policy favoring the building of residential housing."

627.*Payne, Thomas Earl v. the Islamic Republic of Iran*, préc., note 465.

628.*Ebrahimi Shahin Shaine v. the Islamic Republic of Iran*, préc., note 281.para.63

5.2.1.1.1.1 The Effects of Market Circumstances

IUSCT precedent has recognized that assessment of business value must consider general economic conditions, including the economic changes of a revolutionary period, even before looking at expropriation or a business's prospects after expropriation. In the claims it has seen, the value of the expropriated assets never rose after expropriation, but rather declined or evaporated altogether. In the tribunal's jurisprudence, the distinction between the effects of economic changes and the impact of expropriation may be useful in valuation of future prospects and serve as a model for other international investment tribunals.[629]

It is almost axiomatic that valuation of expropriated property must exclude any drop in value flowing from expropriation. In Iran, events before nationalization in 1980– such as the revolution -- are relevant to this value, unlike those that came later. As for methods of valuation, there is certainly no rule of thumb, and much depends on the nature of the property or interest taken as well as on the circumstances of its taking.[630] Such analysis, however, need not factor in risks to future profitability, nor the particular risk of expropriation.[631].

The tribunal has not applied as precedent the effects either of the very act of nationalization nor of events after nationalization. However, tribunal precedent has recognized inclusion of general economic conditions, including the economic changes of a revolutionary period, at least insofar as they are not part of the government's expropriation. In its *American International Group, Inc.* award[632], the tribunal held: "Prior changes in the general political, social and

629.I. MARBOE, préc., note 232. P.230

630.S. RIPINSKY, préc., note 56., C. F. AMERASINGHE, préc., note 304. P.59

631.I. MARBOE, préc., note 225. P.740

632.*American International Group Inc. v the Islamic Republic of Iran*, préc., note 276.p.108

economic conditions which might have affected the enterprise's business prospects as of the date the enterprise was taken should be considered. Whether such changes are ephemeral or long-term will determine their overall impact on the value of the enterprise's future prospects."

These principles also guided the judges in the *Payne* case and the *Phelps Dodge Corp.* award. In the *Payne* case,[633] the claimant sought the fair value of two companies making and servicing electronics parts that the authorities expropriated after the revolution. The claimant argued for valuing the business as a going concern. The tribunal concluded, however, that the claimant had underestimated the harm the revolution and the disruption in Iran-U.S. trade had caused to business prospects. Much of the business related to the government, and the business depended on American spare parts and components it could no longer import. The tribunal rejected the claim of its being a going concern: "36. The effects of the revolution seriously discounted the reliability of past performance for the two companies and the value of their good will, particularly since they are service companies." The tribunal then awarded the fair market value of the claimant's interest in the two companies at the time of the taking --actually on a book-value basis.

The general rule is valuation using information available at the date of valuation, including any value-depressing information that does not relate to government conduct.[634].The underlying logic is that, had the investor sold the asset just prior to expropriation, it would have received the asset's market value at that time. The tribunal has elaborated suitable and convincing guidelines for determining a company's value during political change. In its *AmericanInternational Group, Inc.* award,[635] it rejected a proposed valuation on grounds that the claimants'

633.*Payne, Thomas Earl v. the Islamic Republic of Iran*, préc., note 465.para.36

634.S. Ripinsky, préc., note 56. p.252

635.*American International Group Inc. v the Islamic Republic of Iran*, préc., note 276.p.108

expert appraisals downplayed economic and social changes relevant to sales up through the revolution. In the *Ebrahimi* case,[636] it sought expert assistance in calculating GMC Company's fair market value, as of November 13, 1979. After receiving expert valuation, it decided to exclude the economic effects of revolution (as a reducing indicator):

"The expert's valuation shall be made on the basis of fair market value, taking into account the tangible physical and financial assets of the undertaking and other elements, if any, including but not limited to, contractual and intellectual property rights, commercial prospects, goodwill, and likely future profitability. The effects of the very act of nationalization or effects of events that occurred subsequent to nationalization shall be excluded; however, prior changes in the general political, social, and economic conditions which might have affected GMC's business prospects as of the date it was taken shall be taken into account."

Although more generally this approach excluded the effects of expropriation in valuation of businesses, in some instances revolutionary social and cultural change affected future profitability. In these cases, even without expropriation, there was no foreseeable market. In this context, foreseeability of post-expropriation events refers to those that would have affected market value, meaning: take them into account to the extent that the market might well have 'absorbed" an expectation of those events and their effect on the property's value. This approach has support from some commentators: "Without looking at hindsight, there is a risk that the compensation might not restore the investor with the financial position it would have had in the absence of the taking."[637]

636.*Ebrahimi Shahin Shaine v. the Islamic Republic of Iran*, préc., note 281.footnote.18

637.M. A. ABDALA, préc., note 620.p.556

5.2.1.1.1.2 Eliminating the New-Business Rule

The tribunal tends to ignore lost profits as purely speculative for an unestablished or new business. This 'new business' rule, however, runs contrary to the rules and laws of many countries concerning remedies for breach of contract.[638] The tribunal often uses a number of valuation methods to reach its 'full compensation' standard in expropriation cases vis-à-vis businesses. We saw above that the general compensation rule for an unlawful act requires putting the aggrieved party in the hypothetical position that requires assessing the fair market value of the losses. For startup businesses, without any record of profits, assessing fair market value, in the technical sense, may not be possible, as that would require assuming that the business would generate cash into the future, often an uncertain prospect for a startup.[639] When an enterprise fails to qualify as a going concern, a tribunal may award only the value of its assets.[640]

In the *AIG* award,[641] the arbitral noted operations lasting just over 4½ years; an insufficient basis for projecting future profits except very speculatively.

While projecting future cash flows for start-up and early-stage investments is open to legitimate skepticism, arbiters usually find revenue projections for going concerns adequate for awarding damages when there is clear proof of the fact of damages.[642]

638.J. Y. GOTANDA, préc., note 362., p.100

639.B. SABAHI, préc., note 245., p.129

640.A. MOURI, préc., note 156.p.421

641.*American International Group Inc. v the Islamic Republic of Iran*, préc., note 276.p.108

642.W. H. KNULL, S. T. JONES, T. J. TYLER et R. D. DEUTSCH, préc., note 262 .P.274

In the *CBS Inc.* case,[643]the claimant sought compensation for expropriation in Iran. This firm– part of CBS Iranian Companies--produced records and tapes, mostly of Western music. It asked for future revenue from expropriation in 1978 till early 1979. The tribunal noted its short trading history and lack of profits: "The Tribunal notes, however, that the value of a company is affected not only by turnover, but also by profitability. The CBS Iranian Companies had no history of past profits, apart from a small profit of US$58,000, realized during the third quarter of 1978, and mainly attributable, to an exceptionally popular release."

Further, the judges considered the effects of the Islamic Revolution on the distribution of Western music: "The Claimant's valuations also underestimate the adverse effects of the Islamic Revolution on the music market, and thus on the CBS Iranian Companies' future business. In particular, in view of the policy of the new Iranian Government against music, especially Western music, which constituted a substantial part of the CBS Iranian Companies' field of operation, the expectations for these Companies were greatly diminished."

Some observers have challenged the tribunal's approach. Gotanda submits: "Some tribunals and commentators advocate that lost profits are not appropriate when the claimant is an unestablished or a new business because the lack of an earnings history makes such profits speculative. This new business rule is contrary to the rules and laws of many countries concerning remedies for breach of contract and incorrect from a policy standpoint"[644] However, when the enterprise fails to qualify as a going concern, a tribunal may award just the value of its assets[645].

643.*CBS, Inc. v the Government of the Islamic Republic of Iran*, [1990] case no.197, 25 _IUSCTR_ 131 (Iran_U.S. Claims Tribunal).

644.J. Y. GOTANDA, préc., note 362., p.100

645.A. MOURI, préc., note 156.,p.421

5.2.1.1.2 Discounted Cash Flow (DCF)

Discounted cash flow (DCF) is an accounting method for calculating an enterprise's value to its owner, and differs from its fair market value, which a reasonable person, seeking to maximize gain, would be willing to pay for it. DCF follows the 'income approach,' with which an object's worth does not depend on its historical cost and profit, but is equivalent to its ability to create future financial benefits for its owner. In the other words, a hypothetical willing buyer will normally be interested not in what the owner paid for an object but in future gains from it. This method bases fair market value not on historical data, but on future expectations.[646]When the investment is very recent, or still in the process of being made, there isan obvious and often easier alternative to using of future cash flow to determineFMV[647].

DCF involves three steps of valuation:

•projection of probable future earning

•projection of possible future costs

•estimation of risks and discounting factors and the rate of such discount[648]

Projection of future earnings generally uses the contingencies that the tribunal has recognized as too speculative to rely on. Projecting future cash flows, involves careful judgment of parameters and economic variables into the future, which requires reasonable assumptions.[649] Projection of future costs is relatively realistic, invoking expert reports. The notion, 'DCF value,' is logically prospective, is intrinsically forward-looking, and involves a projection of the cash flow that the owner might have gained in the absence of expropriation.

646.I. MARBOE, préc., note 225.p.737

647.L. T. WELLS, préc., note 243.p.475

648.S. RIPINSKY, préc., note 56.p.195

649.M. A. ABDALA, préc., note 620.p.550

According to World Bank Guidelines for the Treatment of Foreign Direct Investment:

"Discounted cash flow value' means the cash receipts realistically expected from the enterprise in each future year of its economic life as reasonably projected minus that year's expected cash expenditure, after discounting this net cash flow for each year by a factor which reflects the time value of money, expected inflation, and the risk associated with such cash flow under realistic circumstances. Such discount rate may be measured by examining the rate of return available in the same market on alternative investments of comparable risk on the basis of their present value."[650]

Discounted cash flow is the most common and prominent valuation technique for determining fair market value, particularly for entire businesses.[651]It measures a business's value by projecting its net cash flow for a fixed period into the future and then discounting it back to present value as of the date of the injury. The discount rate should reflect the time value of money in the host country and the relative risk for the particular investment. Its principal advantage is that, unlike other methods, it does not depend solely on past costs or historical measures of performance. Rather, it recognizes that the true economic value of a going concern is the stream of revenue that it can generate over its operative life --i.e., the profits it will generate. Consequently, DCF should fully compensate foreign investors by allowing a tribunal to award the claimant an amount that reflects the net present value of both the physical assets that it has lost (*damnum emergens*) and the profits that it has forgone (*lucrum cessans*).

There is no single method to determine the future cash flow and profits of a going concern. Rather, parties and tribunals must infer

650 . Article IV, *world Bank Guideline on the Treatment of Foreign Direct Investment*, préc., note 121.

651.I. MARBOE, préc., note 225.p.736, J. ALBERRO, préc., note 264.p689, A. LO, préc., note 107.p94 future performance from a company's current financial position and its past profits, from market trends, and from industry analysis[652]. Doing so involves significant assumptions and frequently turns into a battle of multiple experts. Likewise, it is often extremely difficult to calculate an appropriate discount rate. As a general matter, the discount rate usually factors in such elements as inflation, lending rates, and market volatility in the host country. The report of an expert witness in the *Phillips Petroleum Co.* case[653] explaining DCF submits that standard economic theory holds that market value of an asset equals its expected future cash flows discounted to present value at the opportunity cost of capital, he writes as follows:

"An asset's market value stems from its expected ability to generate cash returns over time. Market value ultimately depends on the amount, timing, and risk of future cash flows. Prompt, safe cash flows are naturally more valuable than delayed, risky ones ... The relation of future cash flows to current market value is expressed in the discounted cash flow formula, in which forecasted cash flows are discounted to obtain present value. The appropriate discount rate is the opportunity cost of capital, that is, the expected rate of return from investing in other assets of equivalent risk."

The tribunal recognized here that determining the fair market value of any asset inevitably requires looking at all relevant factors and exercising judgment. In the absence of an active and free market for comparable assets at the date of taking, a tribunal must resort to various analytical methods to assist it in deciding the price a reasonable buyer would have been willing to pay for the asset in a free market, had such a transaction been possible at the date of the property's taking.

652.Markus BURGSTALLER et Jonathan KETCHESON, « Should Expropriation Risk Be Taken into Account in the Assessment of Damages? », (2017) 32-1 *ICSID Rev.* 193-215.p.201

653.*Phillips Petroleum Company v. the Islamic Republic of Iran and NIOC*, préc., note 157.

The standard of evidence is particularly critical for entities with from little to no track record. These are 'not going concerns,' a characterization that arbitrators frequently employ when rejecting a DCF analysis and that serves as states' primary weapon against DCF valuations. Whether a company qualifies as a going concern is essentially an evidentiary question of the certainty of cash flows.[654] In some cases, the Iran-U.S. Claims Tribunal has refused to award DCF-based compensation to enterprises lacking a proven record of profits. These denials are consistent with World Bank Guideline, which limit DCF awards to going concerns with proven profitability.

DCF is a technique for measuring a property's value to its owner, because applying DCF will make the owner 'whole' or place it in the same position as if no expropriation or similar measure had occurred, by wiping out all the act's consequences. All three IUCST chambers seem to use it. While the method may find support in other reliable indicators such as comparable sales, it is the most reliable measurement in situations where (as in oil and gas properties) sales of comparable properties may be few or nil.[655]The tribunal announced in its *Phillips Petroleum* award:[656]

"106. Thus, the Claimant is entitled by the Treaty to 'just compensation', representing the 'full equivalent of the property taken'. As the Tribunal, has previously held, where the property taken was a 'going concern', compensation that meets the Treaty standard is compensation that makes the Claimant whole for the 'fair market value' of the property at the date of taking."

654.Joshua B. SIMMONS, « Valuation in Investor-State Arbitration: Toward A More Exact Science », (2012) 30-1 *Berkeley J. Int. Law* 196-250. P.231

655.W. H. KNULL, S. T. JONES, T. J. TYLER et R. D. DEUTSCH, préc., note 262.P.275

656.*Phillips Petroleum Company v. the Islamic Republic of Iran and NIOC*, préc., note 157.para.106

Judge Stewart Myers, in the *Phillips Petroleum* award,[657] confirmed that the market value of an asset equals its expected future cash flows discounted to present value at the opportunity cost of capital and noting that the discounted cash flow analysis has been accepted and applied in the awards of numerous international arbitral tribunals, as well as in cases in national courts.

5.2.1.1.2.1 Discount Factor

Converting projected future net revenues to present value requires taking both aspects, time value and risk, into account. The discounting factor is a rate by which to reduce the hypothetical future net cash flow to arrive at its present value on the date of expropriation and also includes adjustments to account for the relative risk characteristics of the enterprise's future cash flow.[658]

Determining the proper discount rate is a complex task for an arbiter. It requires taking into account probable risks, inflation, and the real rate of interest.[659] Where these factors are subject to extreme fluctuation or simply appear unreliable (as in cases involving non-market economies), it can be extremely difficult for a tribunal to determine a fair and reasonable discount rate. Finally, it is often difficult to obtain the objective data necessary to calculate a business's future revenue stream. Tribunals have broad discretion to decide the evidentiary threshold for future cash flows and differ on what constitutes sufficient evidence. Some employ a 'certainty' standard in DCF analysis that seems stricter than the more common 'reasonable certainty' standard for proving damages.[660] The Iran-U.S. Claims Tribunal outlined the various risks it

---

657.*Id.*

658.A. MOURI, préc., note 156. P.475 also see, M. KANTOR, préc., note 353. P.143

659.S. RIPINSKY, préc., note 56. P.197

660.J. B. SIMMONS, préc., note 654. P.231

had to address in deciding the *Amoco* award:[661]

"242. In the calculation of the proper discount rate, an adjustment must be made specifically to account for the relative risk characteristics of Khemco's future net cash flow. Three series of risks were considered: tax and currency risk, business risk, and force majeure risk. The risk of uncompensated breach or expropriation, on the contrary, was disregarded as irrelevant upon counsel's instruction. The Claimant's expert concluded that tax risk and force majeure risk were higher than the average for Khemco, but that currency risk and business risk were lower."

Although DCF is the theoretically preferred way to calculate damages involving going concerns, its practical application can be problematic. First, it can be extremely difficult to apply, and it can produce quite disparate results, depending on who is performing the analysis. As a practical matter, the claimant and respondent almost always compute two vastly different damages amounts from the DCF method. This divergence relates in many ways to the DCF's principal benefit – that it requires looking forward and projecting future performance.

In the *Phillips Petroleum* case,[662] the claimant's one-sixth interest in a long-term Iranian oil venture was at issue. The tribunal found that Iran had expropriated Phillips Petroleum's interest by terminating a joint operating agreement. It ruled that Phillips was due "just compensation" equal to the "full equivalent of the property taken," noting that the governing treaty required award of "compensation that makes the Claimant whole for the 'fair market value' of the property at the date of taking," that is, what a willing buyer and a willing seller

---

661.*Amoco International Finance Corp. v the Islamic Republic of Iran*, préc., note 161., para.242

662.*Phillips Petroleum Company v. the Islamic Republic of Iran and NIOC*, préc., note 157.para.79

would reasonably have agreed on as a fair price at the time of the taking in the absence of coercion on either party. The tribunal adjusted the valuation from the claimant's expert, substantially lowering the valuation. It based these adjustments not on its own DCF calculation, but rather on an underlying asset valuation neither party advocated:

"111. Any such analysis of a revenue-producing asset, such as the contract rights involved in the present case, must involve a careful and realistic appraisal of the revenue-producing potential of the asset over the duration of its term, which requires appraisal of the level of production that reasonably may be expected, the costs of operation, including taxes and other liabilities, and the revenue such production would be expected to yield, which, in turn, requires a determination of the price estimates for sales of the future production that a reasonable buyer would use in deciding upon the price it would be willing to pay to acquire the asset."

Moreover, any such analysis must also involve an evaluation of the effect on the price of any other risks likely to be perceived by a reasonable buyer at the date in question, excluding only reductions in the price that could be expected to result from threats of expropriation or from other actions by the Respondents related thereto. The tribunal identified the valuation's four principal tasks: calculations variously of the anticipated quantity of oil recoverable, the anticipated price of oil, the anticipated production costs, and the associated risks. Therefore, the tribunal continued in its judgment in the award as follows:

"The Tribunal thinks it preferable to examine first the question of the quantity of oil in place that could reasonably have been expected, to be recoverable, as a technical matter, given the will both to make the necessary investments to that end and to lift all the available oil. The Tribunal will then deal separately and as part of the analysis of the perceived risks with the question of the extent to which a buyer, should reasonably have anticipated that future investment and production might fall short of that maximum level."

As the tribunal explained, with respect to risks, it concluded that a buyer of the claimant's JSA interests in September 1979 would reasonably have seen the risks as much higher than the claimant has assumed. The claimant assumed that the risks were no higher than those for any other investment by a major oil company, and it therefore used a discount rate (4.5 per cent) identical to its calculations of the real cost of capital to such companies. Having accepted the method, however, the tribunal concluded that the claimant's estimates of production and prices and low, 4.5% discount rate failed to take into account risks, such as that of reduced future production as a result of national policy changes flowing from the Islamic Revolution, that it should have factored in, even if one could not quantify them with certainty in either the revenue projections or the discount rate. The tribunal did not, however, explain how the claimant's DCF analysis should have incorporated these risks, nor did it set out its ultimate calculation of the quantum of the award. Without further analysis, the tribunal awarded the claimant U.S.$55 million, against a claim of U.S.$159 million, after "taking into account all relevant circumstances."

Although, recently the Idea pointed out by some authors that country risk of expropriation can be taken into account in a number of ways, depending on the valuation methodology used. Adjusting the discount rate involves adding what is described as a country risk premium[663]. This idea has not found any support in the practice of the Iran_U.S. Claims Tribunal. However. In Starrett award, It is discussed that all sorts of risks normally should be assumed by the foreign investor, stating that:

"Investors in Iran, like investors in all other countries, have to assume a risk that the country might experience strikes, lock-outs, disturbances, changes of the economic and political system and even revolution. That any of these risks materialized does not necessarily

---

663.M. BURGSTALLER et J. KETCHESON, préc., note 652.p.196

mean that property rights affected by such events can be deemed to have been taken. A revolution as such does not entitle investors to compensation under international law.[664]"

5.2.1.1.2.2 Important Issues of Applying DCF Method

Some critics raise valid questions about applying the DCF method. In fact, compensation to a private claimant representing the value of its assets, plus any loss of profits in the period between the trespass (nationalization, breach of contract, or expropriation) and the award, restores to it the value of its business – i.e., returns its 'capital' to it. The claimant can now invest that capital elsewhere, in some other business, in some other country, and seek to earn profits. Why, therefore, should that claimant expect an additional award to cover loss of profits under the terminated contract for the same period during which the same capital is earning a second set of profits elsewhere? On the assumption that the claimant has put the returned capital to good use, in effect, it is claiming a double recovery for loss of profits. Such a claim seems both illogical and unethical.[665] This statement finds some support s in Amoco award[666], where the tribunal stated:

"215. The result of the award of lost profits pursuant to the DCF method would also be absurd, since the Claimant would be able to invest the amounts, including lost profits, received as compensation, and therefore obtain a real rate of return for such an investment, which

---

664.Starrett Housing International, Inc v the Islamic Republic of Iran, Interlocutory Award No ITL 32-24-1 (19 December 1983)16 -IUSCTR _112, p.156

665.Thomas R. STAUFFER, « valuation of assets in international taking », (1996) 17 *Energy Law J.* 459-488.p.461

666.*Amoco International Finance Corp. v the Islamic Republic of Iran*, préc., note 161.para.215

would be tantamount to double recovery. Such an award would also produce an unreasonable rate of return."

Professor Walde, also submits that the reason damages are so important in investment arbitration is that investment arbitration is not pure legal technology. It plays in a political context[667]. It is essentially an issue of double recovery, where the investor obtains first, without risk, its original investment expenditures, and then receives also the returns he might have obtained with the very high-risk, long-term contract.

Challenges to a DCF valuation often relate to the amount of projected cash flows and the appropriate discount rate. DCF future cash flows may look like lost profits, but they involve different concepts. In breach-of-contract cases, lost profits (*lucrum cessans*) are the future gains that a party would have earned if not for the other party's actions, as opposed to actual losses suffered (*damnum emergens*). Awarding the latter is more straightforward and less controversial than granting the former. DCF, as a method of determining fair market value, is analytically distinct from *lucrum cessans*, which is a component of damages. Yet they both face similar evidentiary challenges that require a look into the future.[668] The proper method for addressing breach of contract may be to apply both techniques and then, depending on whether the enterprise has reached profitability or not, award either *lucrum cessans* or *damnum emergens*, respectively, but not both.[669]

In using a DCF method for evaluating damages in a contractual breach, comparisons with precedents involving the evaluation of expropriated business ventures are highly problematic. There is generally no basis to apply the contractual-reliance damages (*damnum emergens*), but only the expectancy damages (*lucrum cessans*). The use of *damnum emergens*and *lucrum cessans* -- a traditional remedy for breach of contract

667.H. PEREZCANO, P. PINSOLLE et T. WALDE, préc., note 48.p.51

668.J. B. SIMMONS, préc., note 654.p.222

669.B. SABAHI, préc., note 263.P.568

– arose when valuation was in its early days and looked to the accounting value of individual items of property. That did not represent market value properly as the combination of all items, the package value including goodwill, and the ability to make profit. Whether market perception, comparable transactions, or DCF help determine value, *lucrum cessans* forms part of the analysis. Then any separate payment for lost profit would amount to double recovery.[670]

Awarding both types of damages is simply inappropriate. The dichotomy of the two is harmful; they are rather complementary. They may have been useful apart, in the law of damages, but simply do not fit compensation for expropriation without this major change.[671] The DCF analysis ignores the amount invested and projects cash flows into infinity (by using the terminal value) or up to the end of the legal entitlement, i.e., the end of a contractual term and discounted to present value.[672]

In the cases where the future revenue is projected, it appears that the actual damage consists not of the sunken costs or physical damage but primarily or even exclusively of the loss of expected profits. The valuation, therefore, must measure these forgone opportunities. It is therefore economic nonsense to distinguish between the assets' value and the profits or revenues they would have generated, and economic nonsense does not produce good law. This dualistic approach of assets versus profits seems endemic to many tribunals and commentators, largely because of misapplication of the concepts of damnunemergens and lucrum cessans.[673] Mark Kantor observes: "If arbitrators are not wary, dividing a compensation analysis into a reliance interest (damnum

---

670.B. SABAHI et T. WALDE, préc., note 227.p.1067

671.I. MARBOE, préc., note 225. P.728

672.S. RIPINSKY, préc., note 56.p.296

673.William C. LIEBLICH, « Determining the Economic Value of Expropriated Income-Producing Property in International Arbitrations », (1991) 8 *J. Int. Arbitr.*,59-80, p.59

emergens) and an expectancy interest (lucrum cessans), but using a single DCF forecast, can result in double counting. The valuation should either rely solely on the DCF valuation or adjust the reliance and expectancy components to back out any double counting.[674]"

In its *Amoco* award, the Iran-U.S. Claims Tribunal reaffirmed *lucrum cessans* as the sole awardable damage in a DCF analysis:[675]

"229. The Claimant's calculation completely leaves aside the net value of the expropriated assets; this value has no place whatsoever in the Claimant's reasoning. Exit damnum emergens. The Claimant's method is instead a projection into the future to assess the amount of the revenues which would possibly be earned by the undertaking, year after year, up to eighteen years later in this Case. These forecasted revenues are actualized at the time by way of a discounting calculation, and capitalized as the measure of the compensation to be paid, as well as the alleged market value of the enterprise. With such a method, lucrum cessans becomes the sole element of compensation."

Although the tribunal did not allow the lost profit in this lawful expropriation, it factored in the forgone revenue. This may seem self-contradictory, but the tribunal was drawing a clear line between lost profit and future prospects. It sees future prospects as part of the company's value and defers from lost profits. Its emerging distinction in this case between the two concepts seemed artificial and not practical to some extents. According to the tribunal, future prospects do not equal lost profits. In the *Amoco* case,[676] it held:

"The owner rights appertain to three categories: corporeal properties (lands, buildings, equipment, stocks), contractual rights (supply and delivery contracts) and other intangible valuables (processes, goodwill and 'future prospects'). Using today's vocabulary, this would

---

674.M. KANTOR, préc., note 353. P.199

675.*Amoco International Finance Corp. v the Islamic Republic of Iran*, préc., note 161.para.229

676.*Id.*para.201

mean 'going concern value', which is not a new concept after all. Only one component relates to the future: 'future prospects.' Since, for the reasons set forth in the preceding paragraph, future prospects do not mean lost profits, we safely can say, using the traditional vocabulary of international arbitration, that all these components pertain to damnum emergens."

This statement confirms the tribunal's new practice: omitting lost profit from the undertaking's value, which already includes future prospects. In other words, for the tribunal, future prospects do not equal lost profit. Those are two different concepts. The first one refers to the enterprise as a going concern, able to earn revenues and continue doing so; this was an element of its value at the time of the taking, while the lost profits were hypothetical earnings from taking to expert opinion. Judge Khalilian, in his separate opinion in the *Petolane*case,[677] confirmed this confusing deduction:

"28. Despite its adjudicating numerous cases of expropriation, the Tribunal has not established any precedent of awarding lost profits during its ten-year judicial activities. The core of the problem in the compensations based on the method known as 'discounted cash flow' is also the fact that lost profits have to be taken into account as the main and essential element in the computation thereof."

There is an exception in the tribunal's practice regarding DCF application.In the *Amoco* case,[678] the judges refused to adopt the DCF approach. This case arose out of the expropriation of the claimant's interests in a joint venture company, Khemco, that produced and marketed natural gas. Khemco had long been active and was a going concern at the time of expropriation. The claimant requested DCF-type compensation. The tribunal denied this request and said that it was

---

677.*Petrolane Inc. v the Islamic Republic of Iran*, préc., note 238.para.28

678.*Amoco International Finance Corp. v the Islamic Republic of Iran*, préc., note 161.para.227

basing its approach on the PCIJ's principle set out in the *Chorzow Factory* award. It construed that award as separating the undertaking's value on the date of the taking (*damnum emergens*) from its lost profits (*lucrum cessans*) and concluded that the Treaty 1955 and general principles of international law did not permit use of DCF to determine damages for a lawful expropriation. Although, contra its usual future prospects against lost profits, here the tribunal considered the lost revenue as lost profit, not future prospects. This is a questionable analysis comparing to the jurisprudence of the tribunal.

Another questionable issue vis-à-vis DCF is that when a company (particularly in oil and gas), can request DCF-style damages, while it could not be considered as going concern based on lack of profitability or historical record? Today, academics tend to say yes. Manuel A. Abdala comments: "However, in the oil and gas sector, neither being a startup company (as opposed to a going concern) nor lacking a historic record of profitability are serious impediments for using the DCF method in estimating damages. The DCF cannot be ruled out simply because the company is a startup, or because the company has not yet established historic records of profitability."[679] None the less the Iran-U.S. Claims Tribunal has absolutely rejected this conclusion. It thinks it reasonable to value an investment on a DCF basis, but only if it is a going concern. Mark Kantor concurred: "If the enterprise being valued is not a going concern, investment tribunals are unwilling to project forward revenues and expenses of operation."[680]

The other major issue with DCF is the duration of the projection. How long should it be? According to Mark Kantor, "If the company at issue is heavily dependent on a particular long term contract, experts often use the same period for their compensation decisions. If no long-term contract or any contemporaneous business forecast is used as

679.M. A. ABDALA, préc., note 620.p.550

680.M. KANTOR, préc., note 353.

a basis, experts often use easy to understand periods of five or ten years."[681] IUSCT practice invokes DCF only where there exists a long-term contract or a substantial project. Otherwise, it says no, and, if the company has a history of profits, caters its award to a going concern. For instance, in the *Starrett* case, it recognized future revenue from the construction project ShahGoli. In oil and gas claims, such as *Phillips Petroleum*, it calculated DCF using the duration of the consortium contracts that were terminated.

5.2.1.2 Asset-Based Method

Asset-based approaches using either replacement value or book values of assets are not likely to be very useful in determining damages in expropriation cases. Both methods outline past investments and thus might not represent future cash flows, thus downplaying both the business's true value and its risk.[682] Although Marboe has regarded the replacement method as a market-value approach, he stated: "However, the replacement value is the appropriate means to achieve full reparation only under the condition that the asset in question is replaceable and that no other damage occurred or can be proven."[683]. The Iran-U.S. Claims Tribunal has frequently employed this method on non-going concerns, where it restricts damage to the investor's actual book-value loss.

5.2.1.2.1 Net Book Value (NBV)

An enterprise's 'net book value' is the value of its assets on its books, minus the liabilities on its books.[684]. This method inherently

681.*Id*,P.178

682.M. A. ABDALA, préc., note 620.p.548

683.I. MARBOE, préc., note 225. P.744

684.A. MOURI, préc., note 156. P.486

looks back.[685]According to World Bank Guidelines on the Treatment of Foreign Direct Investment, "Book value means the difference between the enterprise's assets and liabilities as recorded on its financial statements or the amount at which the taken tangible assets appear on the balance sheet of the enterprise, representing their cost after deducting accumulated depreciation in accordance with generally accepted accounting principles."[686]

In its rulings, the tribunal has advocated the notion of current book value, which adds an inflation factor to the books' asset value. In the *Sedco* case,[687] the claimant calculated the 'current net book value' of IMICO's buildings, equipment, and machinery, calling that figure a better estimate than book value of a fixed asset's actual market value. Book value does not factor in inflation's effect on a property's value, and otherwise reflects only historical cost less an arbitrary rate of depreciation. While the tribunal understood the generally greater fairness of current net book value, it could not agree that the claimant's presentation of it here necessarily reflected the fair market value of IMICO's property on December 15, 1979. Despite the claimant's thoroughly documenting and explaining its valuation method, it had not presented any persuasive evidence to support the fairness of its conclusion.

The majority in the *Sedco*award[688] defined 'current net value' (current cost accounting):

"304. Current cost accounting purportedly presents accurately the present value of an asset. It does so by (1) increasing the historical or book cost of an asset through application of an appropriate price index

685.B. SABAHI, préc., note 263., p.565

686.*world Bank Guideline on the Treatment of Foreign Direct Investment*, préc., note 121. Article IV.

687.*SEDCO, Inc v Iran Marine Industrial CO.*, [1989] case no. 128&129, 21 _IUSCTR- 31 (Iran_U.S. Claims Tribunal).*p.57*

688.*Id.*

to arrive at an estimate of 'current cost new' of the asset, and (2) subtracting from the 'current cost new' a 'current depreciation' amount derived by application of the same price index to the book depreciation of the asset."

The valuation of damages on the basis of past costs and expenses comes very close to restitution. This seems to be a 'solid' valuation approach and has been applied in numerous IUSCT cases where other items of damages seemed too speculative or lacking sufficient evidence[689].

In some circumstances, a claimant has requested merely an enterprise's dissolution value, based on a liquidation of the individual assets at their individual fair market value and discharge of any outstanding liabilities. When it has received such a requested, the tribunal has usually complied. This approach is consistent with the standard of full compensation.[690].The first tribunal award to refer to this valuation technique was in *American International Group, Inc.*: "The book value method is used mainly for liquidation purposes." In fact, the liquidation value is the lowest possible value.[691]

However, if the object of valuation will probably not generate income for the owner, an arbiter could still use a hypothetical liquidation price to calculate fair market value. World Bank Guidelines refers to the liquidation value as[692] "the amounts at which individual assets comprising the enterprise or the entire assets of the enterprise could be sold under conditions of liquidation to a willing buyer less any liabilities which the enterprise has to meet."

689.*Phillips Petroleum Company v. the Islamic Republic of Iran and NIOC*, préc., note 157.para. 160 , *Petrolane- Inc. v the Islamic Republic of Iran*, préc., note 238., para. 108

690.C. N. BROWER, préc., note 275.p.666

691.I. MARBOE, préc., note 225.p.743

692.*world Bank Guideline on the Treatment of Foreign Direct Investment*, préc., note 121., Article IV

The tribunal's *Sedco* award[693] considered liquidation as a subsidiary method to fair market value:

"58. The claimant made it clear that it does not seek to recover the 'going-concern' value of its investment in IMICO. Rather, it seeks its share of IMICO's dissolution value, which it proposes to determine by calculating the value of IMICO's fixed assets, accounts receivable, and liquid assets on the date of expropriation and subtracting IMICO's liabilities on that date. The Tribunal agrees that this basic approach is appropriate to determine IMICO's value in the circumstances of this Case, but it must be carried out in a way that fairly assesses IMICO's probable liabilities and fairly reflects the fair market value of IMICO's individual assets."

'Dissolution value' is the enterprise's value, after collection of all assets and discharge of all obligations. Liquidation is not an independent valuation method. Where the assets are sold, techniques such as net book value may calculate an enterprise's liquidation value.[694] It is an alternative to going-concern value and assumes winding-up of the enterprise. In the *James M. Saghi* award.[695] the tribunal observes:

"90. Valuations that merely calculate the net value of assets and liabilities may be appropriate for determining the dissolution or liquidation value of a company, but are an inadequate method of valuing a going concern such as N.P.I.[Company] Such valuations ignore the future prospects of a going concern and therefore fail to indicate the price that a potential buyer would pay for the company. In addition, asset/liability valuations that ignore certain assets or liabilities do not provide a complete picture of a company's value."

693.*SEDCO, Inc v Iran Marine Industrial CO.*, préc., note 687.

694.A. MOURI, préc., note 156. p.443

695.*Saghi v. the Islamic Republic of Iran*, préc., note 420. Para.90

5.3 Valuation Date

With regard to the valuation date, the tribunals address two issues, namely; i) the date of the expropriation of the claimants' investment by the respondent and, ii) whether the claimants were entitled to choose between a valuation based on the date of expropriation and a valuation based on the date of the award[696]. The date of valuation is important for a variety of reasons; First and foremost, the value of a property or a right respond to changes occurring at the time of valuation. It also affects the date for converting compensation into a foreign currency and the date when interest on the principal amount of compensation is to begin.[697]

UPICC did not provide any indication for the period between the time of non-performance and the date of judgment as the factor that could make change in the sustained harm by the aggrieved party. But, commentators submit that the application of full compensation, entitles a tribunal to assess the damage payable at the date of judgment rather than the date of breach[698]. It seems that this issue lies in the discretion of the tribunal and it should be influenced by the full compensation principle.

Generally, the Iran-U.S. Claims Tribunal deals with three milestones: the date of breach or expropriation, the date of the case's arrival before the tribunal, and the date of the award. The time of expropriation can be very uncertain. The principle of full compensation usually means assessing damages as late as possible to cover all possible

---

696.Irmgard MARBOE, « Yukos Universal Limited (Isle of Man) v The Russian Federation, Calculation of Damages in the Yukos Award: Highlighting the Valuation Date, Contributory Fault and Interest », (2015) 30-2 *ICSID Rev.* 326–335.p.327

697.S. RIPINSKY, préc., note 56.p.243, also, M. A. ABDALA, préc., note 620. p.560

698.E. MCKENDRICK, préc., note 342 à la page 876.

consequences.[699] The valuation date is usually the date of the expropriatory act or related measures (sweeping nationalizations of banks and industry, and so on), or the following day. But de facto expropriation of property or property rights may leave that date uncertain. To establish a date in all such latter circumstances, the tribunal sought for each case a concrete, complete, and definite act of taking or deprivation.

In many of these problematic cases, earlier state measures gave hints of seizure to come and amounted to de facto expropriation. Some authors have criticized the tribunal's valuation dates, especially for creeping expropriations. While the tribunal says that the dates of expropriation and of valuation are the same, Sloane writes, "The crucial point is not that the proposition expressed by the Iran-U.S. Claims Tribunal is necessarily 'wrong'. It may well provide the appropriate standard for discerning the proper moment of expropriation in many cases of indirect expropriations. If application of its standard in practice reduces the amount of compensation due to victims of creeping or consequential expropriations, then, we suggest, the 'moment of expropriation' should be distinguished from the 'moment of valuation' for these purposes."[700]

The tribunal has usually differentiated the date of announcement of nationalization and the date of de facto taking, recognizing the latter as the valuation date and date of expropriation. In the *Amoco* case,[701] it found the expropriation of Amoco's contract rights to be 'complete' on December 24, 1980, when the Iranian minister of petroleum formally notified Amoco's management that it viewed as null and void a 1967 joint venture between Amoco and the Iranian National Petrochemical Company. But the tribunal none the less awarded Amoco

---

699.J. Y. GOTANDA, préc., note 248, p.998

700.W. M. REISMAN et R. D. SLOANE, préc., note 267. P.148

701.*Amoco International Finance Corp. v the Islamic Republic of Iran*, préc., note 161.para.341

compensation based on the value of its interest as of July 31,1979, its date for the de facto taking. According to its award, "181.The Tribunal decides that this fact will be duly taken into account by determining that the date to be considered for the valuation of such compensation will be the date at which measures definitively took effect, rather than the date of the final decision of nationalization."

In the *Thomas Earl Payne* award,[702] the tribunal determined the date the company lost control as the date of expropriation: "24. The Tribunal finds that the Respondent effectively took control of both Irantronics and Berkeh in July/August 1980 by the appointment of the temporary manager pursuant to the Law of 16 June 1979. No dividends were paid nor was any form of communication in respect of those companies sent to the original owners."

In the *International Technical Prods. Corp.* award,[703] the tribunal insisted that the valuation date is not the date of the first action in the series of measures leading to expropriation, but the time when government interference turns into an irreversible deprivation of rights:

"Where the alleged expropriation is carried out by way of a series of interferences in the enjoyment of the property, the breach forming the cause of action is deemed to take place on the day when the interference has ripened into more or less irreversible deprivation of the property. The point at which interference ripens into a taking depends on the circumstances of the case and does not require that legal title has been transferred."

In the *Malek* award,[704] the tribunal repeatedly recognized the irreversible loss of the property as the valuation date:

702.*Payne, Thomas Earl v. the Islamic Republic of Iran*, préc., note 465.

703.*International Technical Products Corp v. the Islamic Republic of Iran*, [1985] case no.302, 9 _IUSCTR_ 206 (Iran_U.S. Claims Tribunal).p.240-41

704.*Malek v. the Islamic Republic of Iran*, [1992] case no.193, 28 _IUSCTR_ 246 (Iran_U.S. Claims Tribunal).p.288

"114. Where the alleged expropriation is carried out by way of a series of interferences in the enjoyment of the property, the breach forming the cause of action is deemed to take place on the day when the interference has ripened into a more or less irreversible deprivation of the property rather than on the beginning date of the events."

Some remarkable tribunal awards accepted the nationalization date (de jure expropriation) as the valuation date. In the *American International Group, Inc.* award,[705] it held: "The relevant date for valuation is that of the nationalization, 25 June 1979."

In contractual disputes that arose from non-performance of obligations, the tribunal took the due date of the obligation as the valuation date. However, for non-payment of the invoices, it used the 30-day lead time as the trade usage for the debtor and placed the valuation date after that. In breaches of contracts, the actual time of taking is crucial, since it is the date from which damages will flow. It is in the claimant's interest to make it as early as possible, and for the respondent's (Iran) as late as possible. Interest on debts was awarded from the date the debt was due and payable' the date of breach. In the absence of specification, the tribunal frequently held that it would presume an invoice was payable 30 days after presentation.

5.4 Summary

The rulings of the Iran-U.S. Claims Tribunal have displayed strong support for the traditional view that international law requires payment of full compensation. Its awards for going concerns have generally involved determination of fair market value, including likely future profits. The type of assessment it chooses depends on the asset's nature and its market. The assessment of damages is in all cases at the discretion of the judge, who cannot refuse to evaluate on the ground of

705.*American International Group Inc. v the Islamic Republic of Iran*, préc., note 276.p.110

the difficulties the process involves: he must allocate damages even if it is not easy to do so.

A variety of valuation methods have been used. Notably, in the most cases the amount awarded have been substantially below the amounts claimed. The Tribunal usually invoking the arriving to such low assessment by a process of 'approximation' or 'taking into account all relevant circumstances in the case. Approximate valuation is applied by the Tribunal in a variety of case ranging from valuation of a going concern to valuation of physical items. Notably, article 7.4.3 of the UNIDROIT Principles submits to sue the court discretion in the cases that the damage determination is not exact. Article states: "Where the amount of damages cannot be established with a sufficient degree of certainty, the assessment is at the discretion of the court."

The tribunal in assessment of the value of the companies as the income-producer entities takes to methods of going concern and discounted cash flaw method. If the given business is not eligible to recognize as income producer, then the tribunal awarded the value based on net book value assessment. While DCF is suitable for an entity, which has an earning history and has attained the status of a going concern, NBV can be used for valuation of recent investments that have not had the time to earn goodwill and reach profitability. In the practice of the tribunal, going concern means an enterprise consisting of income-producing assets which has been in operation for a sufficient period of time to generate the data required for the calculation of future income and which could have been expected with reasonable certainty. In *plelps Dodge, Sola Tiles* and *CBS* cases, future profits were excluded together on the reason that the business had not reached the point of a going concern. However, the assessment of the market value including the future prospects cannot be easily undertaken where the market is affected by revolutionary upheavals. This method as a backward-looking method, is invoking on the historical records of earning of the company. the Tribunal repeatedly exposed that the principle saying that the going concern value of a business enterprise must be valued as of the date of the taking without consideration being given to post-taking events, does not apply to the post-taking impact of a revolution that took place prior to the taking. The generally accepted way for the tribunal to determine the value of a business that has been destroyed by the respondent's breach of contract which would include lost profits, or expropriated is the discounted cash flow (DCF) method. In this method business worth does not depend on its historical cost and profit, but is equivalent to its ability to create future financial benefits for its owner. Regarding future profits, the awards make it clear that while lost future profits are properly recoverable, the concept of future profits as being an element of the value of a business receives its fullest consideration only in the claims concerning the expropriation of oil interests where the income is derived from a right to extract oil pursuant to a long-term contract. The practice of the tribunal respecting application of DCF method renders following critical points that should be noted.

1- The Damnum emergens/Lucrum cessans combination, which was a traditional remedy for breach of contract, needs to be seen as arising at a time when valuation was back ward\historic and based on the accounting value of individual items of property. It is essentially an issue of double recovery, where the investor obtains first, without risk, its original investment expenditures, and then receives also the returns he might have obtained with the very high-risk, long-term contract.

2- based on the interpretation of the ICJ jurisprudence, the Iran-U.S. Claims Tribunal advocated that in in the lawful expropriation (such as the tribunal cases) it is not allowed to award the Lost profit, but insisted to take the lost revenue of the expropriated company into account in case of such lawful expropriation. This principle emerges particularly from the Amoco International Finance Corp. Case where it was understood that the Chorzow Factory Case did not permit the inclusion of lucrum cessans or future profits in the value of the undertaking which can be claimed. The core of the problem in the compensations based on the method known as 'discounted cash flow' is also the fact that lost profits have to be taken into account as the main and essential element in the computation. To come up the given contradiction, the tribunal in Amoco award advocated that the future respects differs from future profits (lucrum cessans). In the practice of the tribunal the future profitability and goodwill which are different from loss of profits may well be elements to be considered in the assessment of such value. In other words, according to the Tribunal, "future prospects" does not equal lost profit (lucrum cessans) and is regarded as part of value of the assets.

The date of valuation is important for variety of reasons; First and foremost, the value of a property or a right is a variable of those changes obtaining at that point of time for which the valuation is to be made. the valuation date also has a certain impact on couple of other issues, namely, the conversion date in the cases that needs to convert the damage currency, also for determination of starting date in calculation of interest. Generally, the tribunal deal with three points as to be determined as the date of valuation in expropriation and contractual claims. In direct expropriation that set out by the official decrees, the valuation date is usually the date of the expropriatory act or related measures. In indirect expropriation, the point at which interference ripens into a taking depends on the circumstances of the case and does not require that legal title has been transferred. In contractual disputes that arose from non-performance of obligations, the tribunal took the due date of the obligation as the valuation date. However, for non-payment of the invoices, it used the 30-day lead time as the trade usage for the debtor and placed the valuation date after that.

Chapter Six

Interest

6.1 General

Interest is a standard form of compensation for the loss of the use of money, so that the borrower awards it without the lender having to prove actual loss. Tribunals presume that the delayed payment of money deprives the injured party of the ability to invest the owned. Two principles about this are part of international law. First, when a respondent engages in a wrongful act, it is liable for all damages that naturally result. Second, the respondent is liable for the loss of the use of money and must compensate by paying interest.[706] One can define interest as a sum paid or payable as compensation for the temporary withholding of money.[707]

Gotanda cites three reasons why the respondent must pay interest to the claimant.[708] First, and most important, the respondent must fully compensate the claimant by restoring it to the position it would have enjoyed if the wrongful act had not occurred. It is right and just to compensate not only for the original injury or loss but also for the passage of time between the date of injury and the date of full reinstatement. Compensation for assets' lost time value has been a regular component of damages since the early days of international law. Lost profits are typically awarded on damaged, expropriated, or

---

706.John Y. GOTANDA et Thierry J. SÉNÉCHAL, « Interest as Damages », (2009) 47-3 *Columbia J. Transnatl. Law* 492-536., p.497

707.*McCollough& Company, Inc. v. Ministry of Post, Telegram and Telephone*, préc., note 446.,para. 29

708.J. Y. GOTANDA et T. J. SÉNÉCHAL, préc., note 700. P.495

destroyed capital assets for the period between the dispossession of the property and the award. Second, awarding interest prevents unjust enrichment of the respondent. Recent decades have seen changes in the awarding of interest in international law. Matters such as the rate of interest and the compounding of interest have roiled international tribunals and scholars. Third, the payment of interest promotes efficiency; it deters respondents from further damage or from delaying resolution of the dispute. Also, a party suffers further damages when its money is withheld, even with no proof of actual damages, because it could have invested the money.[709]

Despite interest's leading role, there is no uniform and rational method for awarding compensatory interest in international arbitration cases.[710]A clear methodology in respect of determining interest is lacking, and past tribunals have not made any distinction between the lawful/unlawful nature of the damaging act, therefore, no clear link is traceable between the nature of the breach and the chosen reference rate[711].

Most jurisdictions consider interest a substantive issue, while some treat it as a procedural matter. In Germany, Switzerland and France interest is considered another part of the substantive claim for damages and, as such, is governed by the law governing the contract[712]. English law regards the liability to pay interest a substantive issue governed by the law of the contract whilst the rate, the period of which it is awarded and the overall amount are considered to be procedural and

709.David J. Branson and Richard E. WALLACE, « Awarding Interest in International Commercial Arbitration: Establishing a Uniform Approach », (1998) 28 *Virjinia J. Int. Law*.919-947, p.923

710.*Id.*

711.Inna UCHKUNOVA et Oleg TEMNIKOV, « A Procrustean Bed: Pre- and Post-award Interest in ICSID Arbitration », (2014) 29-3 *ICSID Rev.* 648–668.p.651

712.P. ASHFORD, préc., note 226, p. 353.

hence governed by the law of the seat. Branson and Wallace assert that "common-law practitioners are likely to view issues of statutes of limitations and legal interest rates as procedural rather than substantive matters and look to the law of the forum. Similarly, there is no agreement as to whether interest laws should be considered procedural or substantive."[713]

According to Westberg, "In international tribunals, generally, the issues pertaining to interest are usually viewed as being procedural in nature and therefore governed by the law of the forum state or the rules of a particular arbitral regime.[714] The UNCITRAL and ICC arbitration rules do not contain any explicit provisions on awarding interest. Their presumption is that the tribunal will determine the applicable law, then answer interest questions from applicable law.[715] In contrast, some arbitration rules contain provisions allowing the arbitrator to award interest, even compound interest. For instance, notable authorities are the World Intellectual Property Organization, WIPO, Arbitration Rules (2014), the London Court of International, LCIA, Arbitration Rules (2014), and the International Arbitration Rules (2009) of the American Arbitration Association's International Arbitration Rules.[716]

713.D. J. BRANSON et R. E. WALLACE, préc., note 709,P.931

714.J. A. WESTBERG, préc., note 135. p.253

715.*ICC Arbitration Rules*, préc., note 210.and *UNCITRAL model law on international commercial Arbitration*, préc., note 210.

716. Arbitration Rules of WIPO, art.62: "(b) The Tribunal may award simple or compound interest to be paid by a party on any sum awarded against that party. It shall be free to determine the interest at such rates as it considers to be appropriate, without being bound by legal rates of interest, and shall be free to determine the period for which the interest shall be paid." available at http://www.wipo.int/amc/en/arbitration/rules/#awa2. And LCIA Rules 2014 art.26.4 states: "Unless the parties have agreed otherwise, the Arbitral Tribunal may order that simple or compound interest shall be paid by any party on any sum awarded at such rates as the Arbitral Tribunal decides to be appropriate

Interest claims often amount to millions of dollars because of lengthy periods a dispute's origins and the final award. Sometimes, an interest award may as large as the principal claim itself.[717] For instance, the Iran-U.S. Claims Tribunal, in the *American Bell International Inc.* case, awarded approximately U.S.$28 million in interest on damages and about U.S.$50 million as simple interest. As time passed, some interest awards bled the principal amount awarded.[718] There is no uniform practice on interest nor on such subsidiary matters as determining interest rates and the period over which interest is due.[719] This inconsistency raises at least two issues for international arbitration. First, is interest a matter of substantive or procedural law? Sometimes when tribunals face substantive law provisions that restrict or prevent payment of interest, they accept an argument that interest is a procedural matter for the tribunal, because of general principles of international commercial arbitration. Second, many nations limit the ability to recover interest, particular Muslim countries that base their civil law on sharia law. Even where the tribunal has complete discretion, there are questions

---

(without being bound by rates of interest practiced by any state court or other legal authority) in respect of any period which the Arbitral Tribunal decides to be appropriate ending not later than the date upon which the award is complied with." Available at http://www.lcia.org/dispute_Resolution_Services/lcia-arbitration-rules-2014.aspx#Article%2026 and the AAA International Arbitration Rules article .31.4 states: "the tribunal may award such pre-award and post-award interest, simple or compound, as it considers appropriate, taking into consideration the contract and applicable law." Available at:
https://www.adr.org/aaa/ShowProperty?nodeId=/UCM/ADRSTAGE2020868&revision=latestreleased

717.J. Y. GOTANDA, préc., note 502.,p.11

718.J. A. WESTBERG, préc., note 135.p.254

719.Andrea GIARDINA, « issues of applicable law and uniform law on interest: basic distinctions in national and international practice », dans Filip DE LY et Laurent LEVY (dir.), *Interest, Auxiliary and Alternative Remedies in International Arbitration*, ICC Publication Department, 2008.131-168, p.133

of the period and rate of interest, and whether it should be simple or compounded. Should the recovering party recover interest from the time of the loss, of the claim, or some other date? Should the period of interest continue to the date of the award, on the basis that one party has had the money when the other should have had it? What should be the rate of interest? Should interest be simple, or compound, to reflect commercial borrowing?[720] This chapter attempts to see how the Iran-U.S. Claims Tribunal has answered these questions.

6.2 Right to Interest under Transnational Instruments

Some arbitral tribunals determine the applicable rate of interest without referring to any national law. Is there a rule in lex mercatoria relating to the fixing of the interest rate?[721] Article 78 of the CISG Convention guides the awarding of interest under the convention, but it is brief and fails to answer crucial questions, so is up to the tribunal to decide in each case.[722]Article 78 of CISG provides: "If either party fails to pay the price or any other sum that is in arrears, the other party is entitled to interest on it, without prejudice to any claim for damages recoverable under Article 74." This provision sets forth the obligation to pay interest and the period it is to cover. It does not explain the date from which interest is to accrue or the rate of interest. Perhaps the most litigated provision of the CISG is Article 78, which concerns the payment of interest[723]. Most authors assume this is the bailiwick of the applicable domestic law or the general of the CISG.[724] A great deal of litigation swirls around this article because, despite its insistence on

720.V. RAMSEY, préc., note 371.p.1233, I. UCHKUNOVA et O. TEMNIKOV, préc., note 711.p.648

721.E. S. DARANKOUM, préc., note 9.p.451

722.L. SONG, préc., note 538.p.730

723.J. Y. GOTANDA, préc., note 249.p.108

724.J. Y. GOTANDA, préc., note 502. p.42

paying interest for arrears, it does not specify how to calculate it.[725]Some commentators see the issue of interest as lying outside the scope of article 78 and therefore subject to the domestic substantive law that the contract or, failing that, the tribunal specifies.[726]Although, article 78 requires paying interest whenever a payment is in arrears, it does not specify how to calculate interest owed. In contrast, the UPICC contain a very detailed provision on interest. It presents the duty to pay interest as a distinct obligation –both the interest in monetary obligation and the interest on damages for non-performance of non-monetary obligations. UPICC article 7.4.9 provides that interest is payable from the time when payment is due.Article 7.4.9 states:

"1) If a party does not pay a sum of money when it falls due the aggrieved party is entitled to interest upon that sum from the time when payment is due to the time of payment whether or not the non-payment is excused."

The first element in right to damage is that the other party must have failed to pay a sum of money when it falls due. The right to interest only applies to a failure to pay a sum of money[727].

Clearly, in cases of non-performance of non-monetary obligations, at the time of non-performance there will usually not have been a monetary assessment of the amount of damages. The assessment will take place after the harm's occurrence, either by agreement between the parties or by the court. The right to recover interest in respect of a failure to perform a non-monetory obligation is regulated by article 7.4.10 UPICC that states: "Unless otherwise agreed, interest on damages for non-performance of non-monetary obligations accrues as from the time of non-performance." With respect to the applicable interest rate, UPICC set forth a hierarchy for determining the appropriate rate,

725.J. Y. GOTANDA, préc., note 104. p.117

726.D. J. B. and R. E. WALLACE, préc., note 709., p.931

727.E. MCKENDRICK, préc., note 342 à la page 908.

starting with "the average short-term lending rate to prime borrowers prevailing for the currency of payment at the place of payment." If no such rate exists, the Principles provide that interest accrues at the average prime rate in the State of the currency of payment, and, in the absence of such a rate, the rate of interest is to be fixed by the law of the State of the currency of payment. UPICC article 7.4.9 states:

"2) The rate of interest shall be the average bank short-term lending rate to prime borrowers prevailing for the currency of payment at the place for payment, or where no such rate exists at that place, then the same rate in the State of the currency of payment. In the absence of such a rate at either place the rate of interest shall be the appropriate rate fixed by the law of the State of the currency of payment."

Although, some tribunals have applied UPICC article 7.4.9 to resolve questions left open by CISG article 78, particularly to fix the rate at which interest accrues, but professor Gotanda submits that this use has been controversial and improper. He pointed out: "there exist differing views on how the rate of interest should be fixed under the CISG and most courts have applied national law to determine the applicable interest rate. Thus, the approach advocated by the UNIDROIT Principles cannot be said to be a universal trade usage[728]." Also, he emphasises on the differentiation between UPICC and CISG approaches in determining of interest rate. He submits article 74 awards the aggrieved party actual damages, including any loss from borrowing money to continue operations upon the debtor's default, therefore the proper interest rate in these cases is borrowing rate[729], while UPICC does not differs between the case that aggrieved party financed from third party and paid higher interest rate, and just awards the aggrieved party the right to interest on lending rate that seemingly is less.

728.J. Y. GOTANDA, préc., note 249 à la page 25.

729.*Id.* à la page 18.

Although UPICC advocated the rate to calculate interest but it seems that the rule that provided in article 7.4.9 is dedicated to non-performance of monetary obligation and in the case of non-performance of non-monetary obligation, article 7.4.10 is silent on the issue of the rate at which interest is payable. Professor McKendrick in his comments on the UPICC points out in the absence of any provision in the UPICC it is presumably necessary to resort to the applicable law for the purpose of identifying the rate of the interest[730].

Public international law accepts the obligation to pay interest. Article 38 of the ILC Draft Articles provides for duty to pay interest:[731]

"1. Interest on any principal sum due under this chapter shall be payable when necessary in order to ensure full reparation. The interest rate and mode of calculation shall be set so as to achieve that result. 2. Interest runs from the date when the principal sum should have been paid until the date the obligation to pay is fulfilled."

In next paragraph, the practice of the Iran_U.S. Claims Tribunal respecting the authority to award interest and the methods of calculating the interest will be examined.

6.3 Interest in the Practice of the Iran-U.S. Claims Tribunal

The Iran-U.S. Claims Tribunal, in the *McCollough & Co, Inc.* case,[732] defines interest as a sum paid or payable for the temporary withholding of money. The tribunal has encountered complicated situations because of the inconsistency in international arbitration about

---

730.E. MCKENDRICK, préc., note 342 à la page 913.

731.International Law Commission, *Draft Articles on Responsibility of States for Internationally Wrongful Acts*, préc., note 118.

732.*McCollough& Company, Inc. v. Ministry of Post, Telegram and Telephone*, préc., note 446., para.29

rules relating to interest. The tribunal reflected such inconsistency in its award in the *McCollough* case:[733]

"97. It is difficult to draw any distinct conclusions from so diverse a practice. The Tribunal can conclude, however, that no uniform rule of law relating to interest has emerged from the practice in transnational arbitration. No comparable rule has taken form governing the rate of interest or the time from which interest is to be computed. This is illustrated by the frequent use of the word 'fair' to qualify the rate chosen, or by the equally frequent references to the discretion of the arbitrator."

The tribunal, from the outset of its work, recognized that it should award interest as a general rule, because the claims had all arisen earlier and full compensation would require interest. Moreover, interest would also have to run until the date of the award, as otherwise those whose claims were not decided first would suffer unfairly. Because the tribunal faced thousands of claims, it could not defend any system of priority as reasonable without such a provision. The Iranian members, not surprisingly, resisted this conclusion, but to no avail, and asked the full tribunal to rule on whether the Claims Settlement Declaration (Algiers Accords) empowered the tribunal to grant interest on its awards. In the inter-state *A-19* case,[734] the full tribunal, after reviewing the contentions about the validity of interest awards, and consequently, the Tribunal concludes that it is clearly within its power to award interest as compensation for damage suffered. The tribunal held:

"12. The Tribunal notes that the Chambers have been consistent in awarding interest as 'compensation for damages suffered due to delay in payment'. Chamber Three observed that interest is awarded as an element of compensation in most legal systems. Indeed, it

---

733.*Id.*para.97

734.*Iran v. United States, Case A19*, [1987] 16 _IUSCTR_ 185 (Iran_U. S. Claims Tribunal).p.290

is customary for arbitral tribunals to award interest as part of an award for damages, notwithstanding the absence of any express reference to interest in the compromise. Given that the power to award interest is inherent in the Tribunal's authority to decide claims, the exclusion of such power could only be established by an express provision in the Claims Settlement Declaration. No such provision exists."

Dismissal of Claims for Interest, a review of the tribunal's jurisprudence shows that the judges have, in some rare examples, denied interest. They have done so where interest would result in a manifest injustice, otherwise be unconscionable, or violate public policy. It would do that also if the debtor presented sufficient proof of bad faith, duress, fraud, or other unreasonable conduct on the part of the claimant.

The tribunal has rejected usurious rates as a contractual condition, as it has irregular rates, such as the one in *Sylvania*[735]: "The rates stipulated in a contract and thus agreed to by the parties are usually accepted by the Tribunal, although it has been stated that unreasonable or usurious rates will not be enforced." How have the judges defined such rates? The *Anaconda-Iran*[736] award is revealing: "The Tribunal further finds no support in either commercial trade usages or otherwise for the conclusion that interest rates higher than 12 percent would amount to usury.

The judges did not have a problem in the *Reading & Bates Drilling Company* award[737] with 18 per cent per annum, as the contract stipulated: "24. The Tribunal has in the past awarded contractually stipulated interest rate. The Tribunal, therefore, awards simple interest at the rate of one and one half (1½) percent per month (18 percent per annum) on the amount of U.S. $53,755." In the *Benjamin R. Isaiah v.*

735.*Sylvania Technical Systems, Inc. v. the Islamic Republic of Iran*, préc., note 556

736.*Anaconda-Iran, Inc. v. the Islamic Republic of Iran*, préc., note 152.p.236

737.*Reading & Bates Drilling Company v the Islamic Republic of Iran*, [1988] case no.10633, 18 _IUSCTR_ 164 (Iran.U.S. Claims Tribunal).p.174

Bank Mellat case,[738] the tribunal denied interest on an award of the amount of a cheque that had bounced. It noted that the bank had tried unsuccessfully to restore its credit facilities with the New York bank so that the cheque could go through:

"The award of interest is certainly permissible in the discretion of the Tribunal. In this case, there is no evidence that the International Bank of Iran or its successor, Bank Mellat, deliberately deprived the Claimant of his money; on the contrary, the evidence indicates that the Bank made unsuccessful efforts to restore its credit facilities with Chase Manhattan Bank so that the check could be paid. In view of the special circumstances in this case, the Tribunal declines to award interest."

In the *Harris International Telecommunication,Inc.* case,[739] the judges argued that the down-payment was sufficient to cover all unpaid invoices:

"161. The Claimant requests 11.89% interest on the amounts owed for services, termination costs and damages and losses. However, the Respondent's down payment was sufficient to cover all of the outstanding unpaid invoices. Consequently, the Tribunal dismisses the claim for interest."

Some experts call for treating interest as a matter of loss of profit; since awards of lost profits correspond to the claimant's actual loss, awards of interest should do the same. Some commentators distinguish between 'interest on damages' and 'interest as damages,' the latter typically referring to the award of interest because the claimant incurred actual costs, usually by borrowing to mitigate damages from the respondent's breach of contract or other wrongful act, although the

---

738.*Isaiah Benjamin v. Bank Mellat*, préc., note 173.

739.*Harris International Telecommunication, Inc. v. the Islamic Republic of Iran*, [1987] case no.409, 17 _IUSCTR_ 31 (Iran_U.S. Claims Tribunal). p.79 para.161

need to borrow could be hypothetical.[740]

Gotanda has suggested that interest is a kind of damage and hence in effect a component of the damage award, not a separate imposition on the award of damages. He argues that this would help end the debates about inconsistent interest rates.[741] This idea derives from the standard of full compensation and treats the interest as a kind of lost profit, i.e., the loss of the use of the money. In another submission, Gotanda suggests that arbiters have awarded interest as damages under the CISG Convention when the breach caused the aggrieved party to borrow money from a financial institution that charges interest.[742]

This approach finds some support in the practice of the Iran-U.S. Claims Tribunal. The tribunal has awarded, as a reasonably incurred expense, interest claimants paid on loans they would not have needed if the respondents had paid the claimants the money owed in a timely manner. The tribunal awarded the interest rate that the claimant paid to its bank. But the judges regarded this grant as the award of incidental damages, and its interest rate did not reflect the claimant's loss.

In the *Uiterwyk* case,[743] the claimant asserted that the respondent's failure to pay the debt in a timely manner forced him to borrow the funds from the bank to finance the rest of the contractual project. The tribunal recognized the claimant's eligibility for an award for the interest on the loan as consequential damage to the claimant:

"117. the Tribunal is persuaded that Uiterwyk did receive the

---

740.Aaron Xavier FELLMETH, « Blow-Market Interest in International Claims Against States », (2010) 13-2 *J. Int. Econ. Law* 423-457.p.423

741.J. Y. GOTANDA et T. J. SÉNÉCHAL, préc., note 700.,p.516

742.John Y. GOTANDA, « The Unpredictability Paradox: Punitive Damages and Interest in International Arbitration », (2009) 10 *J. World Invest. Trade.*, 553-571, p.553

743.*Uiterwyk Corp. v the Islamic Republic of Iran*, [1988] case no.381, 19 _IUSCTR_ 106 (Iran_U.S. Claims Tribunal). p.140

loan proceeds, did expend the proceeds on IEL's behalf, and is entitled to compensation. The Claimants have introduced a variety of evidence supporting their contention that the loan proceeds were received and used to pay IEL's expenses. Had IEL forwarded the funds to cover these expenses, no loan would have been necessary. Under the circumstances, the interest charged to the Claimants was a reasonably incurred expense for which they are entitled to reimbursement."

Although, the Tribunal concludes that the Claimants are entitled to recover the amount of interest charged to them in connection with this loan, but, the tribunal declined to accept the interest rate the claimants paid:

"171. The Claimants seek to recover interest on amounts due to it at the rate of 14 percent. This rate, according to the Claimants, reflects Uiterwyk's actual cost of borrowing. The Tribunal, however, for the reasons stated in Sylvania Technical Systems, Inc. Award, awards interest at the average rate of interest paid on six-month certificates of deposit in the United States."

6.3.1 Interest in the case of excused non-payment

Article 74 of the CISG states that the right to interest for excused non-payments will not prejudice any claim for damages recoverable under this article. It appears that the entitlement to interest is not limited by grounds for release of obligations as provided for by article 79 CISG as the excuses. The only condition for claiming interest is non-payment of the price or any other sum that is in arrears, even if the non-payment is due to force majeure or, in the language of CISG, to impediment.[744] Similarly, UPICC article 7.4.9 states:

"(1) If a party does not pay a sum of money when it falls due the aggrieved party is entitled to interest upon that sum from the time

744.L. SONG, préc., note 538.p.721

when payment is due to the time of payment whether or not the non-payment is excused."

Some IUSCT claims arose because of Iran's exchange-control policy set out after revolution, which prevented transfer of Americans' funds from Iranian banks. Therefore, the tribunal ruled that, if the non-performing party may not obtain the sum because of new exchange controls, interest will still be due not as damages but as compensation for the debtor's enrichment as a result of its non-payment, as it continues to receive interest on the sum that it may not pay.

In the *Stanwick Corp. Intl., Inc.* case,[745] the claimant asked for its funds, which it had deposited in two Iranian banks, Bank Tejarat and Bank Mellat. The respondent argued that the Central Bank of Iran did not approve such a transfer because of exchange-control policies. The tribunal, regardless of the respondent's defences, awarded the amount owed to the claimant, plus interest for the period the bank withheld the money --i.e., a date in 1980 to the date of the award in 1990:

"The depository banks' failure to seek approval is deemed to result in damages equivalent to the amount Stanwick would have received had Bank Markazi approved the exchange. The Tribunal therefore sets 18 May 1980 and 7 June 1980 as the dates on which Bank Mellat and Bank Tejarat, respectively, should have carried out the exchange and transfer of funds. The official exchange rate in effect on those dates was 70.36. Therefore, Bank Mellat is obligated to pay $609,077.58 and Bank Tejarat is obligated to pay $261,310.55 to Stanwick International, Inc. as the holder of the bank deposits."

6.4 Moratory (Delay) v. Compensatory Interest

In principle, between the occurrence of the damage and the actual compensation, there is a time with which the arbitrators do not

745.*The Stanwick Corporation v. the Islamic Republic of Iran,* [1990] case no.66, 24 _IUSCTR_ 102 (Iran_U.S. Claims Tribunal).p.113

concern themselves. This is the period of enforcement of award. Compensatory or pre-award interest is interest as part of an award that compensates a party for loss of the use of money --interest relating to monetary debt. It aims to restore the injured party to the proprietary situation it would have had if the damage relief had occurred immediately.

Moratory (from Latin *moratorius*, causing delay), post-award, or defaultinterest compensates for the loss of the use of the money. However, unlike compensatory interest, it ordinarily accrues from the date of the judgment or award until the damages owed are paid in full. It has two subsidiary purposes: to discourage frivolous appeals and to create an incentive for losing parties to pay the damage promptly.

International tribunals generally do not distinguish between compensatory and moratory interest; they simply award interest from a designated date until payment in full.[746] Typically, they have four ways of granting moratory interest. The first, awards interest at one rate running from an exact date until the date payment is complete. The second awards moratory interest starting with the date of the award. The third, awards compensatory interest and may later add moratory interest, if the debtor falls behind in payments. The fourth grants compensatory and moratory interest, but at different rates.[747]

There is no consistent rule of international law that prescribes the standards for pre- and post-award interest beyond 'full compensation.'[748] Unlike pre-award interest, the claimant need not apply for post-award interest; the tribunal decides it *ex officio*.[749] As one chamber of the Iran-U.S. Claims Tribunal observed, international tribunals have been markedly inconsistent on pre- and post-award interest and in fixing the starting date for interest. In the *McCollough*

746.J. Y. GOTANDA, préc., note 502. P.56

747.*Id.*p.86

748.A. X. FELLMETH, préc., note 740.p.433

749.L. SONG, préc., note 538. P.730

award,[750] The same diversity appears in relation to the date from which interest is calculated, the tribunal summed up the situation:

"95. In some cases, the starting point is fixed at the time when the awarded amounts were due, or, at least, in direct relation with the time when the damage occurred. In yet other cases, the date of the award or of its notification, or a specific date after the award, is determinative. A few awards make reference to the law recognized as applicable to the contract which is the subject matter of the case. Other cases do not refer to any particular system of law or expressly cite the discretion of the arbitrator."

The tribunal awards compensatory and moratory interest at the same rate, starting from the breach or expropriation or other appropriate date and ending with the award. All three chambers use this approach in all cases. In one contract-breaching claim, the *Edgar Protiva* case,[751] the tribunal awarded 8 per cent interest from the date of breach up to and including the date on which the escrow agent instructs the depository bank to effect payment out of the Security Account. In one expropriation claim, the *Faith Lita Khosrowshahi* case,[752] the tribunal granted 8.6 per cent interest from the dates of "the deprivation of their interests. up to and including the date on which the Escrow Agent instructs the Depository Bank to effect payment out of the Security Account."

6.5 Accrual Period in Tribunal Jurisprudence

There has been no consensus among international tribunals as to the time to begin calculating interest. Some have awarded

---

750.*McCollough& Company, Inc. v. Ministry of Post, Telegram and Telephone*, préc., note 446.para.95

751.*Edgar Protiva v the Islamic Republic of Iran*, [1995] case no.316, 31 _IUSCTR_ 89 (Iran_U.S. Claims Tribunal).P.122

752.*Khosrowshahi, Faith Lita v. the Islamic Republic of Iran*, préc., note 462.

compensatory interest from, variously, the date of breach, the date when the respondent receives notification of default, and the date of filing an arbitration request.[753] The transnational instruments offer some instructions on this matter. Article 78 of the CISG Convention insists on interest from the time when payment is due to the time of payment. Article 7.4.10 of the UNIDROIT Principles states: "Unless otherwise agreed, interest on damages for non-performance of non-monetary obligations accrues as from the time of non-performance." Article 38(2) of the ILC Draft Articles says: "2. Interest runs from the date when the principal sum should have been paid until the date the obligation to pay is fulfilled."[754]

In cases over international contracts, the date for calculating interest depends on when the contractual obligation was due. In the *McCollough* award, the judges emphasize the inconsistency of international practice in this matter:

"98. The first principle is that under normal circumstances, and especially in commercial cases, interest is allocated on the amounts awarded as damages in order to compensate for the delay with which the payment to the successful party is made. This delay, however, varies in relation to the date determined to be the time when the obligation to pay arose. This date can be the date when the underlying damage occurred, the date when the debt was liquidated, the date of a formal notice to pay, the date of the beginning of the arbitral or judicial proceedings, the date of the award or of the judgment determining the amount due, or the date when the judicial or arbitral decision reasonably should have been executed.[755]"

753.J. Y. GOTANDA, préc., note 502.p.53

754.International Law Commission, *Draft Articles on Responsibility of States for Internationally Wrongful Acts*, préc., note 118.

755.*McCollough& Company, Inc. v. Ministry of Post, Telegram and Telephone*, préc., note 446.para.98

Generally, the Iran-U.S. Claims Tribunal has fixed the starting date for damages as from the expropriation date. In addition, in all expropriation cases, it awarded interest from the date it found to be the date of taking or deprivation of the property. In the *Phillips Petroleum* case,[756] the Tribunal held:

"92. The first concrete actions [of expropriation] concerning the Claimant's JSA rights were taken with respect to the oil itself following resumption of production in March 1979. 102. Consequently, the Tribunal finds that the Claimant's JSA rights were taken by 29 September 1979, and that the Respondents are liable to compensate the Claimant for its loss as of that date."

In cases of breach of contract, the starting date is the date from which damages will flow; the date of breach. For the tribunal, the breach equals non-performance, including any non-delivery, non-payment, or non- execution of contractual obligations It has frequently held that it would presume an invoice was payable 30 days after presentation. It took the dates of the respective unpaid bills seriously and used them as the date of the breach of contract and the start of interest. In its *Reynolds Tobacco* award, it referred to the time when it became evident that the contracting partner would not pay the bill for the goods duly delivered, ignoring the date of the invoice itself. However, in some cases, it considered 30 days as lead time for the debtor to pay the debt. Actually, the interest begins to accrue 30 days after the invoice date. This was the tribunal's approach in the *Exxon Research* award:[757]

"69. Exxon Research also seeks interest on the amounts awarded under the Seventh Refinery Project calculated as from the date the invoices were issued. It appears more reasonable, however, in the absence of any contractual provisions in this respect, to award interest based on

756.*Phillips Petroleum Company v. the Islamic Republic of Iran and NIOC*, préc., note 157.para.92

757.*Exxon Research and Engineering Co v. National Iranian Oil Company*, [1987] case no.155, 15 _IUSCTR_ 3 (Iran_U.S. Claims Tribunal). P.21

an assumption that NIOC was obligated to pay the invoices within 30 days of presentation."

In another case, relating to the same claimant,[758] the tribunal recognized the 30-day lead time to pay the bill as a usage: "67. Interest will be calculated based on the generally admitted usage that an invoice is payable within 30 days of presentation."

In a few cases, the tribunal awarded interest only from the date it was first demanded. concluded interest only from the date the claim was filed with the Tribunal. In an official claim, the *Atomic Energy Organization of Iran* case,[759] the tribunal awarded interest only from the date reimbursement of advance payment on expired contracts had been demanded, not from the date of contract expiration. In the *Reliance Group* case,[760] it awarded 10 per cent interest to accrue from the "date of the filing of the statement of the claim up to and including the date on which the Escrow Agent instructs the Depository Bank to effect payment out of security account."[761]

6.6 Form of Interest: Simple or Compound

Compound interest exist where "the interest of a sum of money is added to the principal and then bears interest, which thus becomes a sort of secondary principle."[762] Usually in international arbitration,

---

758.*EXXON Corporation v. the Islamic Republic of Iran*, [1987] case no.154, 17 _IUSCTR_ 3 (Iran-U.S. Claims Tribunal).p.17

759*Atomic Energy Organization of Iran v the United States of America*, préc., note 535.

760.*Reliance Group, Inc. v National Oil Company*, préc., note 528., para. 257,274

761.*Id.*, para.384

762.Henry Campbell BLACK, *Black's Law Dictionary: Definitions of the Terms and Phrases of American and English Jurisprudence, Ancient and Modern*, 6th éd., USA, West Publishing Company, 1990.no.286

compound interest is especially problematic.[763] The general principles of law do not yield unambiguous guidance. The norm, until recently, has been to award simple interest. The practice, however, seems to be changing towards compound interest whenever the injured party can prove that that is the only route to making it whole.[764] One commentator reports spreading recognition of this approach among international tribunal.[765] However, the arbitral awards show a trend away from simple to compound interest.[766] There is probably a difference here between commercial and investment arbitration because there is a line of cases in investment arbitration that considers that compound interest is the rule because it is compatible with the principle of restitutio in integrum[767].

Modern economic reality, as well as equity, demand compound compensation for injured parties who have suffered actual compound interest charges. English law regards the issue as a matter of discretion for the tribunal. The point was recently considered in Sempra Metal Ltd. v. Island Revenue Commissioners[768]The court held that the time had come to recognise that money had a value: "the court had a common law

---

763.Natasha AFFOLDER, « Awarding Compound Interest in International Arbitration », (2001) 12-1 *Am. Rev. Int. Arbitr.* 45-93.p.46

764.B. SABAHI et T. WALDE, préc., note 227. p.1107, Thomas Walde submits: "awarding compound interest requires providing evidence that, claimant paid compound interest on borrowed substitute funds to fulfill its obligations toward the other party."

765.C. MCLACHLAN QC, L. SHORE et M. WEINIGER QC, préc., note 270. P.346

766.S. RIPINSKY, préc., note 56.p.380

767.*Middle East Cement Co v Arab Republic of Egypt, ARB/99/6*, préc., note 66., *Wena Hotels Ltd. v. Arab Republic of Egypt, ARB/98/4*, [2000] 6 ICSID Repoprts (ICSID)., *Compañía del Desarrollo de Santa Elena, S.A. v. Republic of Costa Rica, ARB/96/1*, [1997] 5 ICSID Reports 296 (ICSID).

768.Sempra Metal Ltd. v. Island Revenue Commissioners, 2007, 3WLR 354.

jurisdiction to award interest, simple or compound, as damages on claims for the non-payment of debts as well as on other claims for breach of contract. A tribunal is entitled to take into account the prevailing commercial practice of borrowing and investing on a compound basis."

Although, today in investment disputes there is a general consensus that compound interest should be used instead of simple interest in cases where the expropriation is unlawful[769]. As Mann submits, international tribunals and respected commentators have come to recognize this principle.[770]

Here, at last is indication that, if it receives sound justifications, the Iran-U.S. Claims Tribunal may award compound interest. In the *Ebrahimi Shaine* case,[771] Judge Richard Alison noted his objection to simple interest and called for more careful and reasoned treatment.

The tribunal consistently refuses compound interest in contractual and expropriation claims. It generally denies compound interest. In the *McCollough Inc.* case,[772] it followed international arbitration:

"97. Most awards allocate only simple interest, but occasionally compound interest has been awarded and sometimes a percentage is

---

769.A. LO, préc., note 107.p.98

770.F.A. MANN, « Compound Interest as an Item of Damage in International Law », (1988) 21 *Univ. Calif. Davis Law Rev.* 577-586.p.582

771.*Ebrahimi Shahin Shaine v. the Islamic Republic of Iran*, préc., note 281., para.74. Judge Richard Alison presented his dissenting opinion: "Although I do not believe that the 8.6% rate is patently unreasonable, I do believe that legitimate questions can be raised as to its adequacy, particularly in light of the very high interest rates that prevailed during a significant portion of the period since the taking in these Cases and the fact that (in my view, erroneously) the interest is not compounded. I trust that in future cases these issues will receive a more careful and reasoned treatment than they have in this Award."

772.*McCollough& Company, Inc. v. Ministry of Post, Telegram and Telephone*, préc., note 446., para3,96-97 added to the interest in consideration of the rate of inflation. It is difficult to draw any distinct conclusions from so diverse a practice. The Tribunal can conclude, however, that no uniform rule of law relating to interest has emerged from the practice in transnational arbitration."

In the *J.R. Reynolds Tobacco Co.* case,[773] the tribunal rejected a claim that a contractual clause providing for interest on "all sums" that were unpaid justified compound interest:

"The Tribunal, however, does not find that there are any special reasons for departing from international precedents which normally do not allow the awarding of compound interest. As noted by one authority, there are few rules within the scope of the subject of damages in international law that are better settled than the one that compound interest is not allowable."

Even though the judges could have construed "all sums" to include interest and thereby to allow compound interest, the tribunal, because of the ambiguity of the language, interpreted the clause in the light of the international rule just stated and excluded compound interest.

It reached a similar result in the *Anaconda-Iran. Inc.* case,[774] construing otherwise a contract clause that appeared to provide for compound interest, calling it "ambiguous due to the unreasonable result that such a technical application (of the clause) may yield." It begun that conclusion by justifying why it should not award compound interest:

"First of all, the inherent and essential effect of a contractual provision for compound interest is to dissuade the other party from defaulting in fulfilment of its contractual obligations. As in the present case, such a dispute leads to a termination of the contract in question, this purpose is mooted. Secondly the mathematical result of a full

---

773.*R.J ReynoldsTobacco Co. v the Islamic Republic of Iran, partial award*, préc., note 167.

774.*Anaconda-Iran, Inc. v. the Islamic Republic of Iran*, préc., note 152.para.140

application of contractual provisions such as section 7.04, particularly in view of the delays that any adjudication of a dispute involves, is that the interest due could, by far, exceed the principal amounts awarded."

The tribunal concluded that "the awarding of compound interest in the respect case must be deemed to be outside the scope of the possible common intent of the parties, and that, therefore, compound interest pursuant to section 7.04 must be disallowed. This argument is problematic. The tribunal did not explain its disavowal of contractual agreement, while, in practice of the Tribunal it was established to respect the mutual stipulations. Noting that interest awards would double the principal amounts awarded if the compound interest applied, in many claims adjudicated by the U.S.-Iran Claims Tribunal. In fact, international tribunals have imported the Roman-law rule *alterum tantum* into international law to limit interest awards to amounts no greater than the principal due, but more recently they have moved closer to basic economic reasoning and awarded higher interest when appropriate.[775] In the *Starrett Housing Corp.* case,[776] the claimant suffered compound interest charges on its debt and needed compound compensation to become whole. The tribunal again rejected compound interest, relying on a 1943 proposition that the rule against compound interest was "settled."[777] Whether or not such a rule existed before 1943, it was no longer appropriate or justifiable in 1987.

At the hearing, Starrett's attorney read into the record a legal opinion by F.H. Mann on Starrett's entitlement to compound interest. Mann, noting the precedents disallowing awards of compound interest, commented that the international law on compound interest "has never

---

775.J. A. WESTBERG, préc., note 135.p.254

776.*Starrett Housing Corporations, Srarrett System, Inc. and Starrett Housing International, Inc. v. the Islamic Republic of Iran*, préc., note 240.para. 112,234-5.

777.Marjorie M. WHITEMAN, *Damages in International Law*, 3, Washington, United States Government Printing Office, 1943. P.1997 been fully analyzed and is in fact far from clear. This is due to the relatively small number of cases in which the point was considered, to the fact that most of the cases, were decided many years ago when economic conditions and commercial practices were less developed, and to the absence of profound argument and discussion."

As Mann recognized, times change, and so should the law. Significantly, his study found no prohibitory statement in any source of international law; to the contrary, some cases, most notably the *Aminoil* arbitration,[778] had awarded compound interest. In his opinion, both municipal and international law seemed to be awarding compound interest where, as in this case, the other party's wrongful acts have led to compound interest charges against the injured party. Mann stated: "If, as the claimants allege, the non-payment of the compensation on the 31st January 1980 involved them in the payment of interest to banks, then it is a well-known fact that it is their universal practice to charge compound interest with monthly or half-yearly, or possibly but rarely, yearly rates. Such liability would be a loss directly flowing from the non-payment of compensation ... Interest and compound interest paid or not earned was a direct loss or expense to which the victim is entitled."

Nevertheless, the tribunal did not consider the presented statement and eventually rejected the request for compound interest. The tribunal turned down another request for compound interest in the *International Systems and Controls Corp.* case.[779] The claimant in this case argued forcefully for compound interest, but the judges had not decided when the parties settled. The tribunal held:

"120.At the Hearing the Claimant asserted a claim for compound interest based on the language of Article 5 of the Repayment

---

778.*The State of Kuwait v The American Independent Oil Company (Aminoil')*, [1982] 21 International Legal Materials 976-1053 (ad hoc arbitration).

779.*International Systems & Control Corporation v National Iranian Gas Company*, [1990] case no.494, 24 _IUSCTR_ 47 (Iran_U.S. Claims Tribunal). p.83

Agreement which, the Claimant contends, implicitly provides for the accrual of compound interest. The Claimant's witnesses also testified that the use of compound interest is the norm with such agreements, 121.To date the Tribunal has never awarded compound interest."

In the *R.J. Reynolds Tobacco Co.* case,[780] chamber III found no "special reasons" for departing from international precedents, "which normally do not allow the awarding of compound interest." Accordingly, and pursuant to its award in the *McCollough* case, it ruled for simple interest. It awarded interest at a rate applicable to six-month certificates of deposit, but failed to compound this interest, as would be the normal practice with these instruments.

6.7 Interest Rate

Once an international tribunal decides to award interest, it must determine the rate of accrual, which may vary case by case. The economic circumstances and banking environment could change during the period, and a different country might become the basis for computing the interest rate. Article 78 of the CISG Convention offers no help here. In fact, the drafters intentionally left determination of the rate of interest open, as they could not agree on the right approach.[781] As a result, many observers suggest using local law. However, article 7.4.9 of the UNIDROIT Principles states:

"(2) The rate of interest shall be the *average bank short-term lending rate toprime borrowers* prevailing for the currency of payment at the place for payment, or where no such rate exists at that place, then the same rate in the State of the currency of payment. In the absence of such a rate at either place the rate of interest shall be the appropriate rate fixed by the law of the State of the currency of payment."

780.*R.J Reynolds Tobacco Co. v the Islamic Republic of Iran, partial award*, préc., note 167.p.192

781.L. SONG, préc., note 538.p.724

Despite tribunals' lack of consensus, they generally employ one of four methods to select the interest rate: treat interest as a substantive matter and apply the dispute's substantive law; treat interest as a procedural matter and apply the forum's interest rate; suppose the interest rate to comply with the law of the place of payment; or choose a reasonable rate.[782] So far, international jurisprudence has been inconsistent in selecting investment vehicles as references for the applicable interest rate.[783]Although the Iran-U.S. Claims Tribunal has rendered so many awards enforcing interest payment, it has no fixed method to calculate the interest rate. In some cases it has not clarified the interest rate. In some awards, it awarded interest not by fixing a rate, but rather by fixing a sum of money representing interest or by including interest in the award.[784]

The tribunal's statement in Award No. 602-A15(IV)/A24-FT, July 2014, Iran v. The United States,[785] brilliantly clarifies this point. Here the judges deemed it fair and reasonable to award Iran simple pre-judgment interest on all amounts it awarded to Iran at an annual rate (365-day basis) equal to the U.S. average prime-bank lending rate between its determination that those amounts are due up to and including the date of this award. In applying that particular rate, it was also mindful of UPICC article 7.4.9 (2): "The rate of interest shall be the average bank short-term lending rate to prime borrowers prevailing for the currency of payment at the place for payment." The tribunal referred directly to this article in its award:

"288. Accordingly, having considered all relevant circumstances and the submissions made, in the present Cases, the Tribunal deems it fair and reasonable to award Iran simple prejudgment interest on all

---

782.J. Y. GOTANDA, préc., note 502.p.89

783.I. MARBOE, préc., note 232.P.346

784.*Pomeroy Corporation v. the Islamic Republic of Iran*, préc., note 246., *CMI International, Inc, the Islamic Republic of Iran*, préc., note 151.p.271

785.*Iran v United States, A15*, préc., note 461.

amounts awarded to Iran at an annual rate (365-day basis) equal to the average prime bank lending rate in the United States during the period from the dates the Tribunal has determined that those amounts are due up to and including the date of this Award. In selecting the prime bank lending rate in the United States as the rate of interest applicable in these cases, the Tribunal was also mindful of Article 7.4.9 (2) of the UNIDROIT Principles 2010, which provides: The rate of interest shall be............"[786]

6.7.1 An Attempt to Make the Interest Rate Uniform

Adoption of a fixed interest rate by other tribunals would greatly simplify interest calculations for the Iran-U.S. Claims Tribunal. There is no single fixed commercial rate, however, that could fairly cover the range of circumstances arbitral institutions such as the International Chamber of Commerce face.[787] A less common method depends on the rate of return on investments rather than on borrowing costs. One chamber of the Iran-U.S. Claims Tribunal, for example, has used such a method. It has explained this change as ensuring uniformity in interest awards and using a more realistic measure of damages suffered, particularly if the party experiencing delay in payment did not borrow money. In the inter-state *A-19* case,[788] both Governments argue in the alternative that even if the Tribunal has the power to award interest, the Full Tribunal should establish uniform rules governing the circumstances in which interest may be granted, the period during which

786.*Iran v United States, A15, [2014] Award No. 602-A15(IV)/A24-FT published on the tribunal official website en ligne: <http://www.iusct.net/General%20Documents/AWARD/4-AJoint% 20Separate% 20Opinion% 20IR%20Members%2001%2007%202014%20(Final). pdf>.*, préc., note 101.

787.D. J. B. and R. E. WALLACE, préc., note 709.p.945

788.*Iran v. United States, Case A19*, préc., note 728.

interest should be calculated, and the rate to be allowed, then, the full tribunal held:

"13. The determination of the applicable principles of law in any given case, and consequently the question of whether an award of interest is appropriate, must rest with the Chamber concerned, and relates to the exercise by the Chambers of the discretion accorded to them in deciding each particular case. The Tribunal therefore concludes that the alternative request for the establishment of general rules governing the award of interest by the individual Chambers must be denied."

The full tribunal left it to the chambers to determine the interest rate in the light of the circumstances of each case, although the interest rate should be the market rate, which approximates both the rate of return on investment and the interest cost of borrowing funds.[789] As for the full tribunal's asking the chambers to decide on the basis of circumstances, one observer comments "Calculation methodologies for interest differ partly based on evidentiary issues and partly based on different assumptions about the nature of the claimant's injury."[790] However, two approaches, emerged through long practice. In next paragraphs we survey these two approaches which have been followed by the Iran-U.S. Claim Tribunal in this regard.

6.7.2 The McCollough Method

Actually, one of the tribunal's oft-cited awards regarding interest rate appears in the *McCollough & Co., Inc.* case:[791]. "Under the present Award, the Respondent, the United States of America, is obligated to pay the Claimant, the Islamic Republic of Iran, the total

789.D. J. B. and R. E. WALLACE, préc., note 709.p.919

790.A. X. FELLMETH, préc., note 740. P.430

791.*McCollough& Company, Inc. v. Ministry of Post, Telegram and Telephone*, préc., note 446.

sum of (U.S.$842,468.14), plus simple interest at the successive prevailing prime bank lending rates in the United States for the period of non-payment of this Award." As well, "the rate of interest must be reasonable, taking due account of all pertinent circumstances," and the tribunal set forth several criteria:

i)any pertinent contractual stipulations (which, when the exist, are usually followed for the determination of the rates),

ii) the rules and the principles of the law applicable to the contract,

iii) the nature of the facts generating the damage,

iv) the nature and the level of the compensation awarded, particularly, if it extends to the lost profits or includes a profit in the costs to be reimbursed,

v) the knowledge that the defaulting party could have had of the financial consequences of its default for the other party,

vi) the rates in effect in the markets concerned, and

vii)the rate of inflation.

The problem with determining fairness or reasonableness is that arbitrators differ on what is fair.[792] Judge Brower's dissenting opinion here questioned the fairness of the interest award. The chamber awarded interest at 11 per cent per annum, which he found inconsistent with the commercial approach other chambers used. The inherent support of fairness is evident in other tribunal decisions. In the *AmericanBell Int'l Inc.* case,[793] stating that the claimant is clearly entitled to interest at a "reasonable" or "fair" rate, the tribunal wrote: "The Tribunal first notes that in a commercial case like the present one Claimant is clearly entitled to interest at a 'reasonable' or 'fair' rate to compensate for the delays with which the payments due are made. Following to award in *McCollough* case, noting the absence of any contractually agreed-upon interest rate,

792.N. AFFOLDER, préc., note 763.p.77

793.*American Bell International Inc. v the Islamic Republic of Iran*, [1986] case no.48, 12 _IUSCTR_ 170 (Iran_U.S. Claims Tribunal).p.229, para.201

and taking into account such considerations as were put forward in McCollough, the Tribunal determines that a fair rate of interest to be awarded on all amounts due and owing Claimant is 10 per cent per annum."

In the *Faith Lita Khosrowshahi* case,[794] in order to compensate the claimants for the damages flowing from the respondents' failure to compensate them when they took their property, the tribunal considered it fair to award the claimants simple interest at the rate of 8.6 per cent from the dates of the deprivation of their interests.

6.7.3 The Sylvania Method

In the *Sylvania Technical Systems, Inc.* case,[795] chamber I, fixed interest at the average rate of interest on six-month U.S. certificates of deposit from the time the debt arose to the time of the award, which at that time was 12 per cent. Under the principles it outlined in thiscase, successful claimants would receive interest equal to the rate earnable by the claimant had it invested the sum in a commercial investment common in its own country. For successful U.S. claimants, the tribunal customarily uses the average interest rate on six-month certificates of deposit for the period from the day following the date on which payment was due to the date on which the escrow agent instructs the depository bank to effect payment. Accordingly, in *Sylvania*, chamber I awarded the claimant the average rate of interest on six-month U.S. certificates of deposit from the start of the debt to the payment of the award.

794.*Khosrowshahi, Faith Lita v. the Islamic Republic of Iran*, préc., note 462., at 76

795.*Sylvania Technical Systems, Inc. v. the Islamic Republic of Iran*, préc., note 556.

This standard the tribunal further explained and refined in the *First Travel Corp.* case:[796]

"In its award in *Sylvania Technical Systems, Inc.*, this Chamber expressed its intention to develop and apply a consistent approach to the awarding of interest in cases before it. In the absence of a contractually stipulated rate of interest, it is the Tribunal's policy to derive a rate of interest based approximately on the amount that the successful claimant would have been in a position to have earned if it had had the funds available to invest in a form of commercial investment in common use in its own country. Six-month certificates of deposit in the United States are such a form of investment for which average interest rates are available from an authoritative official source."

In the *George E. Davidson* case,[797] the tribunal granted interest to the claimant at the rate of 7.789 per cent, in accordance with the principles it outlined in *Sylvania*, beginning on the date of interference with the property rights, plus simple interest at the rate of 7.789 per cent per annum (365-day basis) from July 1, 1980, up to and including the day on which the escrow agent instructed the depository bank to pay the claimant out of the Security Account. In the *Kenneth P. Yeager* case,[798] the tribunal followed the *Sylvania* method:

"Tribunal considers it appropriate to award interest as of 17 February 1979 in an amount approximately equal to the rate a successful Claimant would have been able to earn had it invested the sums awarded in a form of commercial investment common in its own Country. For successful American claimants, the Tribunal customarily uses the average rates earned on a six-month Certificate of deposit. The average rate for the period relevant to this Award, rounded to the nearest quarter

796.*First Travel Corporation v. the Islamic Republic of Iran*, [1985] case no.34, 9 _IUSCTR_ 360 (Iran_U.S. Claims Tribunal).p.376

797.*George E. Davidson v. the Islamic Republic of Iran*, préc., note 530.

798.*Kenneth P. Yeager v the Islamic Republic of Iran*, [1987] case no.10199, 17 _IUSCTR_ 92 (Iran_U.S. Claims Tribunal)., p.112,para.72

percent, is 10.50 percent."

In the *Aeronutronic Overseas Services, Inc.* case,[799] chamber I followed the *Sylvania* method and expressed its intention to develop and apply a consistent approach to the awarding of interest in cases before it in *Sylvania Technical Systems, Inc.* award:

"65. In the absence of a contractually stipulated rate of interest, it is the Tribunal's policy to derive a rate of interest based approximately on the amount that the successful Claimant would have been in a position to have earned if it had had the funds available to invest in a form of commercial investment in common use in its own country. Six-month certificates of deposit in the United States are such a form of investment for which average interest rates are available from an authoritative official source."

6.7.4 The Interest Rate in Inter-State Claims

The *Atomic Energy Organization of Iran* award[800] involved an official claim in which the successful claimant is a government. The tribunal rejects as inappropriate a commercial investment rate, particularly without evidence as to either government's fiscal practices:

"With respect to the appropriate rate of interest to be applied, developed in *Sylvania* case... in the absence of a contractually stipulated rate of interest, it is the Tribunal's policy to derive a rate of interest based approximately on the amount that the successful claimant would have been in a position to have earned if it had had the funds available to invest in a form of commercial investment in common use in its own country."

799.*Aeronutronic Overseas Service, Inc. v. the Islamic Republic of Iran*, préc., note 527., para.65-67

800.*Atomic Energy Organization of Iran v the United States of America*, préc., note 535.

Once Judge Ameli had observed this practice, his separate opinion in*Iran v. The United States, Case A27,*[801] in 1998 stated: "I would have preferred that for the rate of interest for the post-breach period, that is, from 24 November 1992 to the date of payment, 10% be applied in accordance with the long-established practice of the Tribunal, in intergovernmental claims, the Tribunal has consistently applied this rate."

The tribunal did not respect this precedent in a later award -- No. 602-A15(IV)/A24-FT (July 2014).[802] The Iranian government was successful in a claim against the U.S. government regarding some official claims, and the tribunal factored in the new global financial environment:

"The Tribunal finds that, while an award of simple ten percent interest might have been reasonable at the time those decisions were rendered, it would not be reasonable today in light of the steady decline in interest rates since 1990 as well as the dramatic fall in interest rates as a result of the global financial crisis of 2008."

The tribunal chose for interest the rate of prime bank lending in the United States. In its award the tribunal ruled that, the respondent, the United States of America, is obligated to pay the claimant simple interest at the successive prevailing prime bank lending rates in the United States for the period of non-payment. The tribunal states:

"286. The Tribunal's application of the Average Six-Month CD Rate in determining the *post-judgment* interest in Case No. A27 may have been justified in the circumstances of that particular case, where the Tribunal applied a simple ten-percent annual rate in determining the *pre-judgment* interest awarded to Iran on the ground that "the Second Circuit would likely have awarded such interest if its decision had been

---

801.*Iran v. United States, Case A27,* [1998] 34 _IUSCTR_ 39 (Iran_U.S. Claims Tribunal).p.62

802.*Iran v United States, A15,* préc., note 461.

to grant enforcement of the *Avco* award......, 314. The Tribunal, however, does not deem a similar application of the Average Six-Month CD Rate reasonable in the present Cases[803]."

6.7.5 Agreed Rate of Interest

The parties may, in their contract, stipulate that the effect of the breach shall be the payment of the interest on an agreed rate. Because of party autonomy in international arbitration, an explicit agreement of the parties on interest is invaluable.[804]In its *Reynolds Tobacco* award,[805] the tribunal recognized the priority of party agreement as a general principle of contract law: "Under generally accepted principles of contract law a contractually stipulated rate of interest is normally binding upon the parties." This award sanctioned agreed interest in the form of the LIBOR (London Interbank Offered Rate) plus 2 percentage points.

If parties to a case agreed on a rate of interest, the tribunal would apply it in awarding damages. We can see this in the *McHarg* award:[806] "73. Absent 'special circumstances' this Chamber applies contractually stipulated rates of interest. The Contract here provides for a rate of 6% interest on amounts left unpaid 30 days after the due date. The Tribunal therefore applies that rate to the amounts awarded."

Usually, in contracts that ascertained the interest rate, it has been the prime rate plus an agreed percentage. Prime represents what commercial banks charge their most creditworthy borrowers, such as large corporations, thus taking on a very minor risk.[807]

803.*Id.*

804.I. MARBOE, préc., note 232.p.336

805.*R.J. Reynolds Tobacco Co. v. the Islamic Republic of Iran*, [1985] case no.35, 8 -IUSCTR- 55 (Iran_U.S. Claims Tribunal).

806.*McHarg v the Islamic Republic of Iran*, [1986] case no.10853, 13 _IUSCTR_ 286 (Iran_U.S. Claims Tribunal).p.308,, para.73

807.I. MARBOE, préc., note 232.p. 339

In the *International Systems and Controls Corp.* case,[808] the tribunal held: "Pursuant to the contractual agreement contained in Article 5 of the Repayment Agreement, such interest should be at the rate of one percent (1%) above the Prime Rate of the First National Bank of Chicago applicable to ninety-day commercial loans to substantial and responsible borrowers commencing on 1 September 1978." Then, the tribunal has calculated the contractual rate on the basis of an annual average and expressed the award of interest in such terms.

In the *Anaconda* award,[809] the tribunal selected the agreed rate in the contract: "NICIC shall pay to AI interest at the rate per annum equal to the prime rate then being charged by The Chase Manhattan Bank, plus 2%, on any amount due AI under this Agreement, whether on account of fees or costs, from the date due until said amount, plus accrued interest on said amount, shall have been paid in full."

However, certain circumstances may affect the validity of the agreed rate of interest, even though it is binding. The tribunal does not apply contractual arrangements that it considers unfair. For example, in its *Anaconda* award,[810] the tribunal rejected the stipulated compound interest.

6.8 Summary

The Iran-U.S. Claims Tribunal, in case no. *A-19*, adopted the long-standing principle in international arbitration that awarding interest is inherent in the authority to award just compensation for damages. But it declined to set down uniform rates or time periods for interest, leaving that for each chamber to decide case by case. Regarding

---

808.*International Systems & Control Corporation v National Iranian Gas Company*, préc., note 773., para.123

809.*Anaconda-Iran, Inc. v. the Islamic Republic of Iran*, préc., note 152.para.135

810.*Id.*para.138

appropriate rates, there was general agreement to follow the rate in the contract if parties have specified it.

If not, judicial discretion rules. Chamber I, in its *Sylvania* and later awards, followed the 'investment-rate rule' --the rate that the successful party could have earned had it received payment on time and invested the money in a commercial six-month deposit account in its home country, as per UPICC's article 7.4.9. states "2) The rate of interest shall be the average bank short-term lending rate to prime borrowers prevailing for the currency of payment at the place for payment,". In contrast, chamber III, in its *McCollough* case and subsequent awards, rejected uniform application of any particular rule and determined the rate for each case, in the light of its facts and circumstances.

The tribunal has faced some claims that flowed from Iran's exchange controls, which prevented transfer of Americans' funds from Iranian banks. The judges have, there, accepted force majeure to absolve the banks but still awarded interest on the amounts that they withheld, in accordance with article 7.4.9 of UPICC. The tribunal, however, found no special reasons for departing from international precedents disallowing compound interest, be that in its expropriation or commercial claims. In inter-state claims, it applied 10 per cent interest, following its own long-established practice.

About determining a reasonable rate of interest in inter-state claims, the tribunal has set forth several factors to weigh. In a 2014 award, after noting the global financial environment and the steady decline in interest rates since 1990, which speeded up with the global financial crisis of 2008, it selected the rate of U.S. prime bank lending.

The tribunal awards compensatory (pre-award) and moratory (post-award) interest at the same rate, from the breach, expropriation, or other appropriate date till payment of the award. In taking claims, interest starts at expropriation; in contract disputes, when the contractual obligation was due. This follows article 7.4.10 of UPICC.

states: "Unless otherwise agreed, interest on damages for non-performance of non-monetary obligations accrues as from the time of non-performance." It is the Tribunal's policy to derive a rate of interest based approximately on the amount that the successful claimant would have been in a position to have earned if it had had the funds available to invest in a form of commercial investment in common use in its own country. With respect to the calculation of interest, determining the rate of interest depending on the circumstances of the case, including whether the claimant terminated the contract and whether there was a complete or partial breach. What is reasonable is a question of fact dependent upon the circumstances of a particular case.in fact, the tribunal does not explain how to calculate damages do as circumstances dictate. However, in some areas of valuation, a uniform standard is already developing. For example, as explained in previous sections, there is a general consensus that simple interest should be awarded instead in cases where the expropriation is lawful.

Conclusion

Today, responding the need to uniformity and harmonization in international trade law, the new transnational substantive rules of law has been codified through not only international commercial dealings, standard clauses and arbitral awards, but also from comparative study of legal rules common in most significant legal systems. This codification of the general principles of law, as incorporated into uniform principles such as the UNIDROIT commercial contract principles, can therefore be regarded as set of rules which are being applied as substantive law in concluding contractual relation and also applied as applicable law in international arbitration. The differences between the two types of international investment and international commercial arbitration—one based on a contract and the other on a treaty—have a bearing on the choice of the rules of law that are applied in dispute resolution. Whereas, in investment law the obligations can arise under public international law, national law, or under both international and national law simultaneously, obviously it defers from commercial arbitration that the parties' arbitration are based on the contract law rules. In fact, there has been debate over whether transnational law does really exist, and whether this general principle, which some see as a newlex mercatoria, can serve as the applicable law in international investment arbitration.

This study has reviewed the potential of general principles of law, as codified in UPICC, to be applied in international investment arbitration. In investment arbitration case law, there are some examples of awards that make reference to the UPICC as an expression of generally recognized principles. Although, there are some cases applying the UPICC directly as a source of international law, and some case law showing the use of the UPICC as corroboration in this context. Basically, in these awards the existence of a principle is assumed rather than proven. This is a step towards proving the principle, although it does not seem to meet the strict requirement of a rigorous examination. This study assessed to what extent the UPICC rules have been or may be used as 'rules of law' that govern the international disputes, as a source of international law. The study explores in more detail to what extent are they capable to present the solution for the investment dispute arbitrations?

This study has examined the practice of the Iran-United States Claims Tribunal in applying the principle of compensation from international arbitration and compared it to the general principles of law in the UNIDROIT Principles of International Commerical Contracts (UPICC 2010) and the United Nations Convention on Contracts for the International Sale of Goods (CISG, 1980). The goal is to determine how the tribunal interprets and applies the principle of compensation in arbitration cases and to see whether UPICC can serve as substantive law in international investment arbitration relating to disputes between private parties and a state and to highlight the share values between the practice of Iran_U.S. Claims Tribunal and the rules of transnational instrument. Following the first chapter, which introduces the background and context of the tribunal, five chapters present a case study and comparison of the tribunal's jurisprudence with the transnational instruments. Some of the main findings of this study may be summarized as follows:

In chapter one, it is examined that the tribunal practises a transnational legal process.

The tribunal as an international arbitral body came into force since 1981 in order to decide on nearly 4000 claims that arose in expropriation and contract cancellation by America investors and traders against Iran government. However, because of the lack of confidence between American and Iranian parties, they could not agree on each others' national laws, then they proposed the general principles of law as the applicable law in their claims arbitration process. Therefore, one can conclude that the application of the general principles of law to investment dispute resolution, may be preferred due to the resistance of foreign parties to subject the judgment to the law of the host State. The tribunal, by applying principles of commercial law in deciding many of the commercial cases before it, has contributed significantly to the stabilization and development of a multitude of principles and rules of the lex mercatoria. Also, the tribunal routinely applies general principles of transnational law and in fact has spurred development of that law, the judges holding very similar views regarding content. Tribunal jurisprudence that applies the principle of compensation is often termed investment arbitration, and some authors have even claimed that the tribunal practice *jurisprudence constante* in investor--state arbitration.

In chapter two, it is examined that the tribunal has upheld the traditional approach of full compensation. Therefore, its awards have ruled decisively in favour of traditional, full compensation. Every award that addressed the issue has clearly endorsed that standard of compensation. Whether it looked to customary international law or to the Treaty of Amity of 1955 between Iran and United States, it found various terms, such as 'adequate,' 'equitable,' 'fair,' and 'full,' to express different aspects of one concept. In contractual disputes it usually compensated any actual loss (*damnum*) and lost profit (*lucrum cessans*). However, its application of the compensation principle in claims arising from contracts fits exactly with the rules in UNIDROIT Principles of International Commercial Contracts. Its interpretation of the Permanent International Court of Justice's jurisprudence in the *Chorzow Factory* award has led it to find a fundamental distinction between lawful and unlawful taking in the standard of compensation. Accordingly, it decided that, in lawful expropriation, only *damnum emergens* (loss suffered) would be compensable, and, because in all its cases the expropriation was lawful, it did not award lost profits there. It submits that in unlawful expropriation the claimant can recover the following two items rather than a lawful expropriation claim: the higher value that the investment might have acquired at the date of award, and consequential expenses, particularly, lost profit (*lucrum cessans*). This chapter shows that the tribunal's standard of compensation comports with UPICC and such auxiliary legal principles as unjust enrichment and equity, and the role of the equity in approximation of the quantum of damage in the Tribunal's awards is the same as set out in the UNIDROIT Principles. The principle of undue enrichment finds an obvious field of application in cases where a foreign investor has sustained a loss whereby another party has been enriched, but which does not arise out of an internationally unlawful act which would found a claim for damages. The tribunal frequently, in quantification of the damages, refered to principle of offset of benefits. The principle is in part derived from the basic notion of full compensation in the case of a breach. When applying the standard of full compensation to an award, tribunal is cautious to avoid double compensation – whether through application of a single valuation method or by applying lump sum compensation.

In chapter three, the damage limitations were studied. Damage limitation based on the idea that there must be limits to the recovery of damages, which restricts the liability in damages. Most legal systems acknowledge causation, foreseeability, certainty, and mitigation as criteria for measuring damages. The expectation measure of contract damages, which requires the breaching promisor to pay the promisee an amount of money sufficient to put the promisee in the position it would have been in if the promisor had performed, is delimited subject to several exceptions that tribunal duly applied in its reasoning. First, the award is reduced when a portion of the promisee's loss is attributable to circumstances that the promisor could not ordinarily foresee. This result is due to the rule of consequential damages, also known as foreseeability or Hadley rule which drives from the famous judgment *Hadley v. Baxendale* (1854). Second, the award is reduced when a portion of the promisee's loss is attributable to the promisee's failure to take actions that would have minimized its losses subsequent to the promisor's breach. This result is due to the mitigation rule. Other doctrine hold that the award is reduced when the promisee cannot show that the loss was reasonably certain, in fact, compensation is due only for harm, including future harm, that is established with a reasonable degree of certainty.

The law requires a sufficient link or nexus between the wrongful act and the injury before imposing any obligation to make reparations for that injury. In this analysis, a causal link was a necessary element of the finding of expropriation.

Foreseeability also limits the recoverability of damages. The underlying doctrine is that parties, while completing a contract, should be able to calculate the risks and potential liability they assume by their agreement. Foreseeability should limit the risk of liability to what the party can determine at the conclusion of the contract, thus enabling it to take the risk, acquire insurance, or abstain from concluding the contract. Both transnational instruments incorporate this idea. According to article 7.4.4 of UPICC, the non-performing party is liable only for harm that it foresaw or could reasonably have foreseen while concluding the contract as being likely to result from its non-performance, and article 74 of CISG makes it clear that it is only the party in breach that must foresee. The Iran-U.S. Claims Tribunal has invoked foreseeability in regard to recoverable damages following breach of contract. Judges applied the doctrine in several rulings, such as the *Sea-Co* award.

As for certainty, Usually the claimant must prove lost profits with reasonable certainty. Arbitral tribunals have insisted on a "sufficient (degree of) certainty" in proof of future losses. UPICC requires reasonable certainty, and article 7.4.3 of CISG states: "(1) Compensation is due only for harm, including future harm, that is established with a reasonable degree of certainty." The Iran-U.S. Claims Tribunal's practice limits recovery to certainly provable future damages. The border between direct and indirect damages, or between prospective and merely speculative profits, is seldom clear, and often depends on the arbitrator's subjective estimate. The claim's size need not always be so certain, and the tribunal often deals with approximation. When precise calculation is difficult or impossible, as with inconclusive evidence, tribunals may exercise discretion and estimate. According to CISG article 7.4.3: "(3) Where the amount of damages cannot be established with a sufficient degree of certainty, the assessment is at the discretion of the court."

In limiting damages, the general rule is that a victim must minimize the damage sustained and a debtor must reimburse solely the immediate and direct damages. This concept finds its ultimate source in the principle of good faith. The mitigation doctrine requires the promisee to take steps to reduce the loss from breach after it learns of the breach or acquires reason to know of it. If the promisee fails to take such steps, it will not recover full expectation damages. The reasonableness of measures that were or should have been undertaken is rather to be assessed on a case by case basis. This assessment falls to the discretion of the tribunal and is to be made interpreting the general principles of international trade, especially the principle of good faith in international trade. The aggrieved party cannot sit idly while the losses resulting from the breach of contract accumulate and then expect to be entitled to recover the losses that could have been avoided. Instead, one is generally required to undertake all measures that are reasonable in the circumstances to mitigate the loss resulting from the breach. These principles are strongly applicable in international contracts and provoked in transnational instruments. and CISG Article 77 of CISG states: "A party who relies on a breach of contract must take such measures as are reasonable in the circumstances to mitigate the loss, including loss of profit, resulting from the breach. If he fails to take such measures, the party in breach may claim a reduction in the damages in the amount by which the loss should have been mitigated" Arguably, UPICC has indicated to the application of the principle in article 7.4.8 which states: "(1) The non-performing party is not liable for harm suffered by the aggrieved party to the extent that the harm could have been reduced by the latter party's taking reasonable steps. (2) The aggrieved party is entitled to recover any expenses reasonably incurred in attempting to reduce the harm." IUSCT awards for contract breach or repudiation seem to have recognized and invoked an almost absolute duty to mitigate damages in the same line as proposed in UPICC, forcing the judges to estimate and deduct amounts where the injured party itself had failed to mitigate. The awards we examined indicate that the tribunal factored in profits from resale of goods or the value of retained goods in its efforts to be fair and equitable. In its practice, several awards pointed out the claimant's duty to take reasonable steps to minimize damages. For example, changing the storage and moving goods into a well-maintained place would seem a reasonable measure to mitigate damages. The tribunal's awards frequently announced the anticipatory breach. When a buyer fails to pay and take delivery of goods and the unpaid seller resells the items, the tribunal accepts the substitute transaction as necessary to mitigate damages.

In chapter four, awarding some heads of dameges in practice of the tribunal is studied. The most controversial topics that were discussed in the tribunal were observed in this chapter. The tribunal may consider recoverability of currency devaluation and legal fees as suffered losses. In expropriation cases, where the tribunal has calculated the value of the expropriated property interests in Iranian rials, it has consistently converted that amount to U.S. dollars, using the exchange rate from the time of expropriation. In other types of cases, especially for debts in rials, its practice reveals no firm decision, although it seems to have preferred the rate at the debt's due date. The tribunal has sometimes examined whether, if the claimant had been paid at the due date, it exchanged the amount to its own country's currency. Regarding devaluation of currency, the tribunal believes that the award of interest should s cover such damages.

As for legal costs, it is free to determine which party shall bear them in whole or in part. Because of its broad discretion in this matter, its practice has been less than fully consistent. In deciding the proper amount of such costs to award, it has considered the nature and outcome of the proceedings, including the case's complexity, the degree of the prevailing party's success, and both parties' attitude and demeanour. However, the tribunal awarded no costs at all to the successful claimants in full. If costs are understood as akin to damages, a broad view of allowable items and the recoverable amounts is needed in order to give full compensation to the successful party. The recoverable costs should be considered as similar to an item of damage suffered due to the breaches of contract of the other party, and the amounts claimed should be made subject to proof like any other proof of damage. The tribunal has usually awarded lost profit vis-à-vis expropriated investments or terminated commercial contracts, as part of paying full compensation. But it has often dismissed as speculative or too uncertain claims for lost profits in cases of breach of contract. In expropriation claims with strong indicators of future profitability, it considers lost profit based on future projections, but the mere fact of a project's nearing completion does not demonstrate its future profitability. The tribunal has argued that in lawful expropriation the actual or suffered loss is the only compensable damage and abstained from awarding lost profits, and it has applied that standard in cases arising from the massive nationalizations in Iran following its Islamic Revolution.

In chapter five, the practice of the tribunal regarding the problem of valuation of the damage is studied. Although, the expropriation clauses, stipulated in investment agreements, specifies that the compensation must amount to the value of the investment, but it makes no mention of how to calculate the fair market value of the investment. Therefore, as demonstrated in the chapter, such agreements are often limited as a source of guidance in determining damages. The rulings of the Iran-U.S. Claims Tribunal have displayed strong support for the traditional view that international law requires payment of full compensation. Its awards for going concerns have generally involved determination of fair market value, including likely future profits. The type of assessment it chooses depends on the asset's nature and its market.

A variety of valuation methods have been used. Notably, in the most cases the amount awarded have been substantially below the amounts claimed. The Tribunal usually invoking the arriving to such low assessment by a process of 'approximation' or 'taking into account all relevant circumstances in the case. Approximate valuation is applied by the Tribunal in a variety of case ranging from valuation of a going concern to valuation of physical items. Notably, article 7.4.3 of the UNIDROIT Principles submits to sue the court discretion in the cases that the damage determination is not exact. Article states: "Where the amount of damages cannot be established with a sufficient degree of certainty, the assessment is at the discretion of the court." The tribunal in assessment of the value of the companies as the income-producer entities takes to methods of going concern and discounted cash flaw method. If the given business is not eligible to recognize as income producer, then the tribunal awarded the value based on net book value assessment. While DCF is suitable for an entity, which has an earning history and has attained the status of a going concern, NBV can be used for valuation of recent investments that have not had the time to earn goodwill and reach profitability. The practice of the tribunal respecting application of DCF method renders following critical points that should be noted

1- The Damnum emergens/Lucrum cessans combination, which was a traditional remedy for breach of contract, needs to be seen as arising at a time when valuation was back ward\historic and based on the accounting value of individual items of property. It is essentially an issue of double recovery, where the investor obtains first, without risk, its original investment expenditures, and then receives also the returns he might have obtained with the very high-risk, long-term contract.

2- based on the interpretation of the ICJ jurisprudence, the

Iran-U.S. Claims Tribunal advocated that in in the lawful expropriation (such as the tribunal cases) it is not allowed to award the Lost profit, but insisted to take the lost revenue of the expropriated company into account in case of such lawful expropriation. This principle emerges particularly from the Amoco International Finance Corp. Case where it was understood that the Chorzow Factory Case did not permit the inclusion of lucrum cessans or probable future profits in the value of the undertaking which can be claimed.

In chapter Six, the practice of the tribunal respecting interest issues was studied. The Iran-U.S. Claims Tribunal, in case *A-19*, adopted the long-standing principle in international arbitration that awarding interest is inherent in the authority to award just compensation for damages. But it declined to set down uniform rates or time periods for interest, leaving that for each chamber to decide case by case. It is the tribunal's policy to derive a rate of interest based approximately on the amount that the successful claimant would have been in a position to have earned if it had had the funds available to invest in a form of commercial investment in common use in its own country. Regarding appropriate rates, there was general agreement to follow the rate in the contract if parties have specified it, if not, judicial discretion rules. Chamber I, in its *Sylvania* and later awards, followed the 'investment-rate rule' --the rate that the successful party could have earned had it received payment on time and invested the money in a commercial six-month deposit account in its home country, as per UPICC's article 7.4.9. states "2) The rate of interest shall be the average bank short-term lending rate to prime borrowers prevailing for the currency of payment at the place for payment,". In contrast, chamber III, in its *McCollough* case and subsequent awards, rejected uniform application of any particular rule and determined the rate for each case, in the light of its facts and circumstances. The tribunal has faced some claims that flowed from Iran's exchange controls, which prevented transfer of Americans' funds from Iranian banks. The judges have, there, accepted force majeure to absolve the banks but still awarded interest on the amounts that they withheld, in accordance with article 7.4.9 of UPICC. The tribunal, however, found no special reasons for departing from international precedents disallowing compound interest, be that in its expropriation or commercial claims. In a 2014 award, after noting the global financial environment and the steady decline in interest rates since 1990, which speeded up with the global financial crisis of 2008.The Tribunal finds that, while an award of simple ten percent interest might have been reasonable at the time those decisions were rendered, it would not be reasonable today in light of the steady decline in interest rates since 1990 as well as the dramatic fall in interest rates as a result of the global financial crisis of 2008. This wording indicates that tribunal is delicately aware of the economic environments and is impact on the case circumstances. The tribunal, in its recent awards, takes these changing factors into account.

The examination here of the practice of the Iran-U.S. Claims Tribunal has shown that an international arbitral tribunal operating specifically in an investor--state context can decide cases more efficiently and lawfully by applying general principles of law than by invoking the national law of either disputing party. The tribunal's application of the general principles of law, its extraction of them through comparative analysis of doctrine and customary international law, and its interpretation of them in the rulings and awards it has made in its cases have furthered the goal of codifying the UNIDROIT Principles, even though it was long reluctant to refer directly to the UPICC as a legal source in its awards. This study of tribunal practice shows that it interprets the UNIDROIT Principles carefully, through a comprehensive legal analysis. In most of its cases, general principles of law have figured prominently as sources of international law.

Studying the tribunal's 36 years of jurisprudence shows that the UPICC principles are indeed applicable in commercial disputes, and suggests clearly that they could serve effectively as substantive law in disputes between foreigners and states regarding international investment law. This analysis has demonstrated that international commercial law and international investment law both enshrine, in very similar ways, the principle of compensation and secondary, allied principles, such as duty to mitigation. Although the tribunal's tendency towards applying general principles has long been in line with the goals of codifying UPICC, it would not refer directly to UPICC as a legal source in its awards. However, UPICC's popularity and frequent application in international arbitrations have swayed the tribunal, and in 2014, for the first time, it expressly cited UPICC articles in its reasoning for an award.

This study also shows that the 'practical' criticism that transnational rules are too few in number and often contradictory to be helpful in arbitration rests on an inaccurate assumption. Therefore, there is undoubtedly scope to promote the use of the UNIDROIT Principles in international investment law.

The Iran _United States Claims Tribunal, by consistently applying principles of commercial law in deciding many of the commercial cases before it, has contributed significantly to the stabilization and development of a multitude of principles and rules of the lex mercatoria. This study has shown how tribunal implied the principle of compensation and the allied principles such as duty to mitigate foreseeability, certainty, undue enrichment, duty to pay interest in the investor-state claim and how interpret them in the same line with the rules incorporated in UPICC as the general principles of law. Indeed, the development of a body of international commercial law has made a quantum advance due to the work of the Tribunal, and its jurisprudence in commercial cases represents a veritable horn of plenty for those who are called to research and apply in field of transnational commercial law.

The analysis here reveals the similarity, and often the identity, of the values and preoccupations underlying the UNIDROIT Principles and the legal principles that the Iran_U.S. Claims Tribunal has applied in its 36 years of jurisprudence. It also makes clear that UPICC's compensation rules to restore the original equilibrium between parties -a form of contractual justice–are invaluable not only in private contracts but also in any financial transaction between private and state parties and even in inter-state disputes. Clearly the global values set out in UPICC are superb vehicles for articulating and enforcing universal business contracting. The tribunal routinely applies general principles of transnational law, which it has greatly helped to develop because the judges tend to agree on this. However, the tribunal did not apply UPICC directly in its arguments till 2014, when it finally appeared in a final award issued in an interstate claim. In this award to determine the interest rate, in proposing the prime bank lending rate in the United States as the rate of interest applicable in the investment dispute, the Tribunal was mindful of Article 7.4.9 (2) of the UNIDROIT Principles 2010. This stipulation in tribunal language denotes the tendency of this tribunal to invoking the rules of UPICC as the rules of international law which could be applied independently. The application of UPICC by Iran_U.S. Claims Tribunal supports this statement that, disputes arising out of bilateral or multilateral investment treaties may also prove fertile ground for the application of the UNIDROIT Principles, especially considering the explicit role given to general principles of international law in the resolution of disputes arising under those treaties

By way of concluding remarks, indeed, the tribunal adapted provisions pertaining to the realm of private law, and more specifically to contract law (that is, the provisions of the UPICC), by considering them suitable for application in the field of investment law—a field of international law. More significantly, the UPICC are considered to complement international law. As the arbitral tribunal precedent has shown, the use of the UPICC as a confirmation of a rule that is already part of customary international law appears more acceptable than using the UPICC to add a new rule to international law. Therefore, it may be said that the UPICC have gained full access to international investment arbitration.

Bibliography

Documents

•ALGIERS ACCORDS, Declaration of the government of the democratic and popular republic of Algeria, _IUSCTR_ Vol.1 (1981).

•ALGIERS ACCORDS, *Claims Settlement Declaration*, 19 janvier 1981_IUSCTR_ Vol. 1 (1981).

•Communique regarding the work of the Tribunal, 16/1, 2016, enligne :<https://www.iusct.net/Pages/Public/A-News.aspx>.

•constitution act of the Islamic Republic of Iran, 1982, enligne :<https://www.constituteproject.org/constitution/Iran_1989.pdf?lang=en>.

•FULL TRIBUNAL OF IRAN_UNITED STATES CLAIMS, *tribunal rules of procedure*, 3 mai 1983, en ligne : <http://www.iusct.net/General%20Documents/5tribunal%20rules%20OF%20procedure.pdf>.

•Energy Charter Treaty (opened for signature 17 December 1994, entered into force 16 April 1998).COR-REG-36116-Sr-4622, at https://treaties.un.org/Pages/showDetails.aspx?objid =080000028009ac15 accessed 2 February 2017

•INTERNATIONAL CHAMBER OF COMMERCE, *ICC Arbitration Rules*, amended 2017, enligne : <https://cdn.iccwbo.org/content/uploads/sites/3/2017/01/ICC-2017-Arbitration-and-2014-Mediation-Rules-English-version.pdf>.

•*International Law Commission, Draft articles on Responsibility of States for Internationally Wrongful Acts*,10 Novembre 2001. https://legal.un.org/ilc/texts/instruments/english/commentaries/9_6_2001.pdf

•*North America Free Trade Agreement (NAFTA)*, enligne :

<http://www.international.gc.ca/trade-agreements-accords-commerciaux/agr-acc/nafta-alena/text-texte/11.aspx?lang=eng>.

•*statute of international court of justice*, 1945, enligne : <http://legal.un.org/avl/pdf/ha/sicj/icj_statute_e.pdf>.

•*Treaty of Amity, Economic Relations, and Consular Rights. Signed at Tehran, on 15 August 1955, between Iran and United States,Treaty Series, Volume 284, 1957,1958, Secretariat of the United Nations*, enligne : <https://treaties.un.org/doc/Publication/UNTS/Volume%20284/v284.pdf>.

•UNCITRAL Arbitration Rules 2010.en ligne: http://www.uncitral.org/uncitral /en/uncitral _texts/ arbitration/ 2010 Arbitration _ rules.htm,l accessed 3 May 2017

•UNCITRAL model law on international commercial Arbitration, revised 2010, enligne : <http://www.uncitral.org/uncitral/en/uncitral_texts/arbitration/2010 Arbitration_rules.html>.

•*UNIDROIT principles of international commercial contracts 2010*, International Institute for the Unification of Private Law, Rome, 2010.

•*world Bank Guideline on the Treatment of Foreign Direct Investment*, 1992, volume 2, enligne : <http://documents.worldbank.org/curated/pt/955221468766167766/pdf/multi-page.pdf>.

Books

•ALDRICH, G. H., *The Jurisprudence of the Iran-United States Claims Tribunal*, New York, Oxford University Press, 1996.

•ASHFORD, P., *Hand Book on International Commercial Arbitration*, Second Edition, United States, JurisNet, 2014.

•AVANESSIAN, A., *Iran-United States Claims Tribunal in Action*, Great Bretain, Martinus Nijhoff, 1993.

•BERGER, K. P., *The Creeping Codification of the Next Lex Mercatoria*, Second, Great Bretain, Wolters Kluwer, 2010.

•BLACK, H. C., *Black's Law Dictionary: Definitions of the Terms and Phrases of American and English Jurisprudence, Ancient and Modern*, 6th éd., USA, West Publishing Company, 1990.

•BLACKABY, N. et C. PARTASIDIES, *Redfern And Hunter on International Arbitration*, Sixth, New York, Oxford University Press, 2015.

•BONELL, M. J., *An International Restatement of Contract Law: the UNIDROIT Principles of International Commercial Contracts*, Second, New York, Transnational Publishers, Inc., 1997.

•BORN, G. B., *International Arbitration: Law and Practice*, Second, Wolter Kluwers, 2016.

•BROWER, C. N. et J. D. BRUESCHKE, *The Iran - United States Claims Tribunal*, the Hauge, Martinus Nijhoff Publications, 1998.

•CARON, D. D. et L. M. CAPLAN, *The UNCITRAL Arbitration Rules, A Commentary*, Second Edition, United Kingdom, Oxford University Press, 2013.

•CHENGWEI, L. et M. S. NEWMAN, *Remedies for Non-performance - Perspectives from CISG, UNIDROIT Principles and PECL*, Juris Net Llc, 2008.

•CRAWFORD, J., *Brownlie's Principles of Public International Law*, 8th éd., United Kingdom, Oxford University Press, 2012.

•DUGAN, C. F., D. WALLACE, N. RUBINS et B. SABAHI, *Investor-State Arbitration*, United States, Oxford University Press, 2008.

•GORDON, R. H. F. and M. W., *International Business Transactions*, Second, United States, West Academic Publishing, 2016.

•GOTANDA, J. Y., *Supplemental Damages in Private International Law*, The Hauge, Kluwer Law International, 1998.

•KANTOR, M., *Valuation for Arbitration: Compensation Standards, Valuation Methods and Expert Evidence*, The Netherlands, Kluwer Law International, 2008.

•KHALILIAN, K., *Iran_United States Claims Arbitration*, U.S, Trafford, 2012.

•LILICH, R. B., *The Iran-United States Claims Tribunal, 1981-1983*, United States, the University Press of Virginia, 1984.

•LILLICH, R. B., *the Valuation of Nationalized Property in International law*, IV, United States, University Press of Virgiana, 1987.

•LILLICH, R. B. et D. BARSTOW MAGRAW, *The Iran-United States Claims Tribunal: Its Contribution to the Law of State Responsability*, New York, Transnational Publishers, Inc., 1998.

•MAPP, W., *The Iran-United States Claims Tribunal, The first ten years*, Manchester, Manchester University Press, 1993.

•MARBOE, I., *Calculation of Compensation and damages in international investment law*, United States, Oxford University Press inc., 2009.

•MARQUIS, L., *International Uniform Commercial Law*, England, Ashgate, 2005.

•MCLACHLAN QC, C., L. SHORE et M. WEINIGER QC, *International Investment Arbitration, Substantive Principles*, Great Britain, Oxford University Press, 2008.

•MOHEBI, M., *The International Law Character of the Iran-United States Claims Tribunal*, Boston, Kluwer Law International, 1999.

•MOURI, A., *The International Law of Expropriation as Reflected in the Work of the Iran-U.S. Claims Tribunal*, The Netherland, martinus Nijhoff, 1994.

•NASSER, N., *sanctity of contracts revisited*, Netherlands, Kluwer publishers, 1995.

•RIPINSKY, S., *Damages in International Investment Law*, London, British Institute of International and Comparative Law, 2008.

•ROWAN, S., *Remedies for Breach of Contract, A Comparative Analysis of the Protection of Performance*, United States, Oxford University Press, 2012.

•SABAHI, B., *Compensation and Restitution in Investor_State Arbitration*, New York, Oxford University Press, 2011.

•SAIDOV, D., *The Law of Damages in International Sales*, Hart Publishing, Oxford, 2008.

•SCHREUER, C. H., *The ICSID Convention: A Commentary*, Second, New York, Cambridge University Press, 2009.

•SCHWENZER, I. et C. FOUNTOULAKIS, *International Sales Law*, London, Routledge. Cavandish, 2007.

•SCHWENZER, I., P. HACHEM et C. KEE, *Global Sales and Contract Law*, Great Britain, Oxford University Press, 2012.

•SORNARAJAH, M., *The International Law on Foreign Investment*, New York, Cambridge University Press, 2010.

•WESTBERG, J. A., *International Transactions and Claims involving Government Practice, Case Law of The Iran -United States Claims Tribunal*, Washington, D.C., International Law Institute, 1991.

•WHITEMAN, M. M., *Damages in International Law*, 3, Washington, United States Government Printing Office, 1943.

•ZELLER, B., *Damages under the CISG*, Second, New York, Oxford University Press, 2008.

Monographies

•ABDALA, M. A., « Key Damage Compensation Issues in Oil and Gas International Arbitration Cases », (2009) 24-3 *Am. Univ. Int. Law Rev.* 540-570.

•ADAM KRAMER, « Remoteness: New Problems with the Old Test », dans DJAKHONGIR SAIDOV et RALPH CUNNINGTON (dir.), *Contract Damages Domestic and International Perspectives*, Hart Publication, 2008.

•AFFOLDER, N., « Awarding Compound Interest in International Arbitration », (2001) 12-1 *Am. Rev. Int. Arbitr.* 45-93.

•ALBERRO, J., « Estimating Damages Using DCF: From Free Cash Flow to the Firm to Free Cash Flow to Equity (and Back) », (2015) 30-3 *ICSID Rev.* 689–698.

•ALDRICH, G. H., « What Constitutes A Compensable Taking of Property? The Decisions of the Iran-United States ClaimsTribunal », (1994) 88 *Am. J. Int. Law* 585-610.

•ALEXANDER KOMAROV, « the Limitation of domestic and International contract damagesin domestic legal systems and international instruments », dans DJAKHONGIR SAIDOV et RALPH CUNNINGTON (dir.), *Contract Damages; Domestic and InternationalPerspectives*, United States, Hart Publication, 2008.

•ALFORD, R. P., « The Convergence of International Trade and Investment Arbitration », (2013) 12 *St. Clara J. Int. Law* 36-63.

•AMERASINGHE, C. F., « Issues of Compensation for the Taking of Alien Property in the Light of Recent Cases and Practice », (1992) 41 *Int. Comp. Law Q.* 22-65.

•———, « Some Aspects of the Quantum of Compensation Payable upon Expropriation », (1993) 87 *Am. Soc. Int. Law.* 477-482

•BAMODOU, G., « Exploring the Interrelationship of Transnational Commercial Law, "The New Lex Mercatoria" and International Commercial Arbitration », (1998) 10-7 *Afr. J. Int. Comp. Law* 31-59.

•BEDERMAN, R. B. L. and D. J., « Jurisprudence of the Foreign Claims Settelment Commission: Iran Claims », (1997) 91-3 *Am. J. Int. Law.*

•BERGER, K. P., « The New Law Merchant and the Global Market: A 21st Century View of Transnational Commercial Law », (2000) 91-3 *INT ARB REV.*

•BERNARDINI, P., « UNIDROIT Principles and international investment arbitration », (2014) 19-4 *Unif. Law Rev.* 561–569.

•———, « Private law and general principles of public international law », (2016) 21-2-3 *Unif. Law Rev.* 184-196.

•BJORKLUND, A. K., « Causation, Morality, and Quantum », (2009) 32 *Suffolk Transnatl. Law Rev.* 435-450.

•BJORKLUND, A. K. et A. REINSCH, « introduction: the ILA study group on the role of soft law instruments in international investment law », dans andrea K. BJORKLUND et August REINISCH (dir.),

International Investment Law and Soft Law, United Kingdom, Edward Elgar, 2012, p. 1-9.

•BOCKSTIEGELT, K. H., « Applying the UNCITRAL Rules: The Experience of the Iran-United States Claims Tribunal », (1986) 4 *Int. TAX Bus. LAWYER*.

•BONELL, M. J., « The law governing international commercial contracts and the actual role of the UNIDROIT Principles », (2018) 23-2 *Unif. Law Rev.* 15-41.

•BONELL, M. J., « International Investment Contracts and General Contract Law: a Place for the UNIDROIT Principles of International Commercial Contracts », (2012) 17-1-2 *Unif. Law Rev.* 141–159.

•BROWER, C. N., « Current Developments in the Law of Expropriation and Compensation: A Preliminary Survey of Awards of the Iran-United States Claims Tribunal », (1987) 21 *Int. Lawyer.*

•BROWER, C. N., « The Global Court: The Internationalization of Commercial Adjudication and Arbitration », (1997) 26 *Baltim. Law Rev.*

•BROWER, C. N. et S. W. SCHILL, « Is Arbitration a Threat or a Boon to the Legitimacy of International Investment Law? », (2009) 9 *Chic. J. Int. Law* 471-498.

•BROWER, C. N. et J. K. SHARPE, « The Creeping Codification of Transnational Commercial Law:An Arbitrator's Perspective », (2004) 45-1 *Va. J. Int. LAW* 199-220.

•BRUNETTI, M., « The Iran-United States Claims Tribunal, NAFTA Chapter 1, and the Doctrine of Indirect Expropriation », (2001) 2-1 *Chic. J. Int. Law* 203-212.

•———, « The Lex Mercatoria in Practice: The Experience of the Iran-United States Claims Tribunal », (2002) 18-3 *Arbitr. Int.* 355 et seq.

•BURGSTALLER, M. et J. KETCHESON, « Should Expropriation Risk Be Taken into Account in the Assessment of Damages? », (2017) 32-1 *ICSID Rev.* 193-215.

•CARBONNEAU, T. E., « arbitral law-making », (2004) 25 *Michigan Journal of International law* 1183-1208.

•CARBONNEAU, T. E. et M. S. FIRESTONE, « Transnational Law-making: Assessing theimpact ofthe Vinenna Convention and the Viability of Arbitral Adjudication », (1987) 1 *J. Int. Dispute Resolut.* 51-80.

•CARON, D. D., « The Iran_U.S. Claim Tribunal and Investment: Arbitration: Understanding the Claims Settlement Declaration as a Retroactive BIT », dans Christopher R. DRAHOZAL et Christopher S. GIBSON (dir.), *The Iran_U.S. Claim Tribunal at 25, the cases everyone needs to know for investor-state & international arbitration*, United States, Oxford University Press, 2007.

•CARON, D., « The ILC Articles on State Responsibility: The Paradoxical Relationship Between Form and Authority », (2002) 96 *Am. J. Int. Law.*

•CHRISTOPHER S. GIBSON AND CHRISTOPHER R. DRAHOZAL, « Iran-United States Claims Tribunal Precedent in Investor-State Arbitration », (2006) 23-6 *J. Int. Arbitr.* 521-546.

•CLAGETT, B. M., « The Expropriation Issue Before the Iran-United States Claims Tribunal: is "Just Compensation" Required by International Law or Not? », (1984) 16 *Law Policy Int. Bus.* 813-891.

•CORDERO-MOSS, G. et D. BEHNY, « The relevance of the UNIDROIT Principles in investment arbitration », (2014) 19-4 *Unif. Law Rev.* 570-608.

•CRANSTON, R., « Theorizing Transnational Commercial Law », (2007) 42-7 *Tex. Int. Law J.* 597-617.

•CRAWFORD, J., « The ILC's Articles on responsibility of states for internationally wrongful acts: Retrospect », (2002) 96-4 *Am. J. Int. Law* 874-890.

•CROOK, J. R., « Applicable Law inInternational Arbitration: The Iran-U.S. Claims TRribunal Experience », (1989) 83 *Am. J. Int. Law* 278-311.

•CUNIBERTI, G., « Three Theories of Lex Mercatoria », (2014) 52-6 *Columbia J. Transnatl. Law* 369-434.

•DAI, T., « Assessing Damages in Non-Expropriation Cases Before International Investment Arbitration », (2009) 52 *Jpn. Yearb. Int. Law.*

•DARANKOUM, E. S., « L'application des Principes d'UNIDROIT par les arbitresinternationaux et par les jugesétatiques », (2002) 36 *Rev. Jurid. Thémis* 425-480.

•DENNIS, M. J., « Modernizing and harmonizing international contract law: the CISG and the UNIDROIT Principles continue to provide the best way forward », (2014) 19-1 *Unif. Law Rev.* 114-151.

•DEREK W. BOWETT, « claims between States and private entities: the twilight zone of international law », (1986) 35-4 *catholic university law review* 929-942.

•DOUGLAS, Z., « The hybrid foundations of investment treaty arbitration », (2003) 74 *Br. Year b. Int. Law* 151-289.

•DRAHOZAL, C. R., « Contracting out of National Law: An Empirical Look at the New Law Merchant », (2005) 80-2 *Notre Dame Law REeview* 523-552.

•———, « Private Ordering and International Commercial Arbitration », (2009) 113-4 *Penn State Law Rev.* 1031-1050.

•DUMBERRY, P., « The Role and Relevance of Awards in the Formation, Identification and Evolution of Customary Rules in International Investment Law », (2016) 33-3 *J. Int. Arbitr.* 269-287.

•EISELEN, S., « Unresolved damages issues of the CISG: a comparative analysis », (2005) 38-1 *Comp. Int. Law J. South. Afr.* 32-46.

•ESCARCENA, S. L., « Expropriation and other Measures Affecting Property Rights in the Case Law of the Iran-United States Claims Tribunal », (2013) 31-2 *Wis. Int. Law J.*

•FELLMETH, A. X., « Blow-Market Interest in International Claims Against States », (2010) 13-2 *J. Int. Econ. Law* 423-457.

•FERRARI, F., « Comparative Ruminations on the Foreseeability of Damages in Contract Law », (1993) 53-4 *La. Law Rev.* 1262-1269.

•———, « Hadley v Baxendale v Foreseeability under Article 74 CISG », dans DjakhongirSAIDOV et Ralph CUNNINGTON (dir.), *contract damages. domestic and international perspectives*, United States, Hart Publication, 2008, p. 305-329.

•GAILLARD, E., « Use of General principles of International Law in International Long-Term Contracts », (1999) 27 *Intl Bus. Law* 214-224.

•GAZZINI, T., « General Principles of Law in the Field of Foreign Investment », (2009) 10 *J. World Invest. Trade* 103-119.

•———, « Drawing the Line between Non-compensable Regulatory Powers and Indirect Expropriation of Foreign Investment - An Economic Analysis of Law Perspective », (2010) 7-3 *Manch. J. Int. Econ. Law*.

•GIARDINA, A., « issues of applicable law and uniform law on interest: basic distinctions in national and international practice », dans Filip DE LY et Laurent LEVY (dir.), *Interest, Auxiliary and Alternative Remedies in International Arbitration*, ICC Publication Department, 2008.

•GIBSON, C. S., « Yukos Universal Limited (Isle of Man) v The Russian Federation, A Classic Case of Indirect Expropriation », (2015) 30-2 *ICSID Rev.* 303-314.

•GILLESPIE, K., « U.S. corporations and Iran at the Hague », (1990) 44-1 *Middle East J.* 18-36.

•GOODE, R., « The Codification of Commercial Law », (1988) 14 *Monash Univ. Law Rev.* 135-157.

•GOODE, R., « usage and its reception in transnational commercial law », (1997) 46 *Int. Comp. Law Q.* 1-36.

•GOODE, R., « Rule, practice, and pragmatism in transnational commercial law », (2005) 54-3 *Int. Comp. Law Q.* 539-562.

•GOTANDA, J. Y., « Recovering Lost Profits in International Disputes », (2004) 36 *Georget. J. Int. Law Fall 2004 61-112* 61-112.

•———, « Awarding Damages Under the United Nations Convention on theInternational Sale of Goods: A Matter of Interpretation », (2006) 37 *Goergetown J. Int. Law*.

•———, « Using the Unidroit Principles to Fill Gaps in the CISG », dans DjakhongirSAIDOV et Ralph CUNNINGTON (dir.), *Contract Damages; Domestic and InternationalPerspectives*, Portland, Hart Publication, 2008, p. 107-124.

•GOTANDA, J. Y., « The Unpredictability Paradox: Punitive Damages and Interest in International Arbitration », (2009) 10 *J. World Invest. Trade*.

•GOTANDA, J. Y., « Consistently Inconsistent: The Need for Predictability in Awarding Costs and Fees in Investment Treaty Arbitrations », (2013) 28-2 *ICSID Rev.* 420–437.

•GOTANDA, J. Y. et T. J. SÉNÉCHAL, « Interest as Damages », (2009) 47-3 *Columbia J. Transnatl. Law* 492-536.

•GOTANDA, J. Y., « Damages, Article 74 », dans Stefan KROLL et loukasMISTELIS (dir.), *UN Convention on Contracts for International Sale of Goods*, munchen, Germany, C.H.Beck, 2011.

•GUZMAN, J. H. D. and A. T., « Expropriatory and Non-Expropriatory Takings Under International Investment Law », *UC Berkeley Public Law Leg. Theory Res. Pap. Ser.* 2012.21.

•HACHEM, P., « The CISG and Statute of Limitation », dans Ingeborg SCHWENZER (dir.), *35 years CISG and beyond*, 39, coll. international commerce and arbitration, The Hague, Elven international publishing, 2016.

•HANESSIAN, G., « General principles of law in Iran-U.S. claims tribunal », (1989) 27 *Colum J. Transnatl. Law* 309-352.

•HEPBURN, J., « The UNIDROIT Principles of International Commercial Contracts and Investment Treaty Arbitration: A Limited Relationship », (2015) 64-4 *Int. Comp. Law Q.* 905-933.

•HIRSCH, M., « sources of international investment law », dans Andrea K. BJORKLUND et August REINISCH (dir.), *international investment law and soft law*, United Kingdom, Edward Elgar, 2012.

•JESSUP, P. C., « The Concept of Transnational Law: An Introduction », (1963) 3-1 *Columbia J. Transnatl. Law* 1-17.

•JH DALHUISEN, « legal order and their manifestation: the operation of the international commercial and financial legal order and its lex mercatoria », (2006) 24 *berkeleyjournal of international law* 129-191.

•JOHNSON, V. M., « Codification of the lex mercatoria: friend or foe? », (2015) 21-2 *Law Bus. Rev. Am.* 150-166.

•KAUFMANN-KOHLER, G., « Arbitral Precedent: Dream, Necessity or Excuse? », (2007) 23-3 *Arbitr. Int.* 357-378.

•KNULL, W. H., S. T. JONES, T. J. TYLER et R. D. DEUTSCH, « Accounting for Uncertainty in Discounted Cash Flow Valuation of Upstream Oil and Gas Investments », (2007) 25-3 *J. ENERGY Nat. Resour. LAW* 268-302.

•KOH, H. H., « Transnational Legal Process », (1996) 75 *Neb. Law Rev.* 181--207.

•KOMAROV, A., « Mitigation of Damages », dans Yves DERAINS et Richard H. KREINDLER (dir.), *Evaluation of Damages in International Arbitration*, ICC Publication Department, 2006.

•LANDO, O., « The Lex Mercatoria International Commercial Arbitration », (1985) 34 *Int. Comp. Law Q.* 747-768.

•LIEBLICH, W. C., « Determining the Economic Value of Expropriated Income-Producing Property in International Arbitrations », (1991) 8 *J. Int. Arbitr.*

•LO, A., « Determining Damages in ICSID Arbitration: A Problem of Uncertainty », (2013) 6-1 *Contemp. Asia Arbitr. J.* 75-105.

•LOOKOFSKY, J. M., « Consequential Damages in CISG Context », (2007) 19 *Pace Int. Law Rev.* 63-88.

•MAFI, H., « Controversial Issues of Compensation in Cases of Expropriation and Nationalization: Awards of the Iran-United States Claims Tribunal », (2011) 18-1 *Intl J Humanit.* 83-102.

•MALANCZUK, P., « mixing legal cultures in international arbitration. the Iran_United States Claims Tribunal », dans Vijay K. BHATIA (dir.), *Legal Discourse across Cultures and Systems*, Hong Kong, Hong Kong University Press, 2008.

•MANIRUZZAMAN, A. F., « The Lex MercatoriaAnd International Contracts: A Challenge for International Commercial Arbitration ? », (1999) 14 *AM U INTL REV* 657-697.

•MANN, F. A., « Compound Interest as an Item of Damage in International Law », (1988) 21 *Univ. Calif. Davis Law Rev.* 577-586.

•MARBOE, I., « Compensation and Damages in International Law The Limits of "Fair Market Value" », (2006) 7 *J. World Invest. Trade* 723-759.

•———, « Yukos Universal Limited (Isle of Man) v The Russian Federation, Calculation of Damages in the Yukos Award: Highlighting the Valuation Date, Contributory Fault and Interest », (2015) 30-2 *ICSID Rev.* 326–335.

•MARRELLA, F., « Choice of Law in Third-Millennium Arbitrations: The Relevance of the UNIDROIT Principles of International Commercial Contracts », (2003) 36-4 *Vanderbilt J. Transnatl. Law* 1138-1188.

•MCKENDRICK, E., « Damages », dans Stefan VOGENAUER et Jan KLEINHEISTERKAMP (dir.), *Commentary on the UNIDROIT Principles of International Commercial Contracts (PICC)*, United States, Oxford University Press, 2009.

•MENAKER, A. J., « the enduring relevance of the expropriation jurisprudence of the Iran_U.S. Claims Tribunal for investor-state arbitrations », dans Christopher S. Gibson and Christopher R. DRAHOZAL (dir.), *The Iran-U.S.Claims Tribunal at 25: The Cases Everyone Needs to Know for Investor_State& International Arbitration*, United Stated of America, Oxford University Press, 2007.

•MICHAELS, R., « The Functional Method of Comparative Law », (2005) paper 26 *Duke Law Sch. Fac. Scholarsh. Ser.* 1-47.

•———, « The true lex mercatoria: Law beyond the state », (2007) 14-2 *Indiana J. Glob. Leg. Stud.* 447-468.

•MOSK, R. M., « Lessons FromThe Hague - An Update on the Iran-United States Claims Tribunal », (1987) 14-11 *Pepperdine Law Rev.* 819-826.

•MUSTILL, M., « The New Lex Mercatoria: the First Twenty-Five Years », (1988) 4 *arbitration international* 86.

•PEREZCANO, H., P. PINSOLLE et T. WALDE, « Damages in Investment Arbitration. Are the Standards different from commercial arbitration? The need for consistency », (2005) 39-6 *J. World Invest. Trade.*

•POSNER, E. A., « Contract Remedies: Forseeability, Precaution, Causation, and Mitigation », dans Bouckaert BOUCKAERT (dir.), *The Encyclopedia of Law and Economics*, U.K, Edward Elgar, 2000, p. 162-178.

•PRAENDL, F., « Measure of Damages in International Commercial Arbitration », (1987) 23-6 *Stanf. J. Int. Law* 263-302.

•RADI, Y., « Precedent, 'Jurisprudences Constantes' and Coherence in International Investment Arbitration », (2014) 1 *Belg. Rev. Arbitr.*

•RAJPUT, A., « Problems with the Jurisprudence of the Iran–US Claims Tribunal on Indirect Expropriation », (2015) 30-3 *ICSID Rev.* 589–615.

•RAMSEY, V., « establishing claims for damages, costs and interest in international arbitration », (2011) 26-5 *Am. Univ. Int. Law Rev.* 1211-1239.

•REIFEGERSTE, S. et G. WEISZBERG, « obligation to mitigate loss and the concept of "reasonableness" in international commercial law », *Int. Bus. Law J.* 2004.181-197.

•REINISCH, A., « Expropriation », dans Peter MUCHLINSKI, Federico ORTINO et Christoph SCHREUER (dir.), *the Oxford handbook of International Investment Law*, New York, Oxford University Press, 2008, p. 407-459.

•———, « The relevance of the UNIDROIT Principles of International Commercial Contracts in international investment arbitration », (2014) 19 *Unif. Law Rev.* 609-622.

•REISMAN, W. M. et R. D. SLOANE, « Indirect Expropriation and its Valuation in the BIT Generation », *Yale Univ. Fac. Scholarsh. Ser.* 2004.115-150.

•REMIEN, O., « Public law and public policy in international commercial contracts and the UNIDROIT Principles of International Commercial Contracts 2010: a brief outline », (2013) 18-2 *Unif. Law Rev.* 262-280.

•RIPINSKY, S., « Assessing Damages in Investment Disputes: Practice in Search of Perfect », (2009) 10 *J. World Invest. Trade.*

•RIZNIK, P., « Some Aspects of Loss mitigation in International Sale of Goods », (2010) 14-2 *Vindobona J. Int. Commer. Law Arbitr.* 267-282.

•ROSELL, J., « Arbitration Costs as Relief/ or Damages », (2011) 28-2 *Kluwer Law Int.* 115-126.

•SABAHI, B., « The Calculation of Damages in International Investment Law », dans Philippe KAHN (dir.), *New Aspects of International Investment Law*, Leiden/Boston, Martinus Nijhoff Publishers, 2007.

•SABAHI, B. et T. WALDE, « Compensation, Damages and Valuation », dans Peter Muchlinski and Federico ORTINO (dir.), *The Oxford Handbook of International Investment Law*, New York, Oxford University Press, 2008.

•SAIDOV, D., « Methods of Limiting damages under the Vienna Convention on Contracts for the International Sale of Goods », (2002) 14 *Pace Int. Law Rev.* 308-353.

•———, « Anticipatory Non-Performance and Underlying Values of the UNIDROIT Principles », (2006) 11 *Rev. Droit Unif.*

•———, « Damages: The Need for Uniformity », (2006) 26-7 *J. Law Commer.* 393-403.

•SCHIFF BERMAN, P., « Global Legal Pluralism », (2007) 80-13 *South. Calif. Law Rev.* 1155-1238.

•SCHILL, S. W., « General Principles of Law and International Investment Law », dans Tarcisio GAZZINI et Eric BRABANDERE (dir.),

International Investment Law, the Sources of Rights and Obligations, USA, Martinus Nijhoff Publishers, 2012.

•SCHNEIDER, E. C., « Consequential Damages in the International Sale of Goods: Analysis of Two Decisions », (2014) 16-4 *J. Int. Law* 615-668.

•SCHREUER, C., « The Development of International Law by ICSID Tribunals », (2016) 31-3 *ICSID Rev.* 728–739.

•SEIDL-HOHENVELDERN, I., « L'évaluation des dommages dans les arbitrages transnationaux », (1987) 33 *Annu. Fr. Droit Int.* 7-31.

•SIMMONS, J. B., « Valuation in Investor-State Arbitration: Toward A More Exact Science », (2012) 30-1 *Berkeley J. Int. Law* 196-250.

•SLOANE, W. M. R. and R. D., « Indirect Expropriation and its Valuation in the BIT Generation », *Yale Univ. Fac. Scholarsh. Ser.* 2004.115-150.

•SMUTNY, A. C., « Some Observations on the Principles Relating to Compensation in the Investment Treaty Context », (2007) 22-1 *ICSID Rev.*

•SONG, L., « Award of Interest in Arbitration under Article 78 CISG », (2007) 12-4 *Unif. Law Rev.* 719-732.

•STAUFFER, T. R., « valuation of assets in international taking », (1996) 17 *Energy Law J.* 459-488.

•STEINGRUBER, A. M., « El Paso v Argentine Republic: UNIDROIT Principles of International Commercial Contracts as a reflection of 'general principles of law recognized by civilized nations' in the context of an investment treaty claim », (2013) 18-3-4 *Unif. Law Rev.* 509–531.

•STONE SWEET, A., « The new Lex Mercatoria and transnational governance », (2006) 13-5 *J. Eur. Public Policy* 627-646.

•TALLON, D., « Damages, Exemption Clauses, and Penalties », (1992) 40-7 *Am. J. Comp. Law* 676-686.

•TIETJE, C. et E. SIPIORSKI, « Offset of Benefits in Damages Calculation in International Investment Arbitration », (2012) 29-5 *J. Int. Arbitr.* 545-566.

•TRAKMAN, L. E., « A Plural Account of the Transnational Law Merchant », (2011) 3 *Transnatl. Leg. Theory* 309-345.

•UCHKUNOVA, I. et O. TEMNIKOV, « A Procrustean Bed: Pre- and Post-award Interest in ICSID Arbitration », (2014) 29-3 *ICSID Rev.* 648–668.

•VEKAS, L., « The Foreseeability Doctrine in Contractual Damage Cases », (2002) 43-1-2 *Acta Juridica Hung.* 145-174.

•VOHRYZEK-GRIEST, A. T., « Unjust Enrichment Unjustly Ignored: Opportunities and Pitfalls in Bringing Unjust Enrichment Claims Under ICSID », (2009) 31-3 *Loyola Los Angel. Int. Comp. Law Rev.* 501-580.

•VON MEHREN, A. T., « The Rise of Transnational Legal Practice and the Task of Comparative Law », (2001) 75-5 *Tulane Law Rev.* 1215-1224.

•VON MEHREN, R. B., « The Iran-U.S. arbitral tribinal », (1983) 31-3 *Am. J. Comp. Law* 713-730.

•WALLACE, D. J. B. and R. E., « Awarding Interest in International Commercial Arbitration: Establishing a Uniform Approach », (1998) 28 *Virjinia J. Int. Law.*

•WELLS, L. T., « Double Dipping in Arbitration Awards? An Economist Questions Damages Awarded to Karaha Bodas Company in Indonesia », (2003) 19-4 *Arbitr. Int.* 471-482.

•ZUMBANSEN, P., « Transnational Law », dans Jan SMITH (dir.), *Encyclopedia of Comparative Law*, Edward Elgar, 2006, p. 738-754.